Alcohol & drugs

Drinking days

The European School Survey Project on Alcohol and Other Drugs (ESPAD) surveyed 15-16 year olds across 35 European countries in 2007 to assess trends in the use of alcohol and other substances.

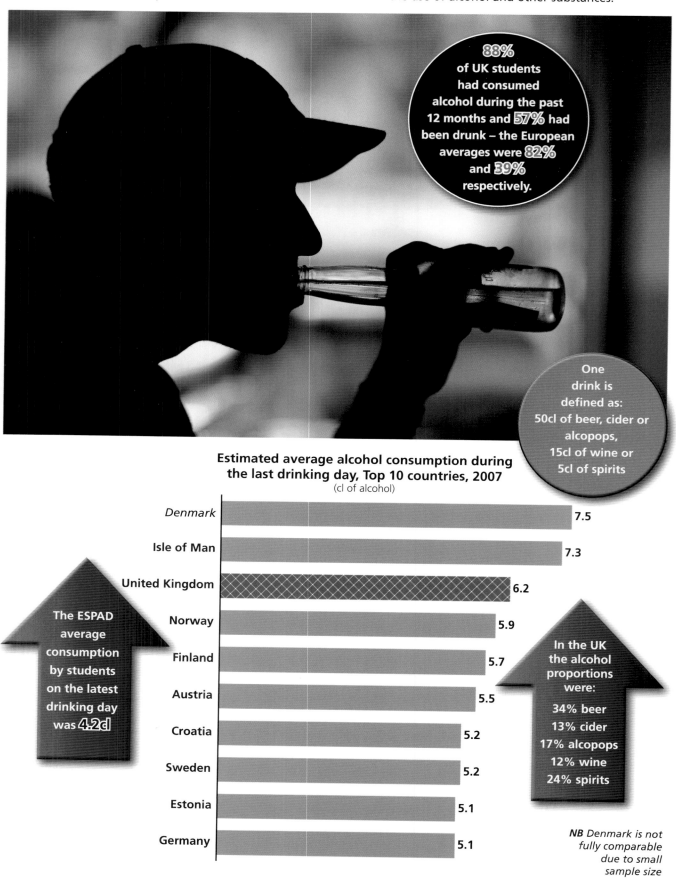

88% of UK students had consumed alcohol during the past 12 months and **57%** had been drunk – the European averages were **82%** and **39%** respectively.

One drink is defined as: 50cl of beer, cider or alcopops, 15cl of wine or 5cl of spirits

Estimated average alcohol consumption during the last drinking day, Top 10 countries, 2007
(cl of alcohol)

Country	cl
Denmark	7.5
Isle of Man	7.3
United Kingdom	6.2
Norway	5.9
Finland	5.7
Austria	5.5
Croatia	5.2
Sweden	5.2
Estonia	5.1
Germany	5.1

The ESPAD average consumption by students on the latest drinking day was **4.2cl**

In the UK the alcohol proportions were:

34% beer
13% cider
17% alcopops
12% wine
24% spirits

NB Denmark is not fully comparable due to small sample size

An average of **43%** of students reported 'heavy episodic drinking' in the 30 days before the survey, ie five drinks or more on a single occasion.

The average for boys was **47%** while girls averaged **39%**. In the UK, Sweden, Faroe Islands, the Isle of Man and Finland, the proportions are relatively equal. In Iceland and Norway the girls' drinking exceeded the boys'.

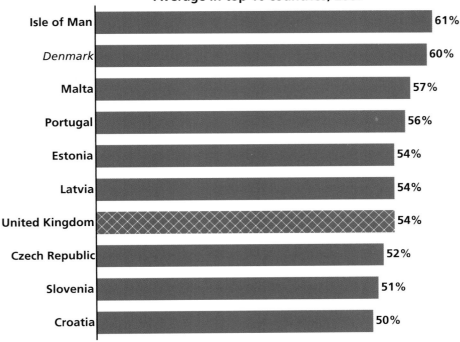

Percentage of students who consumed more than five drinks on one occasion in the last 30 days Average in top 10 countries, 2007

Country	%
Isle of Man	61%
Denmark	60%
Malta	57%
Portugal	56%
Estonia	54%
Latvia	54%
United Kingdom	54%
Czech Republic	52%
Slovenia	51%
Croatia	50%

Happy days?

Students were asked which of five positive and six negative outcomes they thought were likely to arise from drinking.

The **positive** consequences were:

- feeling happy
- having a lot of fun
- feeling relaxed
- feeling more friendly and outgoing
- forgetting their problems

The **negative** ones were:

- harming their health
- having a hangover
- feeling sick
- doing something they might regret
- getting into trouble with the police
- not being able to stop drinking

67% of students associated their alcohol consumption with having fun.

On average about **42%** associated their alcohol consumption with harming health and having a hangover.

Students in the UK seem to be the most positive in their attitudes towards their alcohol consumption.

The countries with the highest positive attitudes are also above average for drunkenness and for amount consumed.

Source: Substance use among students in 35 European countries, ESPAD 2009
http://www.espad.org

Home brew

Is the pub doomed by our changing drinking habits?

A study for the Department of Health surveyed a sample of adults in GB aged 16+ on their drinking habits in 2008.

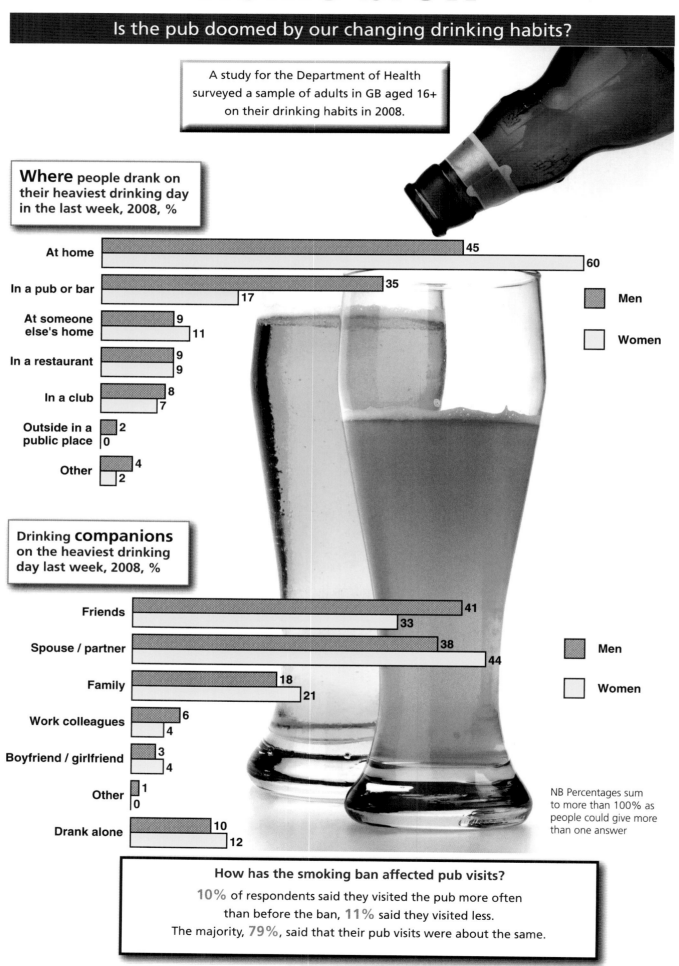

Where people drank on their heaviest drinking day in the last week, 2008, %

	Men	Women
At home	45	60
In a pub or bar	35	17
At someone else's home	9	11
In a restaurant	9	9
In a club	8	7
Outside in a public place	2	0
Other	4	2

Drinking **companions** on the heaviest drinking day last week, 2008, %

	Men	Women
Friends	41	33
Spouse / partner	38	44
Family	18	21
Work colleagues	6	4
Boyfriend / girlfriend	3	4
Other	1	0
Drank alone	10	12

NB Percentages sum to more than 100% as people could give more than one answer

How has the smoking ban affected pub visits?

10% of respondents said they visited the pub more often than before the ban, 11% said they visited less.
The majority, 79%, said that their pub visits were about the same.

Percentage who had bought alcohol from various outlets in the past week

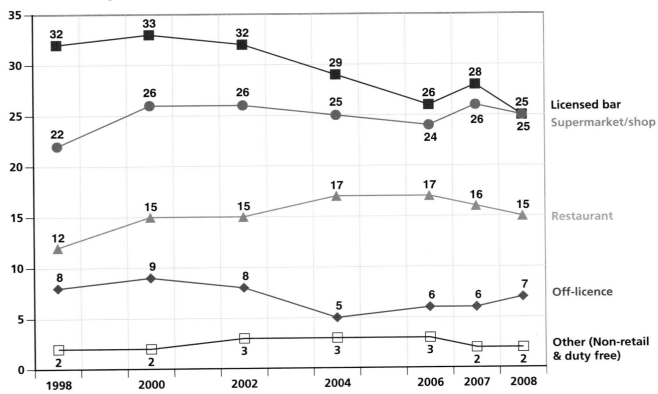

	1998	2000	2002	2004	2006	2007	2008	
Licensed bar	32	33	32	29	26	28	25	
Supermarket/shop	22	26	26	25	24	26	25	
Restaurant	12	15	15	17	17	16	15	
Off-licence	8	9	8	5	6	6	7	
Other (Non-retail & duty free)	2	2	3	3	3	2	2	

In 2008, over **2,000** pubs closed down – a rate of **39 a week** or **6 a day**, compared with **27 a week** or nearly **4 a day** in 2007

Beer sales in pubs are **down** by **16 million** pints a day since 1979.

They are now at their **lowest level** since the Depression of the 1930s, despite a population increase of **36%**

Over **20,000** jobs were lost in pubs during 2008, with **59,000** jobs projected to be lost over the next five years

Source: Drinking: adults' behaviour and knowledge in 2008, ONS © Crown copyright 2009, British Beer and Pub Association
http://www.statistics.gov.uk
http://www.beerandpub.com

Alcohol & drugs 11

Boozy Britain

We are consuming twice as much alcohol as 50 years ago

UK estimated alcohol consumption
(litres of alcohol per person aged over 14, per year)

| Cider | Spirits | Wine | Beer |

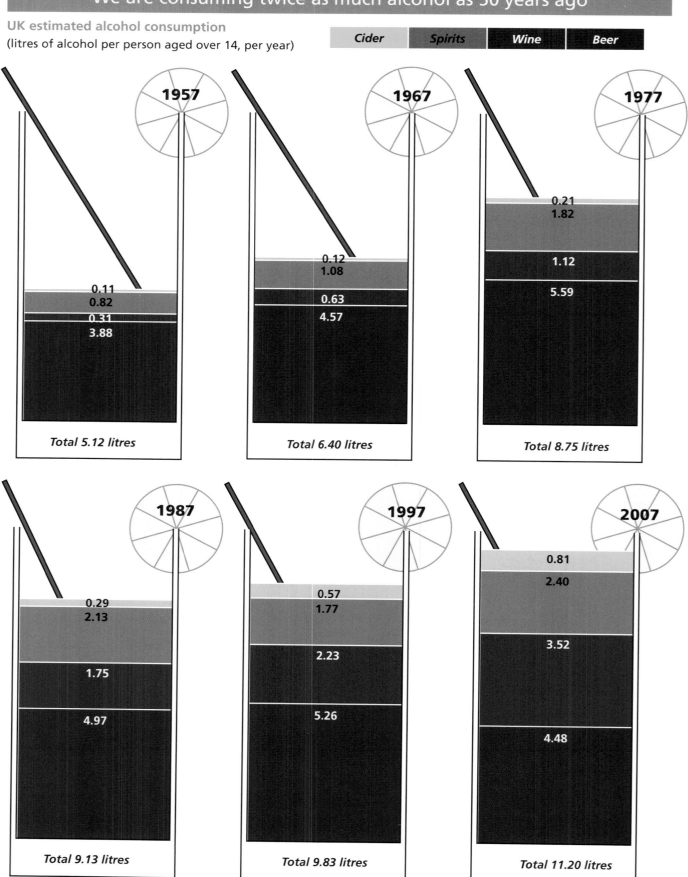

1957
0.11
0.82
0.31
3.88
Total 5.12 litres

1967
0.12
1.08
0.63
4.57
Total 6.40 litres

1977
0.21
1.82
1.12
5.59
Total 8.75 litres

1987
0.29
2.13
1.75
4.97
Total 9.13 litres

1997
0.57
1.77
2.23
5.26
Total 9.83 litres

2007
0.81
2.40
3.52
4.48
Total 11.20 litres

NB It is suggested that unrecorded consumption could add another
2 litres of pure alcohol per person for the years after 1995
Totals may not add up due to rounding

Source: Institute of Alcohol Studies 2008
http://www.ias.org.uk

Dominant drugs

Cannabis continues to dominate the world's illicit drug markets

Top 5 nations for drug usage

Countries with the highest % of population aged 15-64 who have used the drug during the past year

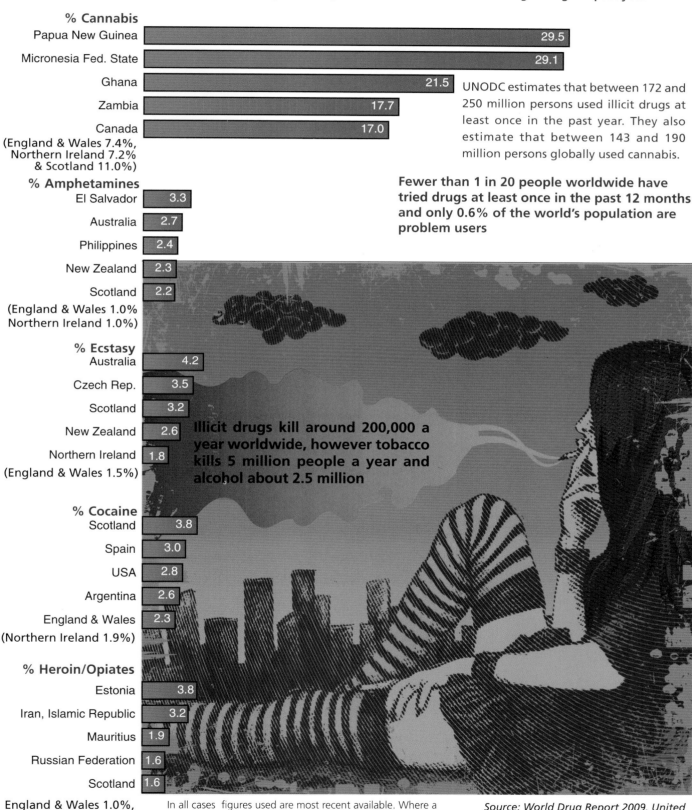

% Cannabis

Papua New Guinea	29.5
Micronesia Fed. State	29.1
Ghana	21.5
Zambia	17.7
Canada	17.0

(England & Wales 7.4%,
Northern Ireland 7.2%
& Scotland 11.0%)

% Amphetamines

El Salvador	3.3
Australia	2.7
Philippines	2.4
New Zealand	2.3
Scotland	2.2

(England & Wales 1.0%
Northern Ireland 1.0%)

% Ecstasy

Australia	4.2
Czech Rep.	3.5
Scotland	3.2
New Zealand	2.6
Northern Ireland	1.8

(England & Wales 1.5%)

% Cocaine

Scotland	3.8
Spain	3.0
USA	2.8
Argentina	2.6
England & Wales	2.3

(Northern Ireland 1.9%)

% Heroin/Opiates

Estonia	3.8
Iran, Islamic Republic	3.2
Mauritius	1.9
Russian Federation	1.6
Scotland	1.6

England & Wales 1.0%,
Northern Ireland 0.10%

UNODC estimates that between 172 and 250 million persons used illicit drugs at least once in the past year. They also estimate that between 143 and 190 million persons globally used cannabis.

Fewer than 1 in 20 people worldwide have tried drugs at least once in the past 12 months and only 0.6% of the world's population are problem users

Illicit drugs kill around 200,000 a year worldwide, however tobacco kills 5 million people a year and alcohol about 2.5 million

In all cases figures used are most recent available. Where a range is stated we have chosen the highest figure.

Source: World Drug Report 2009, United Nations Office on Drugs and Crime
http://www.unodc.org

Drug habit

Are drugs just a part of the social landscape of the UK?

A **third** of us know someone with a drug problem yet **27%** of us
think some drugs should be legalised

Who takes drugs?

27% of UK adults aged 16 +, **33%** of men and **21%**
of women – have taken illegal drugs. That's around
13 million people.

The younger the adults, the more likely they are to
have taken drugs at some point in their lives: **46%**
of the **16-34** age group, but only **5%** of people
over **55**.

18-34-year-olds, on average, first took an illegal
drug when they were **15**. People aged **45+** first
experimented with drugs at **20**. The average age was
17 with men starting slightly earlier than women.

The average age for stopping was **24**.

Do you still take drugs, even if occasionally?

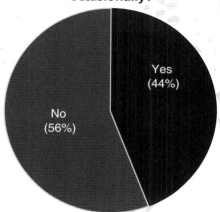

Yes (44%)

No (56%)

Base: All who have ever taken drugs

Why did you first try drugs?

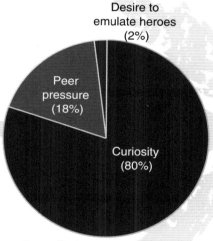

Desire to emulate heroes (2%)

Peer pressure (18%)

Curiosity (80%)

Base: All who have ever taken drugs

Why & what?

People often criticise celebrities for abusing
their position as role models by taking drugs.
However, only **2%** of people put their first
drug-taking experience down to a desire to
emulate heroes.

83% per cent of drug users began by taking
cannabis. Many people oppose the legalisation
of cannabis saying that it leads to taking harder
drugs. Although this isn't the case for most
people, a significant minority went on to try
harder drugs. **35%** went on to try cocaine, **7%**
to try heroin and **6%** to try crack.

How much and where?

44% of those who have tried drugs, still take
them, and fairly regularly too. The average
UK adult spends **£57.56** per month on
alcohol, **£21.74** per month on tobacco and
£12.17 per month on drugs - these figures
include those who do not drink alcohol,
smoke or use illegal substances. Drug users
spend an average of **£70.77** per month on
drugs and tend to spend more on tobacco
and alcohol than the rest of the population.
65% of people taking drugs do so at home
or at a friend's house, with **35%** taking them
at a pub, bar or clubs.

How regularly do you take illegal drugs?

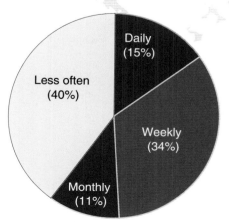

Daily (15%)

Less often (40%)

Weekly (34%)

Monthly (11%)

Base: All who still take drugs

Which of the following drugs have you taken?

Base: All who have ever taken drugs

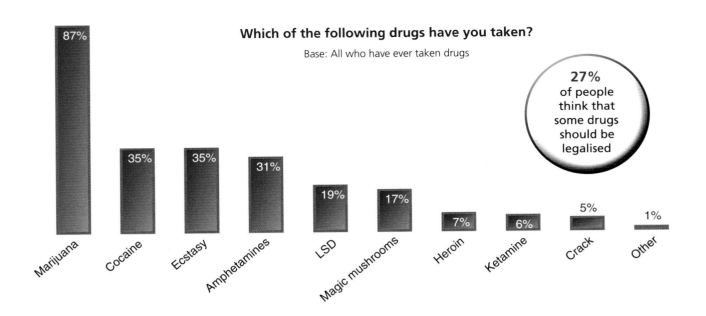

- Marijuana 87%
- Cocaine 35%
- Ecstasy 35%
- Amphetamines 31%
- LSD 19%
- Magic mushrooms 17%
- Heroin 7%
- Ketamine 6%
- Crack 5%
- Other 1%

27% of people think that some drugs should be legalised

Which drugs do you think have the highest level of risk?

Base: All respondents

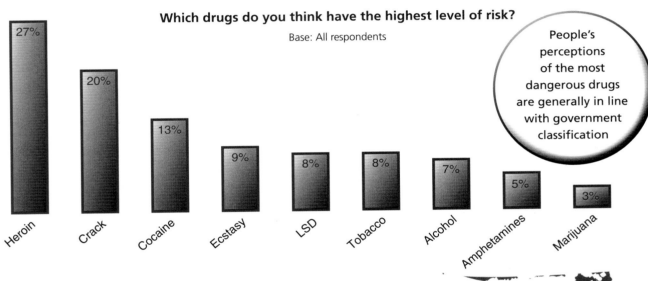

- Heroin 27%
- Crack 20%
- Cocaine 13%
- Ecstasy 9%
- LSD 8%
- Tobacco 8%
- Alcohol 7%
- Amphetamines 5%
- Marijuana 3%

People's perceptions of the most dangerous drugs are generally in line with government classification

A problem or just part of life?

Only **13%** of drug users think they have had a 'problem' with drugs themselves, but **32%** believe they have known someone who has had a serious drug problem.

8% of drug users have used crime to fund their habit. This group and the people who feel that they have had a problem with drugs are more likely to be opposed to drugs being made legal. Perhaps their personal experience has affected their view.

Just say yes on page 96 *of Essential Articles 12*
A chief constable argues that the only solution to the drugs trade is to make it legal

Base: A sample of 1,008 UK adults aged 16+ were interviewed.

Source: The Observer Drugs Poll 2008, The Observer
http://observer.guardian.co.uk/

Animals

Under threat

22% of the world's mammal species are threatened or extinct

The IUCN Red List Categories and Criteria are the world's most widely used system for gauging the extinction risk faced by species.

Each species assessed is put into one of the following categories: **Extinct, Extinct in the Wild, Critically Endangered, Endangered, Vulnerable, Near Threatened, Least Concern** and **Data Deficient**, based on population trend, population size and structure, and geographic range. Species classified as **Vulnerable, Endangered** and **Critically Endangered** are regarded as 'threatened'.

The country with by far the most threatened species is **Indonesia** with **184. Mexico** is the only other country in triple figures with **100** threatened species.

% of species in each IUCN Red List category for all mammal species, 2008

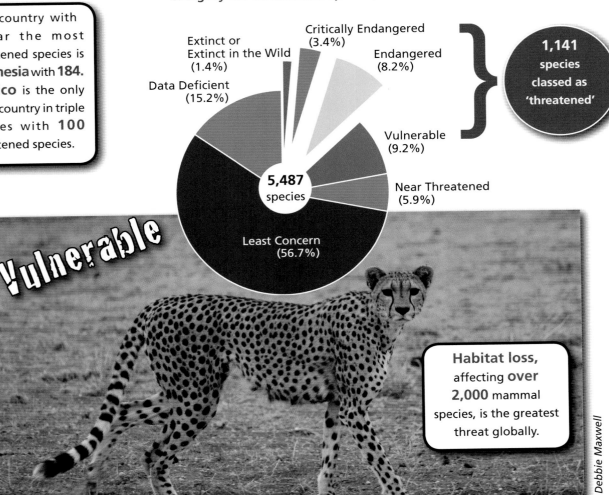

Critically Endangered (3.4%)

Extinct or Extinct in the Wild (1.4%)

Endangered (8.2%)

Data Deficient (15.2%)

1,141 species classed as 'threatened'

Vulnerable (9.2%)

5,487 species

Near Threatened (5.9%)

Least Concern (56.7%)

Vulnerable

Habitat loss, affecting **over 2,000** mammal species, is the greatest threat globally.

Photo: Debbie Maxwell

The known cheetah population is not much greater than **7,000**, and the total population is unlikely to exceed **10,000** mature individuals – this meets the Red List's criteria classing the cheetah as **Vulnerable.**

Cheetahs are considered extinct or possibly extinct in many countries. In northwest Africa the population is probably fewer than **250** mature individuals.

In Asia cheetahs are now known to exist only in Iran.

The effective world population size (percentage of the population likely to reproduce) could be **less than half** of the total population.

Southern Africa is the country with the largest estimated population – it has at least **4,500** adult cheetahs.

The number in Eastern Africa (Ethiopia, southern Sudan, Uganda, Kenya and Tanzania) is estimated at **2,572.**

Source: IUCN Red List 2008

http://www.iucnredlist.org

Shark attack

More people in the water leads to more shark attacks

**Total shark attacks worldwide, by year
(total fatalities in red)**

Year	Attacks	Fatalities
1990	36	2
1991	36	3
1992	49	6
1993	42	11
1994	60	7
1995	69	10
1996	46	3
1997	51	9
1998	51	6
1999	56	4
2000	79	11
2001	68	4
2002	62	3
2003	57	4
2004	65	7
2005	61	4
2006	62	4
2007	71	1
2008	59	4

Where?

Where in the world a shark attacks depends on both the shark population and the number of sea bathers in the area. The USA holds the highest record with 881 total shark attacks, 38 of which were fatal. However, Australia has the highest number of fatalities, 135 out of 345 attacks. In comparison, Europe has had 39 attacks, 19 of which were fatal.

Why?

Most attacks occur in near shore waters, typically inshore of a sandbar or between sandbars where sharks feed and can become trapped at low tide. Areas with steep drop-offs are also likely attack sites. Sharks congregate there because this is where they find their natural food. If people swim or do watersports in those areas, they obviously become potential food items too.

How many?

Worldwide there are probably 70-100 shark attacks each year resulting in about 5-15 deaths. The figure is an estimate because not all shark attacks are reported. Information from Third World countries is especially poor, and in some areas efforts are sometimes made to keep attacks quiet for fear of bad publicity.

In the past the death rate was much higher than today, but readily available emergency services and improved medical treatment has greatly reduced this.

*Source: Florida Museum of Natural History
http://www.flmnh.ufl.edu/*

Who is the hunter?

Most sharks and rays grow slowly, mature late, and produce few young – making them very vulnerable to overfishing

One-third of European sharks are on the IUCN Red List of Threatened Species. 7% of species in the Northeast Atlantic are classified as Critically Endangered, 7% as Endangered, and 12% as Vulnerable, primarily due to overfishing. This means 26% are threatened in the Northeast Atlantic, compared with 18% globally

Blue sharks and spurdog – the two shark species widely considered the world's most abundant in their natural state – have both been seriously overfished in European waters. Their North Atlantic populations are now considered Vulnerable and Critically Endangered, respectively.

Even the world's fastest shark, the shortfin mako, can't out-swim fishing fleets in the tropical seas it inhabits. Makos are widely valued for their high quality meat (fins and skin are also used) and are increasingly sought by vessels fishing for tuna and swordfish.

The lucrative market for shark fins – used in the luxury Asian dish of 'shark fin soup' – is thought to be increasing each year. Scientists estimate that nearly a million makos a year end up in the Hong Kong shark fin trade. Fins are often cut off sharks and the rest of the body is discarded at sea through a process known as 'finning'.

In October 2009, UK Ministers announced a decision to have a complete ban on removal of shark fins at sea. The EU banned finning at sea in 2003, but loopholes make this ineffective. UK Fisheries Ministers have decided to stop issuing permits, which allowed finning, complying with the original intention of the ban – that sharks are landed with their fins naturally attached. Spain and Portugal are now the main obstacles to an effective EU finning ban, since they have more than 250 permits between them.

Shark fins © The Shark Alliance

Giant Devil Ray © The Shark Alliance

Rays are closely related to sharks – and some species are also endangered. Sawfish (shark-like rays with long, tooth-studded snouts) are in serious danger of extinction, with the European population already wiped out.

Giant devil rays are found mainly in deep, offshore waters of the Mediterranean Sea. They produce only a single pup per litter (either every year or every two years). These rays suffer high death rate from being accidentally caught. The giant devil ray is classified as Endangered.

Source: The Shark Alliance, IUCN Red List 2008
http://www.sharkalliance.org
http://www.iucn.org

Butterfly effect

Falling butterfly numbers are an environmental warning

2008 was the poorest summer for butterfly numbers for more than 25 years.

The low breeding rate during the very bad summer of 2007, the wettest on record, had a large impact on butterfly numbers during 2008.

Heavy rain makes it hard for butterflies to survive – they can't fly in the rain and that means they can't reach the nectar they feed on.

Species causing particular concern include one of the UK's rarest butterflies, the High Brown Fritillary – there are now fewer than 50 colonies in the entire country, many of them small.

Butterflies are important as an indicator species, alerting us to underlying problems with the environment.

If butterfly numbers are falling, inevitably other wildlife is also suffering. British butterflies have been declining steadily for years and the recent wet summers have accelerated these declines.

For 12 species, 2008 was their worst year since records began in the mid 1970s.

The list includes several butterflies which were once familiar in gardens but their numbers have dwindled in recent years.

The Orange-tip and the Small Tortoiseshell have declined drastically over the last decade.

Some butterflies are rapidly becoming extinct in parts of the country

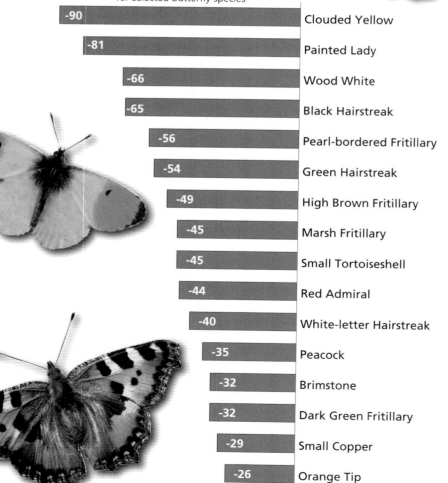

How UK numbers have fallen

% change between 2007 and 2008 for selected butterfly species

Species	% change
Clouded Yellow	-90
Painted Lady	-81
Wood White	-66
Black Hairstreak	-65
Pearl-bordered Fritillary	-56
Green Hairstreak	-54
High Brown Fritillary	-49
Marsh Fritillary	-45
Small Tortoiseshell	-45
Red Admiral	-44
White-letter Hairstreak	-40
Peacock	-35
Brimstone	-32
Dark Green Fritillary	-32
Small Copper	-29
Orange Tip	-26

Source: Centre for Ecology & Hydrology
http://www.ceh.ac.uk

Plan Bee

The bees knees

Honey bees (Apis mellifera) are the world's most important pollinators. Many crops, especially fruits, cannot develop without pollination.

Most flowering plants cannot self-pollinate, so have evolved to attract bees and other insects to do the job for them.

Been and gone

A survey of members of the British Beekeepers Association found that our bees are in continuous decline. 'Normal' losses are considered acceptable at around **7-10%**. Last winter however, **33%** of the UK's **274,000** colonies – **90,000 colonies – did not survive the winter.** Each colony contains approximately **20,000** bees.

The US has reported similar percentage losses as the UK, and losses have been reported in other countries.

What's bugging them?

No-one knows for certain what is causing the losses but theories include:

- pests (such as varroa mites), viruses, bacteria and fungi;
- pesticides, which are picked up by bees as they pollinate sprayed crops;
- genetic narrowing of the species through breeding of bees that are more docile and produce good honey yields, but are more susceptible to pests and disease;
- lack of nutrition and loss of habitats – related to urban sprawl and farming methods;
- bad weather, including spells of particularly wet weather or sudden cold spells

Similar losses of livestock in other areas of farming, such as beef or dairy, would be seen as disastrous.

Bee aware

- Of the world's **115** most important **food crops, 87 require pollination.**
- These crops provide **35% of the calories** we consume yearly and most of the vitamins, minerals and antioxidants.
- **Seven of the nine** crops that provide **at least half of vitamin C** to the human diet, require insect pollination.
- Five major fruit crops are completely reliant on insect pollination.

If we lose bees we lose these:

Apples   Asparagus
     Blackberries   Broccoli
Cabbage
     Citrus   Celery
                    Garlic   Cherries
Leeks   Mustard   Onions
     Peaches   Pears
Tangerines   Tea   Plums

Source: British Beekeepers Association;
Plan Bee, The Co-operative;
New Internationalist, Sept 2009
http://www.britishbee.org.uk/
http://www.theco-operative.coop
http://www.newint.org

Seabird shortage

More than half a million seabirds have disappeared from the UK coastline this decade

In the UK the number of breeding seabirds increased from around **4.5 million** in the late 1960s to **7 million** by the end of the 1990s but reports show that since 2000, the number of seabirds breeding around the UK has **declined by over 9%** – but in Scotland where the majority of the UK's seabirds are found, numbers have **declined by 19%**.

The cause of the decline is thought to be shortage of food – this has led to lower numbers of adults surviving from one year to the next and not enough chicks being produced and surviving to replace them.

The species that are most affected are those that feed on shoals of small fish such as sand eels which are also declining perhaps due to **over-fishing** and **increasing sea temperatures.**

Sea temperatures have been rising around the UK since the 1980s by around **0.2°C - 0.9°C per decade** which affects the amount of plankton – the floating organisms that sand eels and other small fish feed on.

There are **25** species of seabirds breeding in the UK. **12** of the 19 species monitored are in **decline.**

For example, a survey of breeding pairs of puffins carried out in summer 2008 found that numbers were down by a third to **36,500 pairs**, compared to **55,674** in the survey in 2003. Research in summer 2009 will aim to explain why puffin numbers have fallen so dramatically by using GPS technology to track their movements.

Change in the seabird population 2000-2008
(species declining)

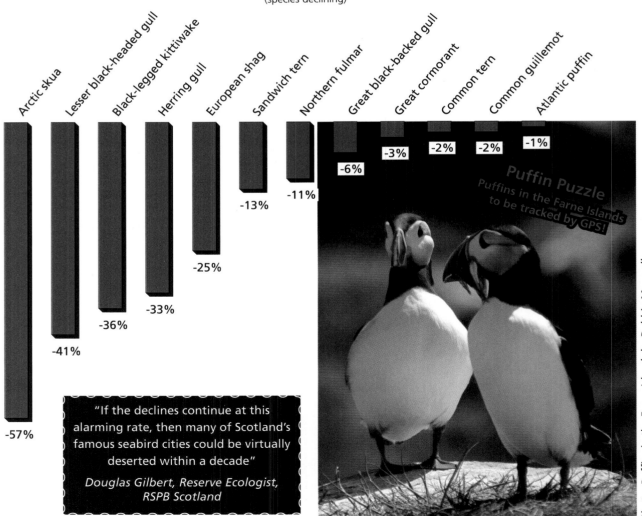

Arctic skua -57%
Lesser black-headed gull -41%
Black-legged kittiwake -36%
Herring gull -33%
European shag -25%
Sandwich tern -13%
Northern fulmar -11%
Great black-backed gull -6%
Great cormorant -3%
Common tern -2%
Common guillemot -2%
Atlantic puffin -1%

Puffin Puzzle
Puffins in the Farne Islands to be tracked by GPS!

> "If the declines continue at this alarming rate, then many of Scotland's famous seabird cities could be virtually deserted within a decade"
>
> *Douglas Gilbert, Reserve Ecologist, RSPB Scotland*

Photo: Puffins in the Farne Islands by Debbie Maxwell

Source: UK Seabirds in 2008 – JNCC © Crown copyright 2009, National Trust, RSPB

http://www.jncc.gov.uk
http://www.nationaltrust.org.uk
http://www.rspb.org.uk

Britain &
its citizens

Population change?

Baby boom

The estimated resident population of the UK was 61,383,000 in mid-2008, up by 408,000 on the previous year.

Children aged under 16 represented around one in five of the total population, around the same proportion as those of retirement age.

It is thought that for the first time in nearly a decade natural changes to the population caused by shifts in birth and death rates have overtaken immigration as the biggest factor affecting population growth.

Passing through

Over the last thirty years, the rate of re-migration from the UK (that is, return or onward migration by non-British nationals) has been about half that of immigration (3,186,200 out compared with 6,189,900 in).

However, since 1975 at least 61,000 immigrants have left the UK each year – with numbers rising steadily in the last decade to a peak of 194,000 in 2006. This is expected to rise further due to the UK recession. Emigration of immigrants is therefore a growing phenomenon.

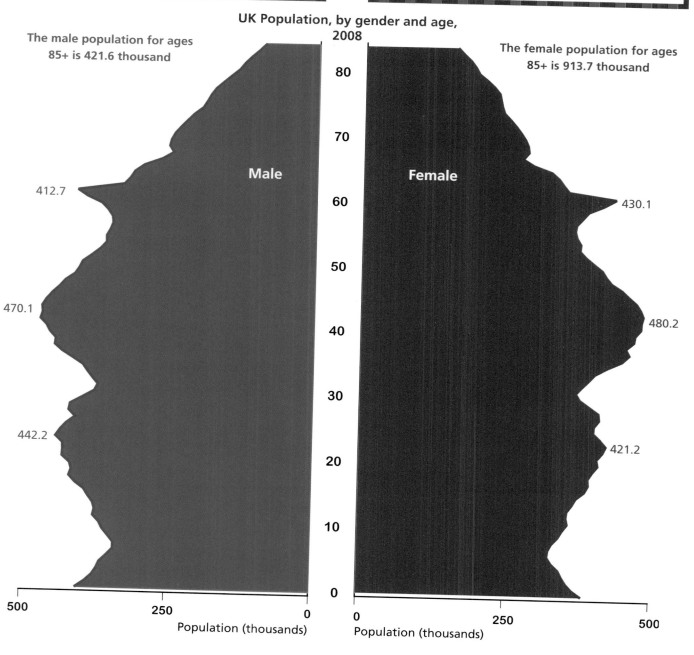

UK Population, by gender and age, 2008

The male population for ages 85+ is 421.6 thousand

The female population for ages 85+ is 913.7 thousand

Male

Female

412.7

430.1

470.1

480.2

442.2

421.2

Population (thousands)

Population (thousands)

Source: ONS; Shall we stay or shall we go?, IPPR 2009
http://www.statistics.gov.uk
http://www.ippr.org.uk/

Delaying the inevitable

Within the UK, life expectancy varies by country. England has the highest life expectancy at birth, while Scotland has the lowest

Life expectancy at birth 2005-07	Men	Women
UK	77.2	81.5
England	77.5	81.7
Wales	76.7	81.1
Northern Ireland	76.2	81.2
Scotland	74.8	79.7

Life expectancy at birth, UK

(years)

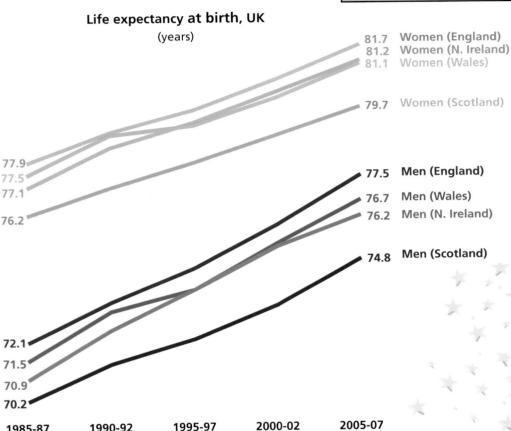

81.7 Women (England)
81.2 Women (N. Ireland)
81.1 Women (Wales)

79.7 Women (Scotland)

77.9
77.5
77.1

76.2

77.5 Men (England)

76.7 Men (Wales)
76.2 Men (N. Ireland)

74.8 Men (Scotland)

72.1
71.5
70.9
70.2

1985-87   1990-92   1995-97   2000-02   2005-07

Life expectancy **at age 65** – the number of years someone reaching 65 in 2005-07 could expect to live – is higher for England than for the other countries of the UK and also higher for women than men.

Life expectancy at age 65 2005-07	Men	Women
UK	17.2	19.9
England	17.3	20.0
Wales	16.9	19.6
Northern Ireland	16.8	19.7
Scotland	16.0	18.7

...and premature deaths from the 'big killers' have plummeted

Premature or 'early' deaths are classed as those deaths before the age of 75.

In England and Wales, **cancer** deaths have dropped from **150.8** per 100,000 people in 1993 to **114.74** in 2007

Deaths from **coronary heart disease** have dropped from **108.68** per 100,000 in 1993 to **42.31** in 2007

Deaths from **strokes** have dropped from **28.29** per 100,000 in 1993 to **13.87** in 2007

Source: ONS © Crown copyright 2008;
Compendium of Clinical and Health Indicators

http://www.statistics.gov.uk
http://www.nchod.nhs.uk/

Race relations

Families are changing Britain's racial profile

Around 85% of individuals in the period surveyed (2004-2008) described themselves as White British. The largest minority group was the Indian group with 2% of the population – Pakistanis made up 1.6%, Black Africans 1.2%, Black Caribbeans 1%, Bangladeshis 0.6% and Chinese 0.4%. From 2001 mixed ethnicity groups began to be measured with the four mixed groups making up 1.1% of the population between them.

Across generations there are indications of increases in diversity. Almost 20% of children under 16 were from minority groups, and nearly 3% of children under 16 were from one of the mixed ethnicity groups.

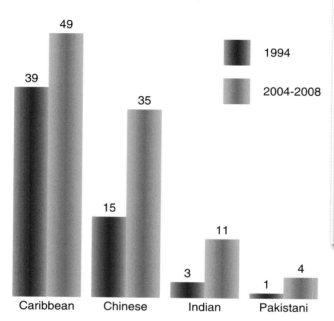

Proportion of children with one white parent, by ethnic origin of other parent, UK, %

	1994	2004-2008
Caribbean	39	49
Chinese	15	35
Indian	3	11
Pakistani	1	4

The percentage of children in minority ethnic groups who also have a white parent has risen – in 1994 39% of children with Caribbean heritage also had a white parent. This has risen to 49%

Mixed race individuals and households containing people of different racial backgrounds mean that many families have mixed or multiple heritages, ie links to different ethnicities through parents and grandparents.

The increase in mixed ethnicity families is a positive indication that barriers are being broken down between races in the UK.

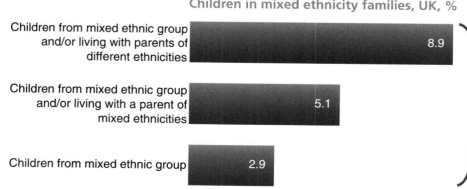

Children in mixed ethnicity families, UK, %

Children from mixed ethnic group and/or living with parents of different ethnicities	8.9
Children from mixed ethnic group and/or living with a parent of mixed ethnicities	5.1
Children from mixed ethnic group	2.9

9% of UK children live in a family with mixed or multiple heritage

While half of all Caribbean men in relationships have a partner from a different ethnic group, other groups have remained more segregated. Pakistanis and Bangladeshis, in particular, are entering mixed-race relationships at a much slower rate. It has been suggested that this could be to do with religion – both groups are predominantly Muslim – or the fact that they tend to live in more insular communities.

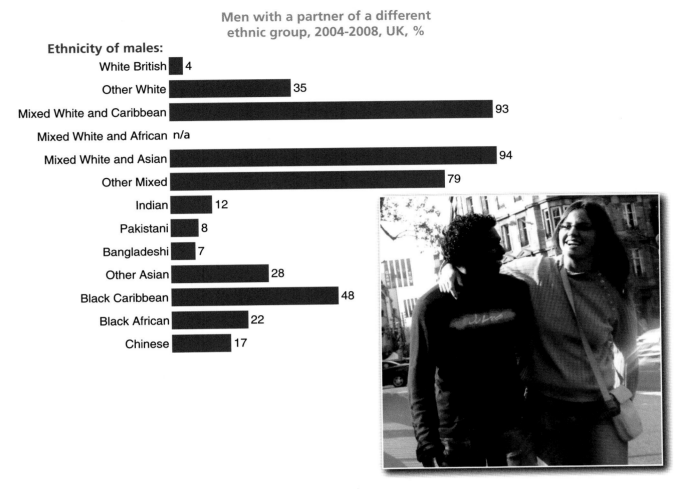

Men with a partner of a different ethnic group, 2004-2008, UK, %

Ethnicity of males:

Ethnicity	%
White British	4
Other White	35
Mixed White and Caribbean	93
Mixed White and African	n/a
Mixed White and Asian	94
Other Mixed	79
Indian	12
Pakistani	8
Bangladeshi	7
Other Asian	28
Black Caribbean	48
Black African	22
Chinese	17

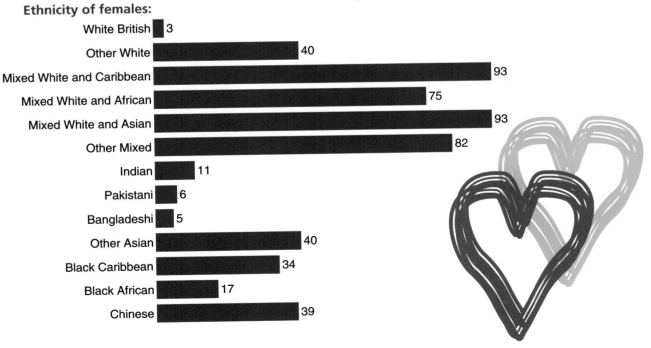

Women with a partner of a different ethnic group, UK, 2004-2008, %

Ethnicity of females:

Ethnicity	%
White British	3
Other White	40
Mixed White and Caribbean	93
Mixed White and African	75
Mixed White and Asian	93
Other Mixed	82
Indian	11
Pakistani	6
Bangladeshi	5
Other Asian	40
Black Caribbean	34
Black African	17
Chinese	39

Source: Ethnicity and Family: Institute for Social and Economic Research, 2008
http://www.equalityhumanrights.com
http://www.intermix.org.uk

Sense of belonging

Proportion of people who feel they belong strongly to their neighbourhood and to Great Britain by ethnicity, 2008-09

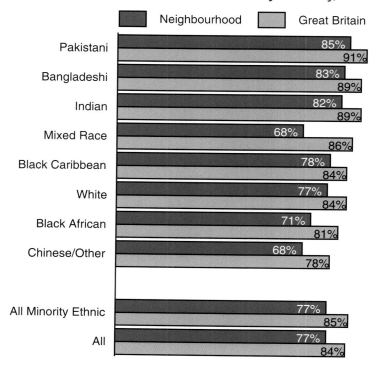

Legend: ■ Neighbourhood   ■ Great Britain

Ethnicity	Neighbourhood	Great Britain
Pakistani	85%	91%
Bangladeshi	83%	89%
Indian	82%	89%
Mixed Race	68%	86%
Black Caribbean	78%	84%
White	77%	84%
Black African	71%	81%
Chinese/Other	68%	78%
All Minority Ethnic	77%	85%
All	77%	84%

Cohesion

The fact that 84% of respondents tended to think that their local area was a place where people from different backgrounds got on well together represents an increase from 2007-08 (**82%**).

This varies by age group, for example, **91%** of those aged **75 years** and over thought their local area was cohesive compared to **80%** of those aged **25-34 years.**

Proportion of people who have mixed with people from different ethnic or religious backgrounds in the last month, 2008-09

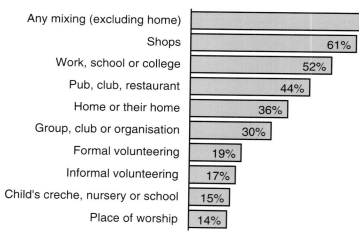

Any mixing (excluding home)	81%
Shops	61%
Work, school or college	52%
Pub, club, restaurant	44%
Home or their home	36%
Group, club or organisation	30%
Formal volunteering	19%
Informal volunteering	17%
Child's creche, nursery or school	15%
Place of worship	14%

Meaningful interaction with people from different backgrounds

In 2008-09, **81%** of people mixed socially at least once a month with people from different ethnic or religious backgrounds.

This is unchanged since 2007-08 when it was first measured. Young people were more likely than older people to mix with people from different ethnic and religious backgrounds. For example, **93%** of people aged **16-24 years** had mixed in this way compared with **50%** of people aged **75 years** and over.

Source: Citizenship survey 2008-09
http://www.communities.gov.uk

Bad manners Britain

More than half of us believe that the biggest problem in the country today is rudeness

86.2% of respondents from a survey of **2,800** adults in 2008 said that Britons are ruder now than 10 years ago. **67%** say that it is the root cause of anti-social behaviour

While driving in their own vehicle, **49.4%** of respondents admitted to shouting abuse, swearing or gesturing rudely at another road user and **17%** admitted to doing it when children were present.

More than **90%** of people believe that many parents are failing to pass on basic manners to their children. **73.8%** of people said that manners should be taught as part of the school curriculum.

GET OUT OF MY WAY YOU *!@**! IDIOTS

Only **6.8%** of people admitted to being abusive whilst travelling on public transport, however **45.5%** said they had been a victim of rude behaviour such as swearing, shouting or spitting while using public transport.

When asked where they experienced rude behaviour **53.5%** of respondents said in the street, **17.6%** said on public transport, **7.6%** said the workplace. Only **1.9%** said in the home

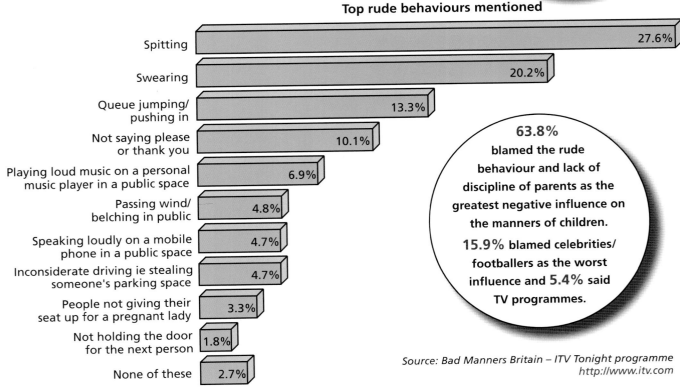

Top rude behaviours mentioned

Behaviour	%
Spitting	27.6%
Swearing	20.2%
Queue jumping/ pushing in	13.3%
Not saying please or thank you	10.1%
Playing loud music on a personal music player in a public space	6.9%
Passing wind/ belching in public	4.8%
Speaking loudly on a mobile phone in a public space	4.7%
Inconsiderate driving ie stealing someone's parking space	4.7%
People not giving their seat up for a pregnant lady	3.3%
Not holding the door for the next person	1.8%
None of these	2.7%

63.8% blamed the rude behaviour and lack of discipline of parents as the greatest negative influence on the manners of children. **15.9%** blamed celebrities/ footballers as the worst influence and **5.4%** said TV programmes.

Source: Bad Manners Britain – ITV Tonight programme
http://www.itv.com

Moving on up

What is social class?
Social Class is often grouped as follows:

People are graded according to economic and status differences. Some people are wealthier than others and some are given greater importance than others

AB: Ranging from the **upper class** (the ruling class and/ or the rich) to the **upper middle class** (managers and professionals on high pay)

C1/C2: Ranging from **lower middle class** (routine white-collar workers in offices/banks etc) to the **'new' working class** (better-paid manual workers, those who are self-employed)

DE: Ranging from **'traditional' working class** (less skilled, less well-paid manual workers) to the **underclass** (the poor and unemployed)

What do we think about social class and social mobility?
A recent survey of over 2,000 people in Britain asked about perceptions of social class and the opportunities within society to improve. On average half of us believe that opportunities for social mobility are 'about right', though there is a difference between different social classes.

To what extent do you agree/disagree that people have equal opportunities to get ahead?

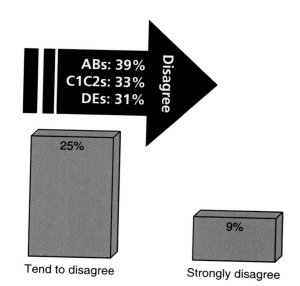

Agree
ABs: 51%
C1C2s: 57%
DEs: 50%

Disagree
ABs: 39%
C1C2s: 33%
DEs: 31%

- Strongly agree: 11%
- Tend to agree: 42%
- Tend to disagree: 25%
- Strongly disagree: 9%

Note: 12% neither agreed nor disagreed or didn't know.

Opportunity v Income

While there is a difference among social classes about equal opportunities to get ahead, nearly **7 out of 10** people believe that parents' income plays too big a part in children's life chances. **74%** of people believe that differences in income in Britain are too large.

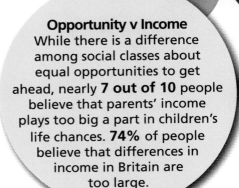

Personal social mobility

The way people view their own wealth now, depends on how wealthy they thought their family was when they were growing up. People were asked "Out of every 100 households, how many households did you think were wealthier than your own families when you were growing up?" and then asked, 'How many do you think are wealthier now?" The table shows the results.

- The main diagonal shows the percentage of people who have experienced class stability. They occupy the same income position and, in effect, social class as they did when they were growing up. For example, 8% believe that approx 51-75 households were wealthier than their own when they were growing up, and the same number are wealthier now they are adults.

- Those in grey below the main diagonal have experienced **downward social mobility**. For example 7% thought only 1-25 households were wealthier than their own when they were growing up, but believe 26-50 households are wealthier than them now.

- Those in blue have experienced **upward social mobility**. For example 12% felt that 51-75 households were wealthier than their families when growing up, but only 26-50 are now.

How many households out of 100 do you think were wealthier than your own WHEN GROWING UP?

		Number of households			
		1-25	**26-50**	**51-75**	**76-100**
Number of households	**1-25**	7%	5%	2%	2%
	26-50	7%	26%	12%	6%
	51-75	2%	9%	8%	5%
	76-100	1%	4%	2%	5%

(Left axis: How many households out of 100 do you think are wealthier than your own NOW?)

(Right axis: Upward social mobility)

Downward social mobility

Source: Social Mobility, The Sutton Trust, 2008

http://www.suttontrust.com

Feeling good?

How do you measure well-being?

The New Economic Forum is 'an independent think-and-do tank' dedicated to challenging current economic thinking and to 'put people and the planet first'. It argues that measures of well-being are needed 'because the economic indicators which governments currently rely on tell us little about the relative success or failure of countries in supporting a good life for their citizens.'

Their working model is built on two headline measures: personal well-being and social well-being, reflecting crucial aspects of how people experience their lives

Personal well-being measures people's experiences of their positive and **negative** emotions, **satisfaction, vitality, resilience & self-esteem** and sense of **positive functioning** in the world.

Social well-being measures people's experiences of supportive relationships and sense of **trust & belonging** with others. The survey results were converted so that they can be easily compared; each indicator is scored out of 10, and 5 is always the European average.

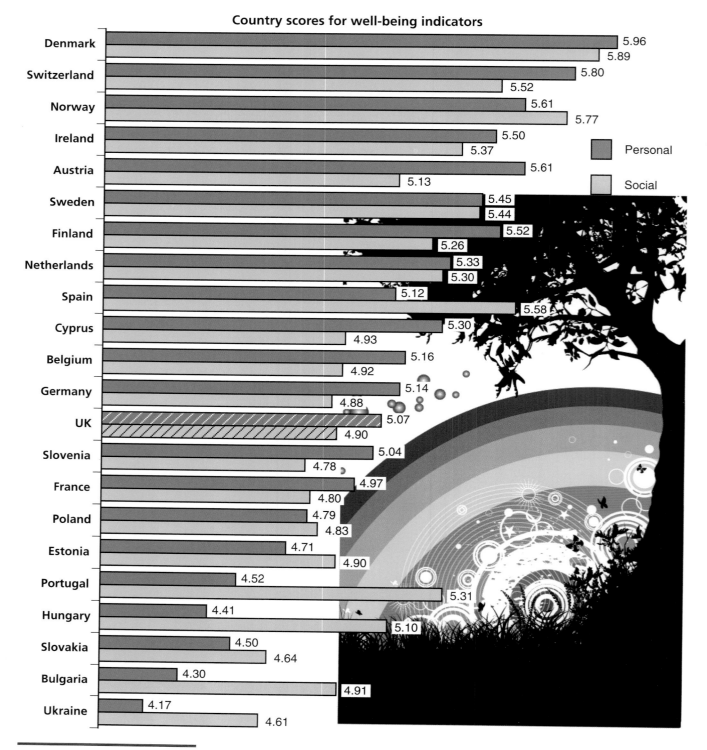

Country scores for well-being indicators

Country	Personal	Social
Denmark	5.96	5.89
Switzerland	5.80	5.52
Norway	5.61	5.77
Ireland	5.50	5.37
Austria	5.61	5.13
Sweden	5.45	5.44
Finland	5.52	5.26
Netherlands	5.33	5.30
Spain	5.12	5.58
Cyprus	5.30	4.93
Belgium	5.16	4.92
Germany	5.14	4.88
UK	5.07	4.90
Slovenia	5.04	4.78
France	4.97	4.80
Poland	4.79	4.83
Estonia	4.71	4.90
Portugal	4.52	5.31
Hungary	4.41	5.10
Slovakia	4.50	4.64
Bulgaria	4.30	4.91
Ukraine	4.17	4.61

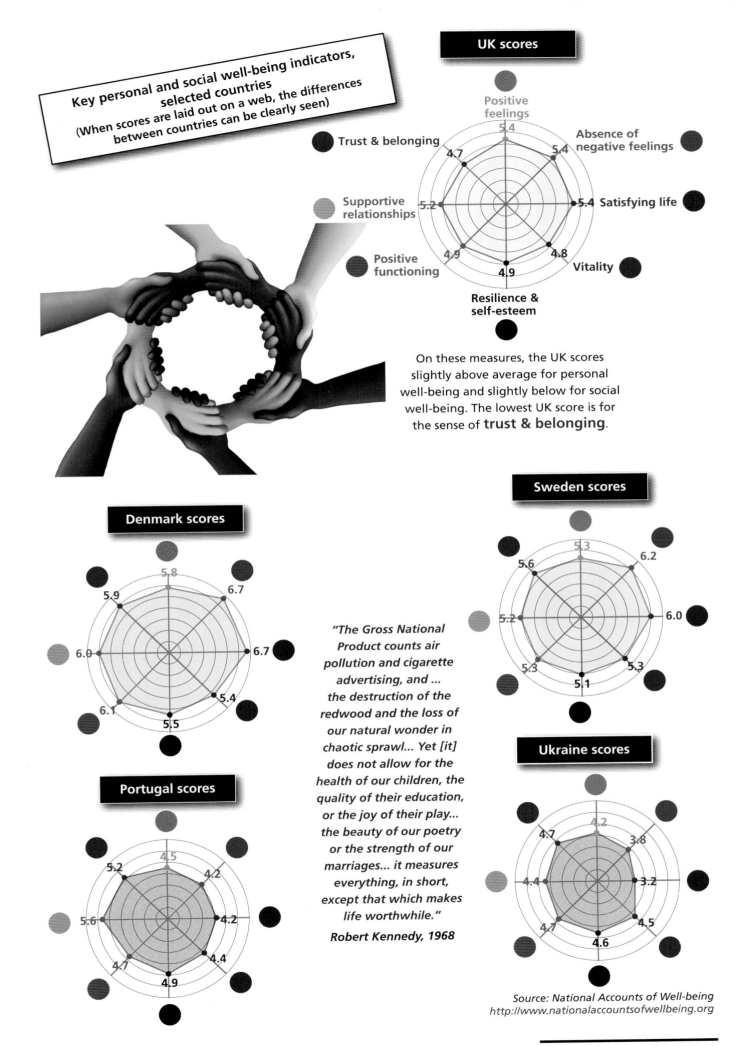

Key personal and social well-being indicators, selected countries
(When scores are laid out on a web, the differences between countries can be clearly seen)

UK scores

- Positive feelings — 5.4
- Absence of negative feelings — 5.4
- Satisfying life — 5.4
- Vitality — 4.8
- Resilience & self-esteem — 4.9
- Positive functioning — 4.9
- Supportive relationships — 5.2
- Trust & belonging — 4.7

On these measures, the UK scores slightly above average for personal well-being and slightly below for social well-being. The lowest UK score is for the sense of **trust & belonging**.

Denmark scores

- 5.8
- 6.7
- 6.7
- 5.4
- 5.5
- 6.1
- 6.0
- 5.9

Portugal scores

- 4.5
- 4.2
- 4.2
- 4.4
- 4.9
- 4.7
- 5.6
- 5.2

Sweden scores

- 5.3
- 6.2
- 6.0
- 5.3
- 5.1
- 5.3
- 5.2
- 5.6

Ukraine scores

- 4.2
- 3.8
- 3.2
- 4.5
- 4.6
- 4.7
- 4.4
- 4.7

"The Gross National Product counts air pollution and cigarette advertising, and ... the destruction of the redwood and the loss of our natural wonder in chaotic sprawl... Yet [it] does not allow for the health of our children, the quality of their education, or the joy of their play... the beauty of our poetry or the strength of our marriages... it measures everything, in short, except that which makes life worthwhile."
Robert Kennedy, 1968

Source: National Accounts of Well-being
http://www.nationalaccountsofwellbeing.org

A life worth living?

The Prince's Trust YouGov Youth Index is the first large-scale study of its kind, investigating how young people feel about the state of their lives today and how confident they are about their future.

While the majority of young people are relatively content, there is a significant core of young people for whom life has little or no purpose – with those not in education, employment or training (NEET) most likely to feel this way.

■ All young people **▢ NEETs**

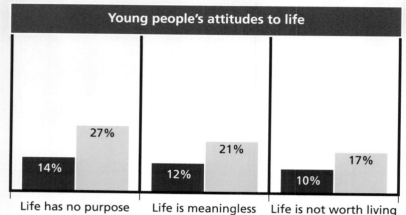

Young people's attitudes to life

	Life has no purpose	Life is meaningless	Life is not worth living
All young people	14%	12%	10%
NEETs	27%	21%	17%

The survey asked young people specifically about their emotions – a clear majority (71%) were often or always happy.

However, a significant group appear to be regularly stressed, depressed and/or anxious. Again, those young people who are NEET are more likely to feel this way more of the time.

Young people's emotions

% often or always

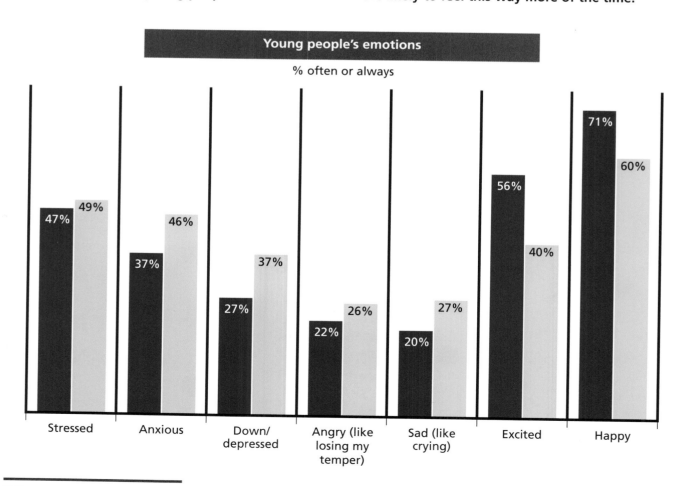

	Stressed	Anxious	Down/ depressed	Angry (like losing my temper)	Sad (like crying)	Excited	Happy
All young people	47%	37%	27%	22%	20%	56%	71%
NEETs	49%	46%	37%	26%	27%	40%	60%

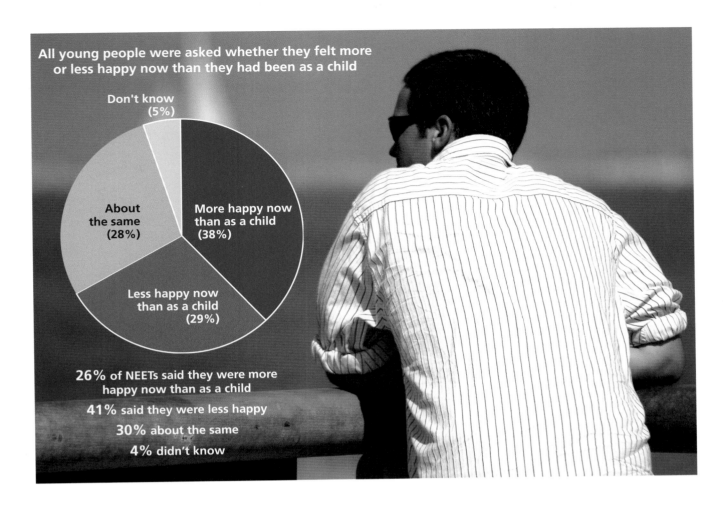

All young people were asked whether they felt more or less happy now than they had been as a child

- Don't know (5%)
- About the same (28%)
- More happy now than as a child (38%)
- Less happy now than as a child (29%)

26% of NEETs said they were more happy now than as a child

41% said they were less happy

30% about the same

4% didn't know

Young people were asked which two areas of life they considered to be most important to their overall wellbeing

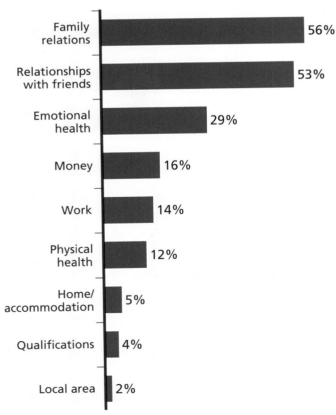

- Family relations — 56%
- Relationships with friends — 53%
- Emotional health — 29%
- Money — 16%
- Work — 14%
- Physical health — 12%
- Home/accommodation — 5%
- Qualifications — 4%
- Local area — 2%

Those that were unhappy with their emotional health were asked why this was the case. Some of the main responses were:

73% feel stressed, anxious, depressed or in a bad mood

64% feel low from time to time for no particular reason

43% don't feel like they've got anything to look forward to

40% don't have anyone to talk to about their problems

28% said they don't have enough support in life in general

Of those that were unhappy in their local community:

62% said there is no sense of community

54% don't feel safe walking around at night

51% said there is nothing to do in the area

Base: 2,004 16-25 year-olds, Great Britain

Respondents could choose more than one answer so percentages do not add up to 100%

Source: Hold your head up, The Prince's Trust YouGov Youth Index 2009
http://www.princes-trust.org.uk/wellbeing

Olympic cheer

While all age groups back the games coming to London, young adults emerge as the cheerleaders for the 2012 Olympics

A random sample of 1,002 adults aged 18+ were interviewed when Britain had just triumphed in the swimming, cycling, rowing and sailing in the 2008 Beijing Olympics

Base: All respondents
Figures may not add up to 100% due to rounding

Do you think the Olympic games will be good or bad for Britain?
(all respondents)

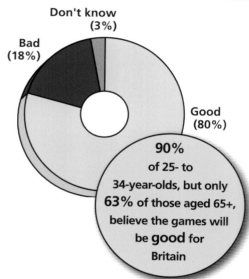

Don't know (3%)
Bad (18%)
Good (80%)

90% of 25- to 34-year-olds, but only **63%** of those aged 65+, believe the games will be **good** for Britain

Are you pleased that the Olympic games will be taking place in London?
(all respondents)

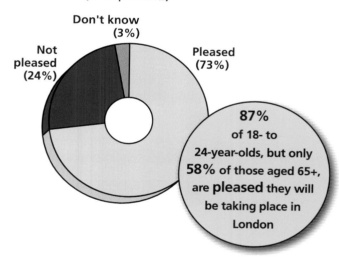

Don't know (3%)
Not pleased (24%)
Pleased (73%)

87% of 18- to 24-year-olds, but only **58%** of those aged 65+, are **pleased** they will be taking place in London

Do you think the London Olympics are likely to be more or less successful than Beijing?
(all respondents)

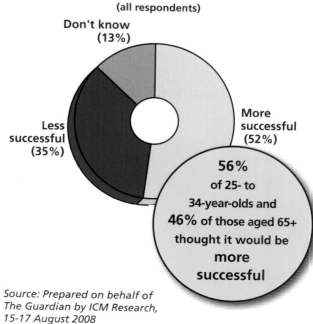

Don't know (13%)
Less successful (35%)
More successful (52%)

56% of 25- to 34-year-olds and **46%** of those aged 65+ thought it would be **more successful**

Would you support or oppose extra taxpayers' money being used by the government to help Britain's best athletes prepare for the 2012 Olympics?
(all respondents)

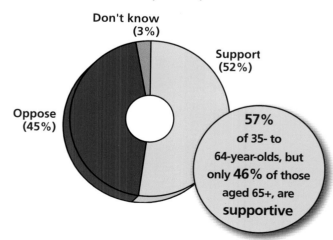

Don't know (3%)
Support (52%)
Oppose (45%)

57% of 35- to 64-year-olds, but only **46%** of those aged 65+, are **supportive**

Source: Prepared on behalf of The Guardian by ICM Research, 15-17 August 2008

http://www.icmresearch.co.uk/media-centre-polls.php

The place to be

PlaceIndex scores **60** of Britain's major cities, providing them with the opportunity to see how they are perceived by the general public and how far this perception is from reality.

Respondents were asked to choose, *for example*, which cities they felt had a good atmosphere and which had a bad atmosphere – the proportion who said bad was then subtracted from the proportion who said good to give an index score.

The cities were ranked on the following **11 key indicators:**

- atmosphere
- cultural experience
- friendliness/helpfulness of locals
- ease of getting around
- variety of shops
- quality restaurants
- the 'buzz' that a city generates
- whether the city is considered a safe investment
- whether it is considered expensive
- whether it is considered safe
- whether people would recommend the city to others

All 11 indicators combine to form an overall desirability score.

Rank	MOST desirable cities	Index Score
1	Edinburgh	32
2	York	31
3	London	23.1
4	Cambridge	22.4
5	Bath	22.2
6	Oxford	21.5
7	Liverpool	17.3
8	Chester	17.2
9	Manchester	17
10	Newcastle upon Tyne	16.4

EDINBURGH ranks as safe to visit, easy to get around and the local people are helpful and friendly

As well as its entertainment and leisure offerings, it is also considered a city worth investing in

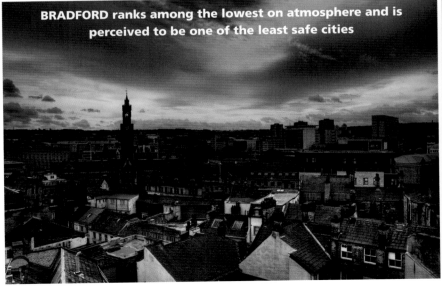

BRADFORD ranks among the lowest on atmosphere and is perceived to be one of the least safe cities

Rank	LEAST desirable cities	Index Score
51	Newport	-1.4
52	Leicester	-1.6
53	Wakefield	-1.6
54	Medwary Towns	-2.8
55	Preston	-2.9
56	Sunderland	-3.9
57	Hull	-4.2
58	Wolverhampton	-6.5
59	Salford	-7.7
60	Bradford	-10.1

Base: interviews with a representative sample of 10,000 respondents in July 2009

Source: YouGov – PlaceIndex
http://www.yougov.com

Education

Costly lesson

The UK spends less per student than many other developed countries

Annual expenditure per student, (US dollars)

Country	Secondary education	Primary education
Luxembourg	18,845	14,079
Switzerland	12,861	8,469
Norway	10,995	9,001
United States	10,390	9,156
Austria	9,751	8,259
Denmark	9,407	8,513
France	8,927	5,365
Greece	8,423	5,146
Iceland	8,411	9,254
Australia	8,408	5,992
Sweden	8,198	7,532
Japan	7,908	6,744
Netherlands	7,741	6,266
Belgium	7,731	6,648
Italy	7,648	6,835
Germany	7,636	5,014
Ireland	7,500	5,732
Finland	7,324	5,557
Spain	7,211	5,502
UK	7,167	6,361
Korea	6,645	4,691
Portugal	6,473	4,871
New Zealand	6,278	4,780
Czech Republic	4,847	2,812
Hungary	3,806	4,438
Poland	3,055	3,312
Slovak Republic	2,716	2,806
Mexico	2,180	1,913

The amount per student is calculated by dividing each country's expenditure on each level of education by the number of full-time students.

The OECD groups 30 member countries sharing a commitment to democratic government and the market economy to work together to address the economic, social and governance challenges of globalisation as well as to exploit its opportunities.

Figures are latest available, 2005 onwards. Figures not available for Canada and Turkey

Source: Education at a Glance 2008, OECD
http://www.oecd.org

Good sport

PE and sport play an important role in school life...

... but are youngsters doing enough?

The average number of sports provided by schools during 2007/08 was **17.5** with football, dance, gymnastics, athletics and cricket the most widely available and provided by **90%** of schools.

A Public Service Agreement target (PSA) was set in 2004 – the percentage of school children in England who spent a minimum of **2 hours** each week on high quality PE and school sport within and beyond the curriculum should be **85% by 2008.**

21,631 schools in the School Sport Partnership Programme were surveyed – the results were used to measure progress towards the PSA target. The survey found that **90%** of students in partnership schools participated in at least **2 hours** of high quality PE and out of hours school sport in a typical week – **exceeding** the PSA target by **5%.**

But this level of participation falls short of other countries eg in Queensland, **Australia,** students have between **3** and **4 hours** each week of PE as part of their curriculum.

Percentage of pupils who participated in at least two hours of high quality PE and out of hours school sport in a typical week, 2007/08

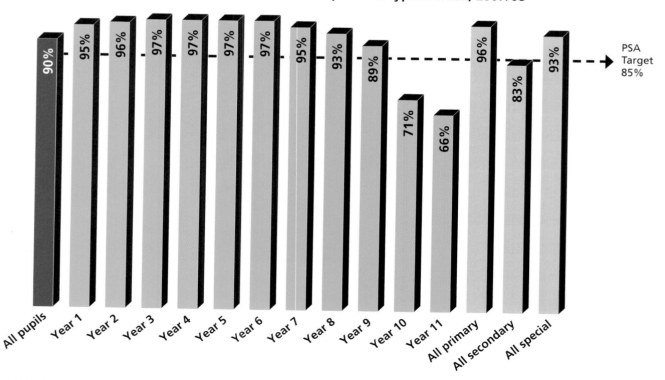

All pupils	Year 1	Year 2	Year 3	Year 4	Year 5	Year 6	Year 7	Year 8	Year 9	Year 10	Year 11	All primary	All secondary	All special
90%	95%	96%	97%	97%	97%	97%	95%	93%	89%	71%	66%	96%	83%	93%

PSA Target 85%

Total curriculum time that all pupils in each year group spend taking part in PE in a typical week

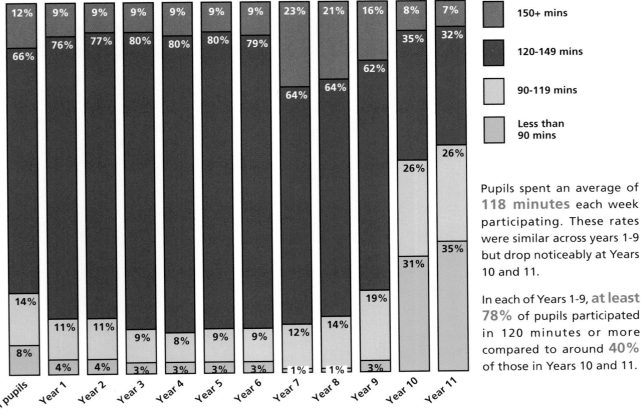

Legend:
- 150+ mins
- 120-149 mins
- 90-119 mins
- Less than 90 mins

	All pupils	Year 1	Year 2	Year 3	Year 4	Year 5	Year 6	Year 7	Year 8	Year 9	Year 10	Year 11
150+ mins	12%	9%	9%	9%	9%	9%	9%	23%	21%	16%	8%	7%
120-149 mins	66%	76%	77%	80%	80%	80%	79%	64%	64%	62%	35%	32%
90-119 mins	14%	11%	11%	9%	8%	9%	9%	12%	14%	19%	26%	26%
Less than 90 mins	8%	4%	4%	3%	3%	3%	3%	1%	1%	3%	31%	35%

Figures may not add up to 100% due to rounding

Pupils spent an average of **118 minutes** each week participating. These rates were similar across years 1-9 but drop noticeably at Years 10 and 11.

In each of Years 1-9, **at least 78%** of pupils participated in 120 minutes or more compared to around **40%** of those in Years 10 and 11.

Pupils achieving 2 hours of PE/ school sport target, 2007/08

90%

12%	'Top-up' out of hours school sport
78%	Curriculum time

Overall **12%** of pupils achieve their two hours of PE and school sport through a 'top up' of out of hours school sport including lunch time or break time activities, rather than through curriculum PE.

In Years 1-9 the two hour target is mainly achieved through curriculum time alone. However, for Years 10 and 11, there is a much greater emphasis on out of hours school sport. Even so, a much smaller proportion of pupils in these year groups achieve the two hour target.

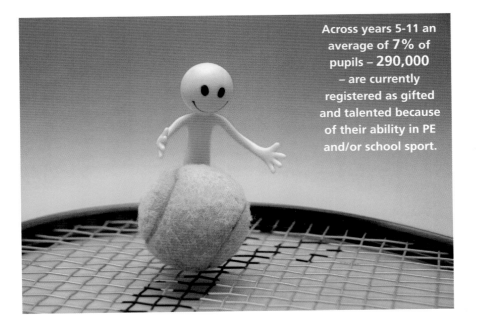

Across years 5-11 an average of **7%** of pupils – **290,000** – are currently registered as gifted and talented because of their ability in PE and/or school sport.

The Government has set a new target of five hours of PE and school sport for all young people by 2012

Source: Department for Children, Schools and Families – School Sport Survey 2007/08 © Crown copyright 2008, Ofsted

http://www.dcsf.gov.uk
http://www.ofsted.gov.uk

Lost for words

The number of students taking languages is in decline

In September 2004, learning a language stopped being a compulsory part of the curriculum for pupils in Key Stage 4 in England and Wales. Even prior to that only **80%** got as far as taking the GCSE and the take-up had been going down since 2000.

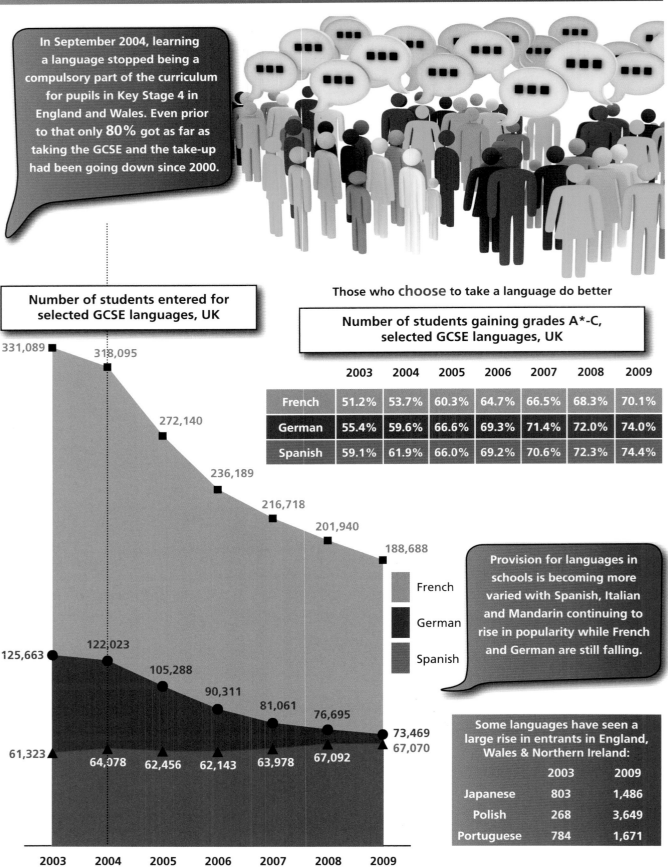

Number of students entered for selected GCSE languages, UK

French
German
Spanish

331,089
318,095
272,140
236,189
216,718
201,940
188,688

125,663
122,023
105,288
90,311
81,061
76,695
73,469
67,070

61,323
64,078
62,456
62,143
63,978
67,092

2003 2004 2005 2006 2007 2008 2009

Those who **choose** to take a language do better

Number of students gaining grades A*-C, selected GCSE languages, UK

	2003	2004	2005	2006	2007	2008	2009
French	51.2%	53.7%	60.3%	64.7%	66.5%	68.3%	70.1%
German	55.4%	59.6%	66.6%	69.3%	71.4%	72.0%	74.0%
Spanish	59.1%	61.9%	66.0%	69.2%	70.6%	72.3%	74.4%

Provision for languages in schools is becoming more varied with Spanish, Italian and Mandarin continuing to rise in popularity while French and German are still falling.

Some languages have seen a large rise in entrants in England, Wales & Northern Ireland:

	2003	2009
Japanese	803	1,486
Polish	268	3,649
Portuguese	784	1,671

Source: Joint Council for Qualifications, CiLT – The National Centre for Languages
http://www.jcq.org.uk/national_results/gcses/
http://www.cilt.org.uk

Uni-fund

Over half of students receive financial support from their parents to help them through their studies

Keeping it in the family...

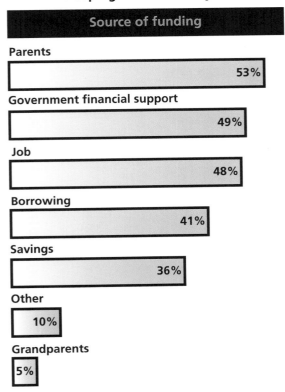

Source of funding	
Parents	53%
Government financial support	49%
Job	48%
Borrowing	41%
Savings	36%
Other	10%
Grandparents	5%

Students still rely on their parents even when they leave home to go to college or university.

Parents are still key contributors to students, even with the additional funding that is available to them.

Scottish students' parents are the most generous...

Regional breakdown of parental funding

Region	%
Scotland	60%
Wales	56%
UK	53%
Northern Ireland	38%
London	56%
North East	55%
South East	54%
South West	52%
Yorkshire & Humberside	52%
West Midlands	51%
East Midlands	51%
North West	50%
Eastern	44%

Parents provide more funding in their child's third year of study...

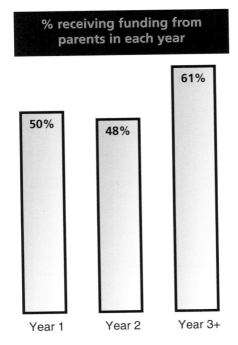

% receiving funding from parents in each year

Year 1	Year 2	Year 3+
50%	48%	61%

Base: 60,000 panelists on Opinionpanel's Student Panel, May 2008

Source: HBOS plc, 2008
http://www.hbosplc.com

University class

Background plays a large part in deciding about higher education

Class act

Based on a survey of 2,387 11-16 year olds in England and Wales, **73%** said they're likely to go into Higher Education. While **26%** of young people from households with two working parents were 'highly likely' to go into higher education, this dropped to **15%** of those from households where no parents worked.

Those who said they were unlikely to go into Higher Education were asked why

Reason	%
I prefer to do something practical rather than study from books	52%
I want to start earning money as soon as possible	50%
I can get a well-paid job without a degree	30%
I do not enjoy learning	25%
I do not need a degree to do the job(s) I am considering	25%
I'm not clever enough	22%
I don't like the idea of it	22%
I won't get good enough exam results	20%
I don't know enough about it	16%
I'm worried about getting into debt as a student	13%
People like me are not expected to go to university	9%
My family can't afford to pay for me as a student	7%
Most of my friends are not planning on going to university	7%
My parents did not go to university	6%
My family want me to start earning money as soon as possible	6%
Someone from a university talked to me about higher education and it put me off	6%
My teachers are encouraging me to do something else	4%
Other/don't know/ not stated	18%

A young person's ambitions are shaped by those around them – family, friends, teachers and other role models, as well as the local environment and the school or college they attend.

What shapes our dreams? And why?

Exam grades and intelligence are not at the top of the list of reasons why young people choose not to go to university.

When teachers were asked why bright students often don't go to university, they said that the main reason was the desire to enter employment, followed by a lack of interest in academic study.

Some students take negative feelings – dislike of formal education and a sense of failure – and turn them into a positive: a desire to get a job.

Some young people are not aware that higher education can lead to higher earnings in the long term. Those from poorer families may also not be in a position to give up several years of immediate earnings in order to study.

What about the parents?

Parents and carers have perhaps the biggest influence on young people's decisions about Higher Education. Parents who were highly educated and from higher social groups were much more likely to believe that their own children would go on to gain a degree and a graduate level job.

Percentage of parents who believe their child will attain a degree

Average

All — **23%**

> Students from manual and unskilled parental backgrounds are more likely to want to leave education and find employment.

By Social Class

ABs — **34%**

C1/C2s — **21%**

DEs — **14%**

Social Class definitions:

AB	Upper middle/middle class
C1/C2	Lower middle/skilled working class
DE	Working class/those on lowest level of subsistence

> Parents from D/E groups were a lot more likely than A/Bs to describe their time at school as a negative experience.

By own qualification level

Degree — **35%**

A level — **30%**

GCSE — **10%**

No formal qualifications — **19%**

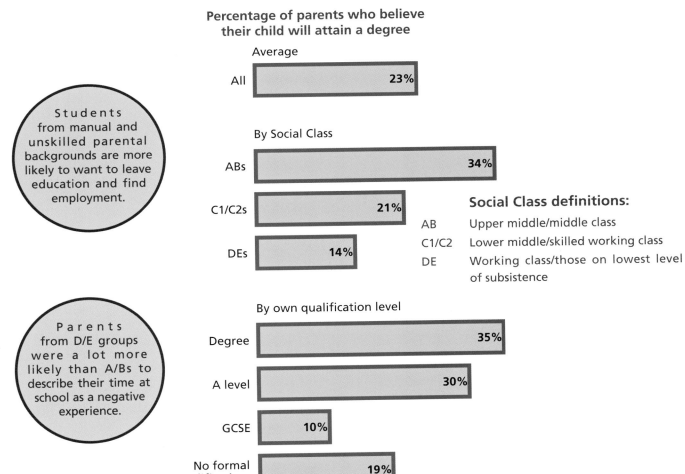

Source: *Increasing Higher Education participation amongst disadvantaged young people and schools in poor communities, The Sutton Trust 2008*
http://www.suttontrust.com

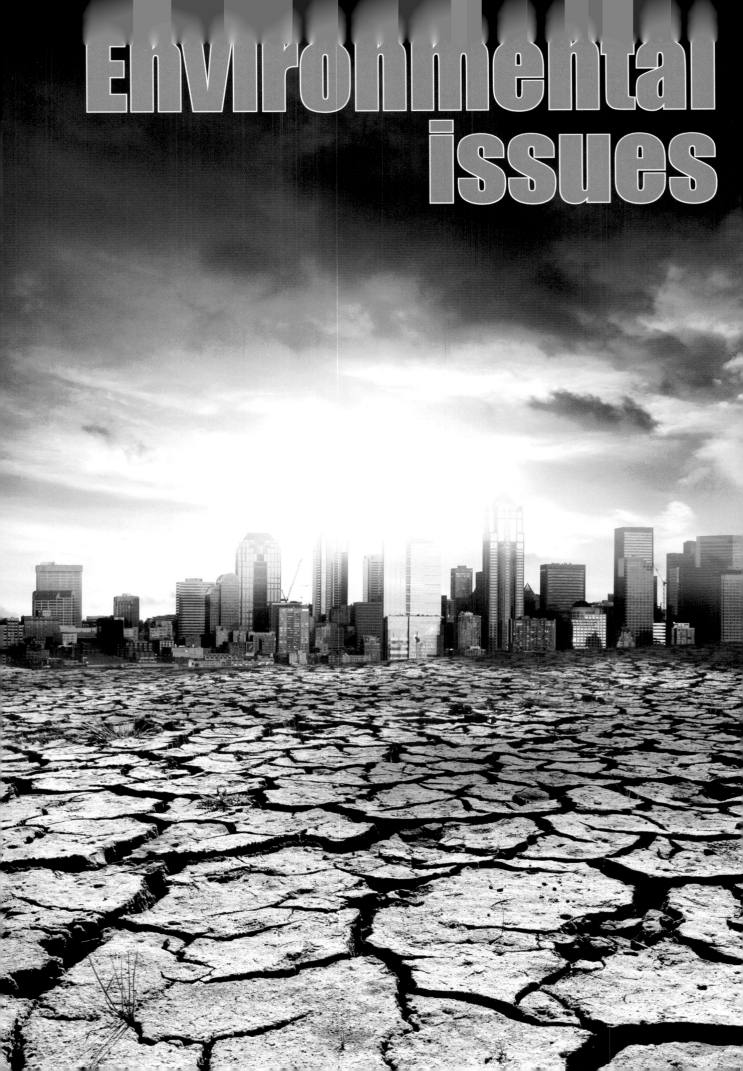

Environmental issues

Rainforest risk

We are losing great natural treasures just as we are beginning to understand their value

Why does deforestation matter?

- Nearly half of the world's species of plants, animals and micro-organisms will be destroyed or severely threatened over the next 25 years due to destruction of the rainforests –that's about **137** plant, animal and insect species every single day
- Currently, **121** prescription drugs sold worldwide come from plant-derived sources – **25%** of our medicines are derived from rainforest ingredients – we risk losing undiscovered medicines when we destroy forests
- Rainforests support over **1 billion** of the world's poorest people
- Forests hold the largest stored amount of carbon on earth. Deforestation is estimated to be responsible for **18%** of greenhouse gas emissions and this will worsen as more forests are destroyed

Rainforests once covered **14%** of the earth's land surface; now they cover a mere **6%** and could be gone in less than **40 years**.

Why is it happening?

Forests are destroyed or degraded by activities such as logging and conversion to agricultural land – especially cattle farming.
If, as expected, the world's average temperature rises by **2°C** (compared to before industrialisation) then there will be less rainfall in the jungle and fewer saplings will mature as older trees die. Fewer trees will mean less evaporation, so less rainfall – the process will feed on itself.

The example of the Amazon

The Amazon is the world's largest river basin and the source of **one-fifth** of all free-flowing fresh water on Earth. It discharges around **40,000** gallons of water into the Atlantic Ocean every second.

Its rain forests are the planet's largest and most luxuriant, and home to - amazingly - one in ten known species on Earth.

The Amazon rainforest contains vast stores of carbon

It contains nearly **40,000** plant and tree species, the world's richest diversity of birds, freshwater fish and butterflies – its thousands of different trees are home to more species of primates than anywhere else on earth.

More than **350** indigenous and ethnic groups have lived in the Amazon for thousands of years.

According to Greenpeace, around 80% of the area deforested in Brazil is now cattle pasture – using more resources, creating more greenhouse gases and taking land from tribal groups.

http://www.worldwildlife.org
http://www.greenpeace.org.ukl

Source: WWF, Greenpeace

A silent crisis –

We are already feeling the effects of climate change – but worse will follow

Human activities, in particular greenhouse gas emissions, are recognised as the main cause of climate change. We are beginning to see the effects of this change all around the globe on food, health, poverty, water, human displacement, and security.

The Global Humanitarian Forum estimates that every year climate change leaves **over 300,000** people dead, **325 million** people seriously affected, and economic losses of **US$125 billion. 4 billion** people are vulnerable, and **500 million** people are at extreme risk because of it.

THE IMPACT OF CLIMATE CHANGE IS ACCELERATING

Thousands of deaths

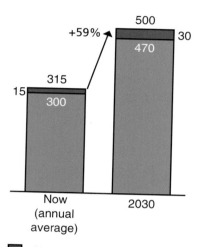

Millions affected

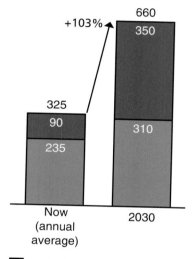

- Weather-related disasters
- Gradual environmental degradation

TO UNDERSTAND THESE NUMBERS, WE CAN COMPARE THEM WITH OTHER GLOBAL DISASTERS

Thousands of deaths, annual average 2004-08

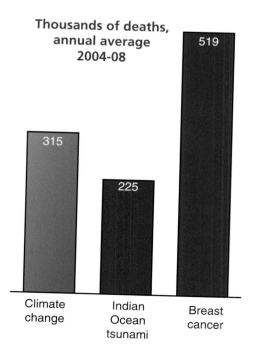

Millions affected, annual average 2004-08

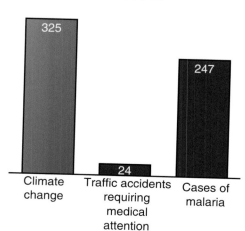

– and a dire warning

Already Australia has seen a full decade of drought. Large tracts of the United States are exposed to stronger storms and severe water shortages — leading to crop loss, job loss, fires, and deaths.

However, the first hit and worst affected are the world's poorest groups. **99%** of all casualties occur in developing countries. In contrast only **1%** of global emissions come from the **50** least developed nations. Those who suffer most from climate change have done the least to cause it.

Even the most ambitious climate agreement will take years to slow or reverse global warming. Emissions are still steadily increasing, and the world population is set to grow by **40%** by 2050.

There is an approximate 20 year delay between emission reductions and the halting of their warming effect so if we do not reverse current trends by close to 2020, we may have failed. Global warming will pass the danger level.

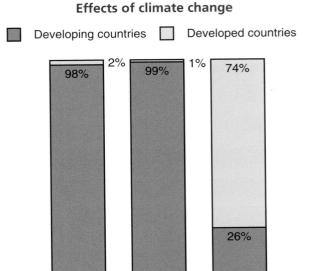

Effects of climate change

Developing countries　　Developed countries

Affected 219 million	Deaths 36 thousand	Economic losses US $64 billion
98% / 2%	99% / 1%	74% / 26%

HOW DOES IT ALL WORK?

INCREASED EMISSIONS

CAUSE AND EFFECT

Climate change effects

- Rising surface temperatures
- Rising sea levels
- More acidic oceans
- Changes in local rainfall and river run-off patterns
- Accelerated species extinction rates
- Loss of biodiversity and ecosystem services

PHYSICAL CHANGES

Gradual environmental degradation

- Melting glaciers
- Shore retreat
- Build up of salt in soil
- Spread of deserts
- Water pressure

Extreme events

- Floods
- Droughts
- Storms
- Cyclones
- Heatwaves

Risk of large scale tipping point events such as

- Melting ice sheets
- Dieback of forests
- Shutdown of streams

HUMAN IMPACT

Food security
Reduction in crop yield and hunger

Health
Malnutrition, diarrhoea, malaria, cardiovascular problems

Poverty
Income loss in agriculture, fisheries and tourism

Water
Scarcity of fresh water (quantity and quality)

Displacement
Voluntary and involuntary movement of people

Security
Risk of instability and armed conflict

Source: The Anatomy of a Silent Crisis, Global Humanitarian Forum, 2009

http://www.ghf-ge.org

Our green world

Concern for the environment is high, but what changes do we make?

The Our Green World study interviewed **13,128** people across **17** countries in 2008, to discover their views about environmental issues and what they do to preserve the environment.

Environmental problem most concerned with (%)

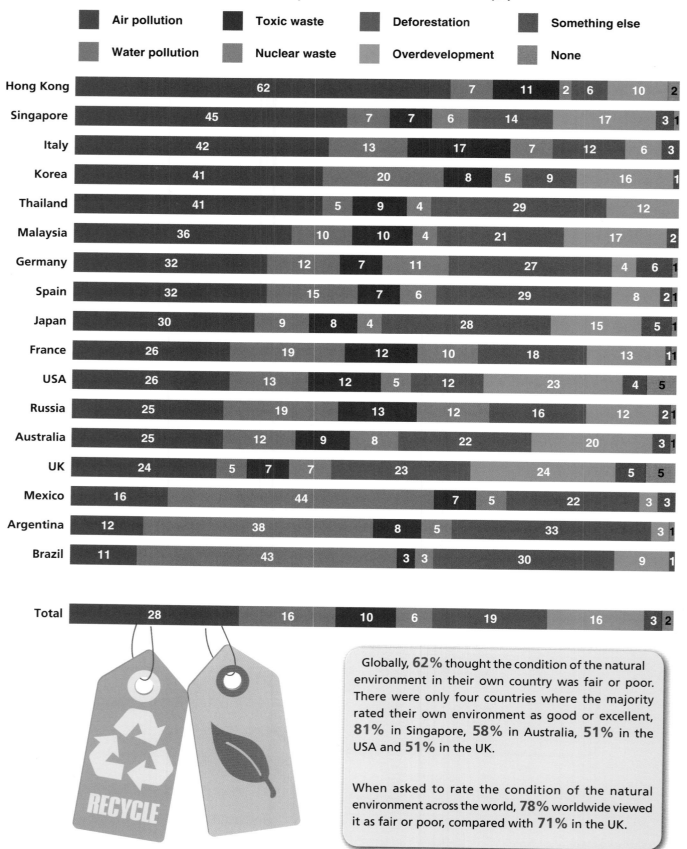

Legend:
- Air pollution
- Water pollution
- Toxic waste
- Nuclear waste
- Deforestation
- Overdevelopment
- Something else
- None

Country	Air pollution	Water pollution	Toxic waste	Nuclear waste	Deforestation	Overdevelopment	Something else	None
Hong Kong	62	7	11	2	6	10	2	
Singapore	45	7	7	6	14	17	3	1
Italy	42	13	17	7	12	6	3	
Korea	41	20	8	5	9	16	1	
Thailand	41	5	9	4	29	12		
Malaysia	36	10	10	4	21	17	2	
Germany	32	12	7	11	27	4	6	1
Spain	32	15	7	6	29	8	2	1
Japan	30	9	8	4	28	15	5	1
France	26	19	12	10	18	13	1	1
USA	26	13	12	5	12	23	4	5
Russia	25	19	13	12	16	12	2	1
Australia	25	12	9	8	22	20	3	1
UK	24	5	7	7	23	24	5	5
Mexico	16	44	7	5	22		3	3
Argentina	12	38	8	5	33		3	1
Brazil	11	43	3	3	30		9	1
Total	28	16	10	6	19	16	3	2

Globally, **62%** thought the condition of the natural environment in their own country was fair or poor. There were only four countries where the majority rated their own environment as good or excellent, **81%** in Singapore, **58%** in Australia, **51%** in the USA and **51%** in the UK.

When asked to rate the condition of the natural environment across the world, **78%** worldwide viewed it as fair or poor, compared with **71%** in the UK.

RECYCLE

Environmental actions we take (worldwide, %)

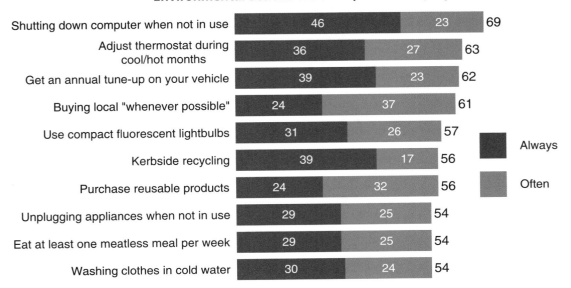

Action	Always	Often	Total
Shutting down computer when not in use	46	23	69
Adjust thermostat during cool/hot months	36	27	63
Get an annual tune-up on your vehicle	39	23	62
Buying local "whenever possible"	24	37	61
Use compact fluorescent lightbulbs	31	26	57
Kerbside recycling	39	17	56
Purchase reusable products	24	32	56
Unplugging appliances when not in use	29	25	54
Eat at least one meatless meal per week	29	25	54
Washing clothes in cold water	30	24	54

Globally, **40%** said they had made recent changes in their lifestyle to benefit the environment, compared with **51%** in the UK.

UK respondents were the least willing to pay extra for environmentally friendly products – **45%**, compared to the global average of **59%** – and to contribute more towards the cost of recycling – only **28%**, compared to the global average of **51%**.

Environmental actions we don't take (worldwide, %)

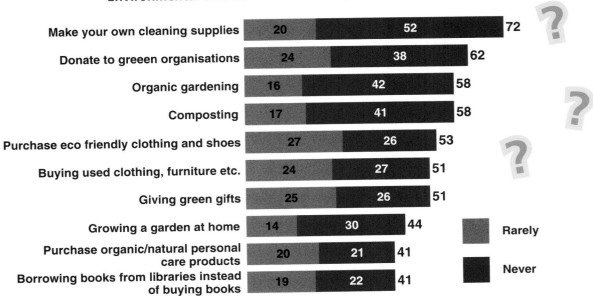

Action	Rarely	Never	Total
Make your own cleaning supplies	20	52	72
Donate to greeen organisations	24	38	62
Organic gardening	16	42	58
Composting	17	41	58
Purchase eco friendly clothing and shoes	27	26	53
Buying used clothing, furniture etc.	24	27	51
Giving green gifts	25	26	51
Growing a garden at home	14	30	44
Purchase organic/natural personal care products	20	21	41
Borrowing books from libraries instead of buying books	19	22	41

Source: Our Green World, TNS, 2008
http://www.tnsglobal.com

Posh polluters

GreenAware maps the relationship between household carbon emissions and green behaviours in the UK. GreenAware categorises everyone into Green Segments – 10 distinct groups according to attitude to and understanding of the environment and climate change. At the top are 'Eco-Evangelists' – people most likely to support "green" causes and who believe in the power of consumer action to make a difference to climate change. At the bottom are the 'Wasteful & Unconvinced' – people who have no interest in changing lifestyles and are more wasteful as a result. You would think that those who had the least interest in environmental issues would be those who polluted the most... but this isn't the case.

Most polluting and least polluting Local Authorities
(number above or below the index)

In the top 10 are the authorities that contain the households with the biggest carbon footprint. They are among the most prosperous places in the country – and they contain the highest number of 'Eco-Evangelists'. In the bottom 10 are the authorities with the smallest carbon footprint. These feature many of the poorest areas and a high level of 'Wasteful and Unconvinced'.

Most polluting

Chiltern (133.78)
South Bucks (133.00)
Surrey Heath (131.32)
South Oxfordshire (126.58)
Hart (126.12)
Uttlesford (126.08)
Mole Valley (125.71)
Windsor and Maidenhead (125.40)
Elmbridge (124.99)
Wokingham (123.94)

100 = UK Average

Least polluting

Sunderland (84.95)
Middlesbrough (84.17)
Barking and Dagenham (83.76)
Newham (83.63)
Merthyr Tydfil (83.31)
Hull (82.63)
Glasgow, City of (82.31)
South Tyneside (81.76)
Wear Vallley (80.03)
Blanau Gwent (77.89)

Carbon emissions per household by postcode were calculated by looking at official figures on energy use, travel and general consumption including food.

People in wealthy areas eat more exotic and environmentally unfriendly food, such as prawns flown from Malaysia, green beans from Kenya and organic pears from New Zealand.

They fly more often and take foreign holidays in more distant locations, drive more "gas guzzling" 4x4s, have more cars per household and live in bigger houses which cost more to heat and light.

Most Polluting Postcode Sectors
(Average tonnes CO2 per household)

WD3 4 Rickmansworth (36.42)

CR3 7 Woldingham (36.22)

RG9 3 Shiplake (35.67)

SL9 7 Oxford Road, Gerrards Cross (35.65)

AL5 2 Hatching Green, Harpenden (35.28)

Least Polluting Postcode Sectors

NE6 2 Newcastle upon Tyne (14.95)

NW1 3 Stanhope St, London (14.91)

WC1H 8 Cromer St, London (14.91)

NE4 7 Newcastle upon Tyne (14.86)

TS18 2 Stockton-on-Tees (14.09)

The Most Polluting

The most polluting postcodes cover the most affluent people in the UK. They have a high income, interest in current affairs and are well educated. They include highly qualified professionals, senior executives and business owners with families as well as retired professionals without children. They live in wealthy, high status suburban and semi-rural neighbourhoods as well as in retirement properties.

They tend to live in large detached homes with four or more bedrooms. These households often have two or more cars and take at least two holidays a year with regular weekend breaks also being popular.

The Least Polluting

Many of the people who live in this sort of postcode will be on a low income, although the type of person varies greatly. They range from single elderly people with a low income and education level living in council flats, home owning Asian families with a high income and education level to ethnic minorities with a very high education level but very low income.

Unemployment is relatively high and people tend to work in routine jobs. The average household income levels for these areas are among the lowest in the country.

Housing in these neighbourhoods ranges from small one or two bedroomed council flats to families who own their own home.

People tend to rely on public transport, walking and the occasional taxi to get around. They are unlikely to go on holiday but will go to bingo and spend money on scratch cards.

Source: Green Aware: The first carbon footprint measure for UK consumers, Experian

http://www.experian.com
http://www.upmystreet.com

Good choice

"Put your money where your mouth is" – but how many of us are prepared to do this for the sake of the environment?

We spent **£35.5 billion** on ethical purchases in 2007 – this is up **15%** over the previous year, but is still a small proportion of the total annual consumer spend of more than **£600 billion**

Every household in the UK spent **£707** in line with their ethical values, up from **£630** in 2006.

Spending on:

- **ethical food and drink** (organic products, Fairtrade goods and free-range eggs) was up **14%** to **£5.8 billion**

- **green home expenditure** (energy-efficient electrical appliances, green mortgage repayments, small renewables such as micro-wind turbines and green energy) **was up 13% to £6.7 billion**

- **eco-travel and transport** (environmentally friendly transport, responsible tour operators, public transport and sales of green cars) saw very little change and was up just **1%** to **£1.6 billion**

- **ethical personal products** (humane cosmetics and eco-fashion eg Fairtrade cotton) was up **4%** to **£1.4 billion**

- **community** (local shopping and charity donations) was up by **18%** to **£4.2 billion**

- **monies in ethical finance** (ethical banking and investments) was up **15%** to **£15.6 billion**

People have become more confident of their ability to make companies behave responsibly

% of people undertaking the following at least once during the year

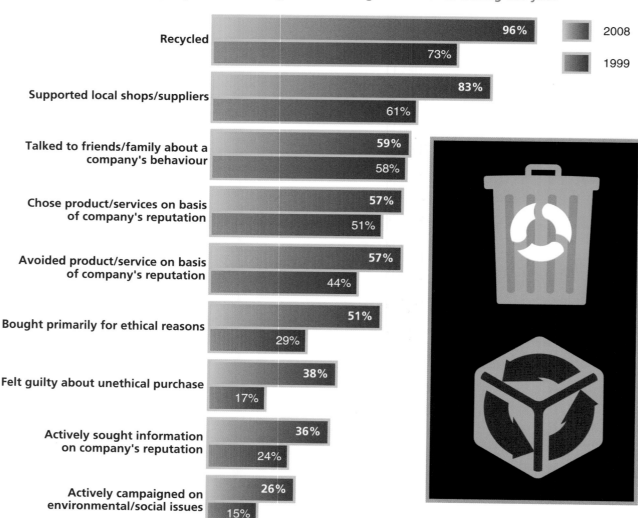

	2008	1999
Recycled	96%	73%
Supported local shops/suppliers	83%	61%
Talked to friends/family about a company's behaviour	59%	58%
Chose product/services on basis of company's reputation	57%	51%
Avoided product/service on basis of company's reputation	57%	44%
Bought primarily for ethical reasons	51%	29%
Felt guilty about unethical purchase	38%	17%
Actively sought information on company's reputation	36%	24%
Actively campaigned on environmental/social issues	26%	15%

Source: The Co-operative Ethical Consumerism Report 2008
http://www.goodwithmoney.co.uk

McLitter

A quarter of streets are littered with fast food rubbish

Keep Britain Tidy surveyed 10 areas of England (Newcastle-upon-Tyne, Leicestershire, Liverpool, Birmingham, Manchester, South West, Leeds, Southampton, Sheffield and London) in December 2008. They wanted to find out which brands created the most litter and to begin working with fast-food companies to reduce the amount of cast off food cartons, drink cans, pizza boxes and chip wrappers in the streets.

The survey revealed that most rubbish is either dropped at lunchtime – when workers make the daily dash out of the office for a bite to eat – or after dark when pubs and clubs have closed and the midnight munchies set in.

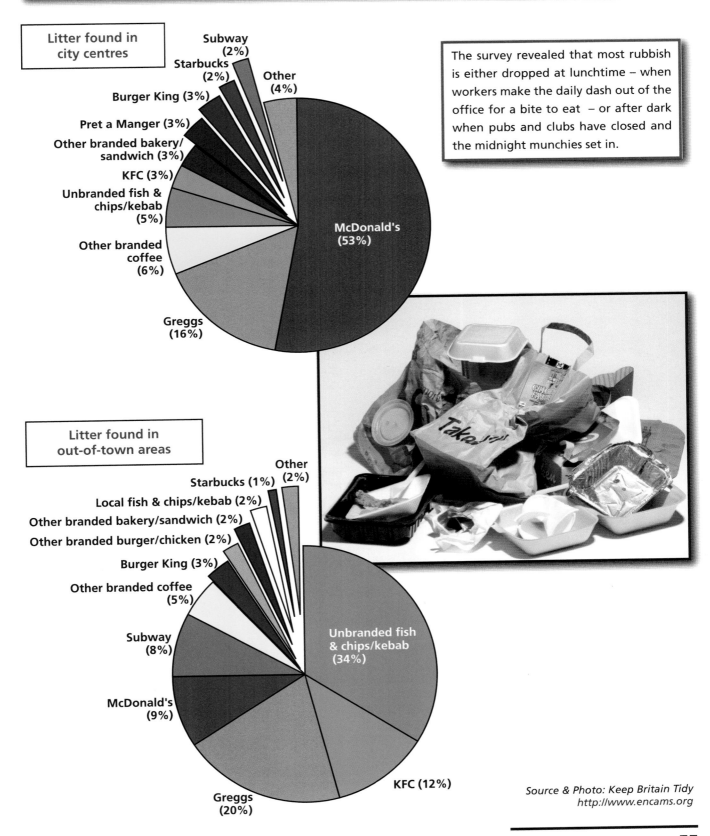

Litter found in city centres

- Subway (2%)
- Starbucks (2%)
- Other (4%)
- Burger King (3%)
- Pret a Manger (3%)
- Other branded bakery/sandwich (3%)
- KFC (3%)
- Unbranded fish & chips/kebab (5%)
- Other branded coffee (6%)
- Greggs (16%)
- McDonald's (53%)

Litter found in out-of-town areas

- Starbucks (1%)
- Other (2%)
- Local fish & chips/kebab (2%)
- Other branded bakery/sandwich (2%)
- Other branded burger/chicken (2%)
- Burger King (3%)
- Other branded coffee (5%)
- Subway (8%)
- McDonald's (9%)
- Greggs (20%)
- KFC (12%)
- Unbranded fish & chips/kebab (34%)

Source & Photo: Keep Britain Tidy
http://www.encams.org

War...

Britain dumps more household waste into landfill than most other countries in the EU (around two thirds of its municipal waste goes to landfill; only Portugal and Greece put more there).

A War on Waste study investigated food packaging and how it is made up, for example whether the packaging is recyclable.

29 common food items representing a regular shopping basket were purchased from eight retailers: ASDA, Co-op, Lidl, Marks & Spencer, Morrisons, Sainsbury's, Tesco and Waitrose.

The Co-op provided the most information about what packaging was made from.

M&S had most items labelled as having recycled content.

M&S provided the most information about whether packaging was recyclable.

The range of recyclable packaging was 57.8% to 66.8%, so there remains scope for improvement across all retailers.

The best examples had less weight of packaging with a higher percentage being recyclable.

Weight of packaging (g) and proportion of packaging that was recyclable, by retailer

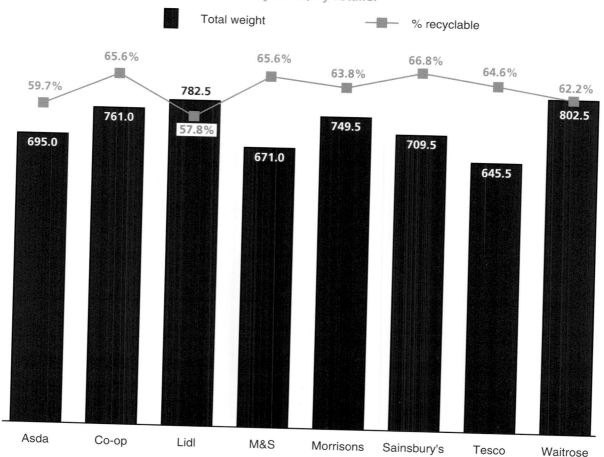

	Total weight	% recyclable

Retailer	Total weight	% recyclable
Asda	695.0	59.7%
Co-op	761.0	65.6%
Lidl	782.5	57.8%
M&S	671.0	65.6%
Morrisons	749.5	63.8%
Sainsbury's	709.5	66.8%
Tesco	645.5	64.6%
Waitrose	802.5	62.2%

...on waste

Best packaging – Tesco

a low weight and a higher recyclable content

Of the **645.5g** of packaging, **35.4% could not be recycled**

Worst packaging – Waitrose

a high weight and a relatively low recyclable content

Of the **802.5g** of packaging, **37.8% could not be recycled**

Photos: Paul Milsom of Milsom photography
Source: Project conducted by BMRB for the LGA – War on Waste food packaging study

http://www.lga.gov.uk/research

Dirty beaches

Our beaches are disappearing under a growing tide of rubbish

Beachwatch is the biggest voluntary beach clean and litter survey in the UK and is organised every year by The Marine Conservation Society

In 2008...

5,219 volunteers surveyed 374 beaches in the UK
176km of UK coastline were cleaned and surveyed

Volunteers collected 385,659 pieces of beach litter and filled over 3,000 bags

Top 10 litter items found
(items per km)

Litter item	Items per km
Plastic pieces (over 1cm)	319
Plastic pieces (under 1cm)	169
Polystyrene pieces	142
Plastic rope	127
Plastic caps and lids	125
Sweet wrappers	114
Cotton bud sticks	100
Fishing net (under 1cm)	89
Glass pieces	76
Glass bottles	71

The average density of litter found has risen by over 110% since 1994

The top 10 litter items found accounted for 60.7% of all litter found

Small plastic pieces have remained the number one item found on UK beaches since 1998

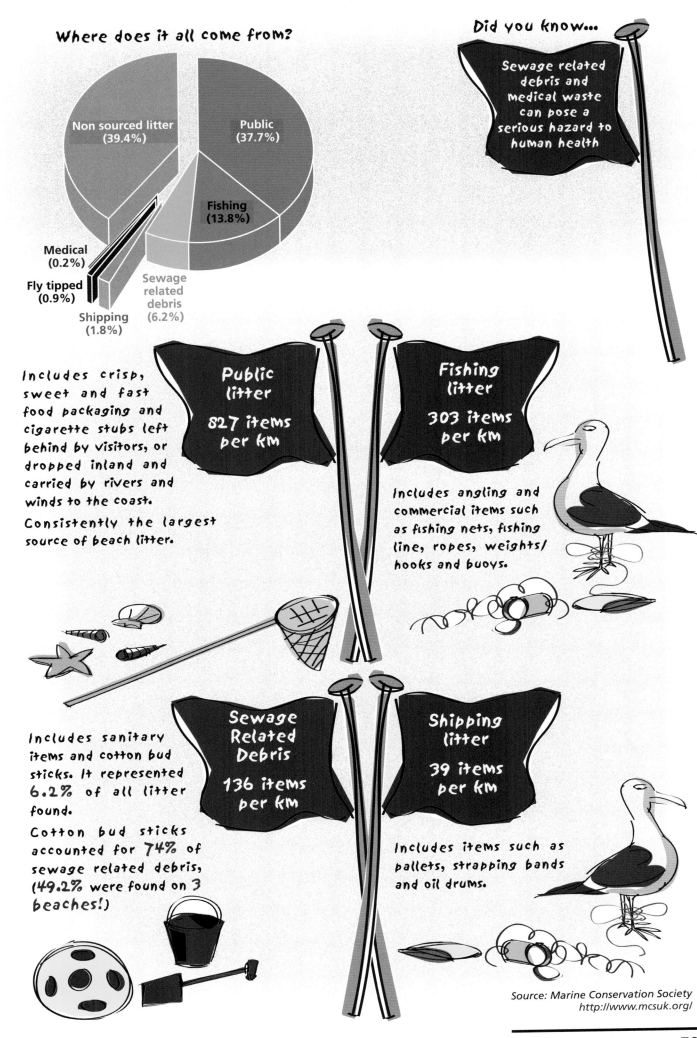

Where does it all come from?

Non sourced litter (39.4%)

Public (37.7%)

Fishing (13.8%)

Medical (0.2%)

Fly tipped (0.9%)

Shipping (1.8%)

Sewage related debris (6.2%)

Did you know...

Sewage related debris and medical waste can pose a serious hazard to human health

Includes crisp, sweet and fast food packaging and cigarette stubs left behind by visitors, or dropped inland and carried by rivers and winds to the coast.

Consistently the largest source of beach litter.

Public litter
827 items per km

Fishing litter
303 items per km

Includes angling and commercial items such as fishing nets, fishing line, ropes, weights/hooks and buoys.

Includes sanitary items and cotton bud sticks. It represented 6.2% of all litter found.

Cotton bud sticks accounted for 74% of sewage related debris, (49.2% were found on 3 beaches!)

Sewage Related Debris
136 items per km

Shipping litter
39 items per km

Includes items such as pallets, strapping bands and oil drums.

Source: Marine Conservation Society
http://www.mcsuk.org/

Family & relationships

For better, for worse

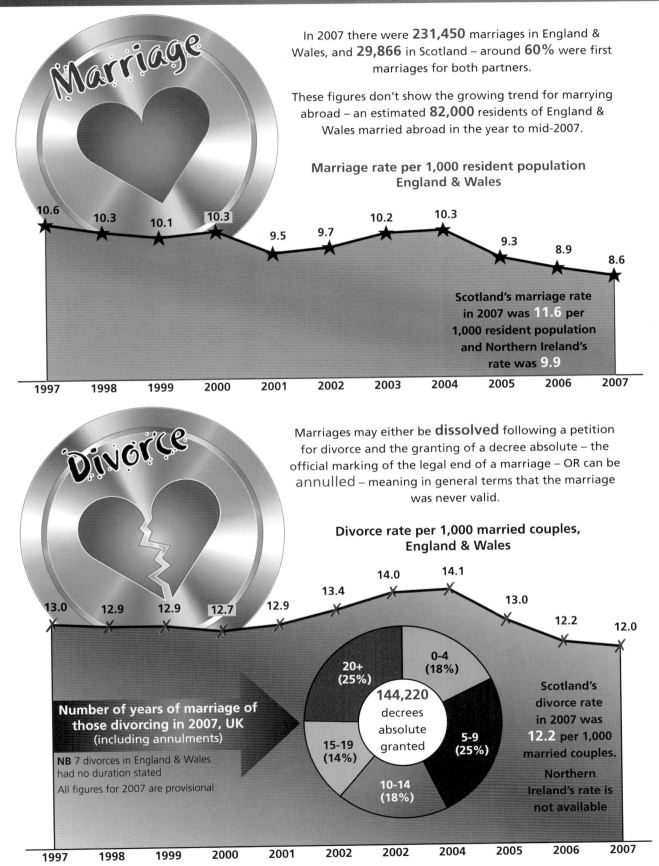

In 2007 there were **231,450** marriages in England & Wales, and **29,866** in Scotland – around **60%** were first marriages for both partners.

These figures don't show the growing trend for marrying abroad – an estimated **82,000** residents of England & Wales married abroad in the year to mid-2007.

Marriage rate per 1,000 resident population England & Wales

10.6 · 10.3 · 10.1 · 10.3 · 9.5 · 9.7 · 10.2 · 10.3 · 9.3 · 8.9 · 8.6

1997 · 1998 · 1999 · 2000 · 2001 · 2002 · 2003 · 2004 · 2005 · 2006 · 2007

Scotland's marriage rate in 2007 was **11.6** per 1,000 resident population and Northern Ireland's rate was **9.9**

Marriages may either be **dissolved** following a petition for divorce and the granting of a decree absolute – the official marking of the legal end of a marriage – OR can be annulled – meaning in general terms that the marriage was never valid.

Divorce rate per 1,000 married couples, England & Wales

13.0 · 12.9 · 12.9 · 12.7 · 12.9 · 13.4 · 14.0 · 14.1 · 13.0 · 12.2 · 12.0

Number of years of marriage of those divorcing in 2007, UK (including annulments)

NB 7 divorces in England & Wales had no duration stated
All figures for 2007 are provisional

144,220 decrees absolute granted

- 20+ (25%)
- 0-4 (18%)
- 5-9 (25%)
- 10-14 (18%)
- 15-19 (14%)

Scotland's divorce rate in 2007 was **12.2** per 1,000 married couples.

Northern Ireland's rate is not available

1997 · 1998 · 1999 · 2000 · 2001 · 2002 · 2002 · 2004 · 2005 · 2006 · 2007

Source: Annual Abstract of Statistics © Crown copyright 2009

Baby mothers

For the first time in five years, teen pregnancies have risen

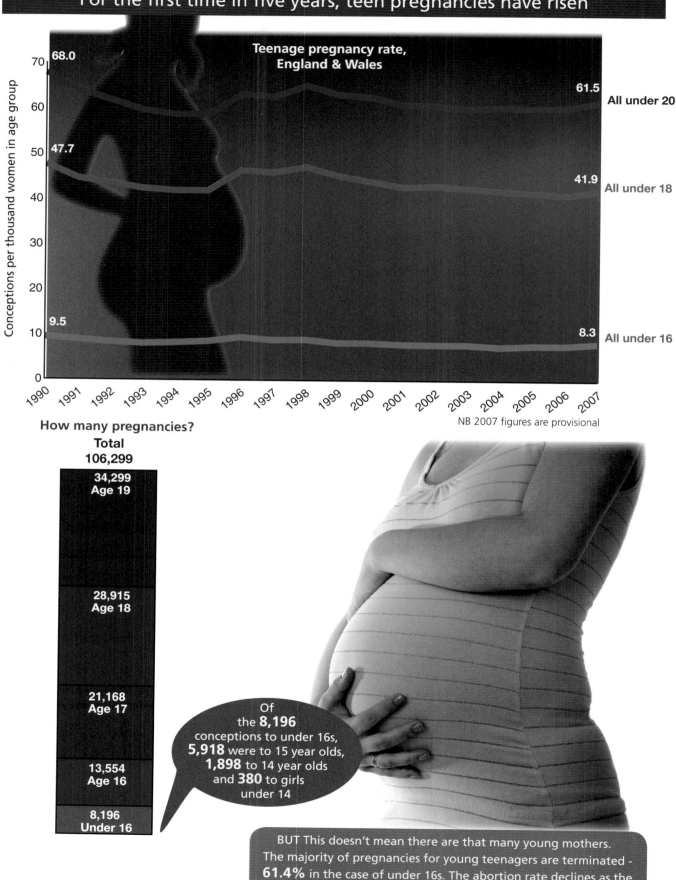

Teenage pregnancy rate, England & Wales

Conceptions per thousand women in age group

- 68.0
- 47.7
- 9.5

- 61.5 — All under 20
- 41.9 — All under 18
- 8.3 — All under 16

1990 1991 1992 1993 1994 1995 1996 1997 1998 1999 2000 2001 2002 2003 2004 2005 2006 2007

NB 2007 figures are provisional

How many pregnancies?

Total 106,299

- 34,299 Age 19
- 28,915 Age 18
- 21,168 Age 17
- 13,554 Age 16
- 8,196 Under 16

Of the **8,196** conceptions to under 16s, **5,918** were to 15 year olds, **1,898** to 14 year olds and **380** to girls under 14

BUT This doesn't mean there are that many young mothers. The majority of pregnancies for young teenagers are terminated - **61.4%** in the case of under 16s. The abortion rate declines as the age of conception increases: **50.6%** at 16, **45.2%** at 17, **39.5%** at 18 and **36%** at 19.

Source: Office for National Statistics
© Crown copyright
http://www.statistics.gov.uk

Creating families – the waiting game

Infertility is estimated to affect around **3.5 million** people in the UK – **one in six or one in seven** UK couples have difficulty conceiving.

It is the most common reason for women aged 20-45 to see their GP, after pregnancy itself.

Couples having fertility problems and desperate to have a family may choose a fertility treatment such as **IVF – in vitro fertilisation** – this literally means 'fertilisation in glass' giving us the familiar term 'test tube baby'.

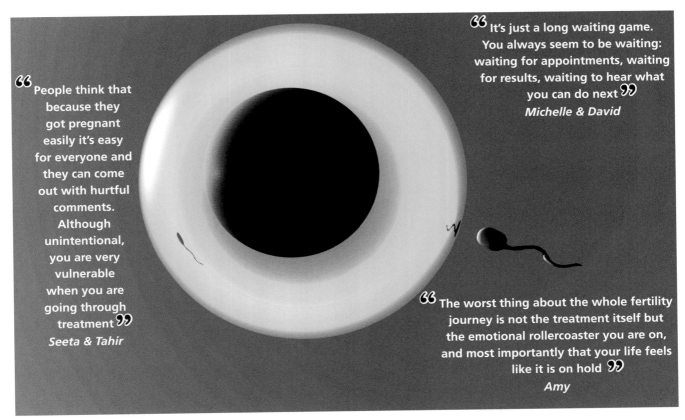

66 People think that because they got pregnant easily it's easy for everyone and they can come out with hurtful comments. Although unintentional, you are very vulnerable when you are going through treatment 99
Seeta & Tahir

66 It's just a long waiting game. You always seem to be waiting: waiting for appointments, waiting for results, waiting to hear what you can do next 99
Michelle & David

66 The worst thing about the whole fertility journey is not the treatment itself but the emotional rollercoaster you are on, and most importantly that your life feels like it is on hold 99
Amy

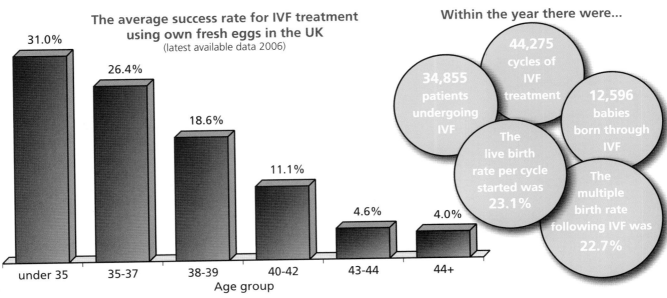

The average success rate for IVF treatment using own fresh eggs in the UK
(latest available data 2006)

- under 35: 31.0%
- 35-37: 26.4%
- 38-39: 18.6%
- 40-42: 11.1%
- 43-44: 4.6%
- 44+: 4.0%

Age group

Within the year there were...

- 34,855 patients undergoing IVF
- 44,275 cycles of IVF treatment
- 12,596 babies born through IVF
- The live birth rate per cycle started was 23.1%
- The multiple birth rate following IVF was 22.7%

Source: © Human Fertilisation & Embryology Authority 2009

http://www.hfea.gov.uk

Creating families – donors

Since 1991, there have been around 2,000 babies born each year following treatment using donated eggs, sperm or embryos

The term 'donation' applies to the gifting of sperm, eggs or embryos for use in fertility treatment or research.

For those who are unable to conceive without the help of a third party, donation may represent the **only** hope to have children of their own.

A donor may specify the number of families he or she is willing to help create, up to a **maximum of 10 families.**

Children born following donor treatment, UK

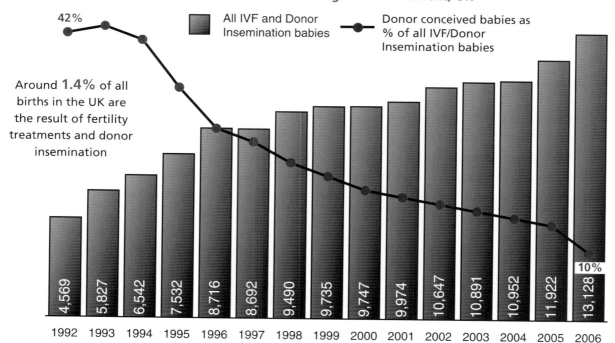

All IVF and Donor Insemination babies

Donor conceived babies as % of all IVF/Donor Insemination babies

42%

Around **1.4%** of all births in the UK are the result of fertility treatments and donor insemination

10%

Year	Babies
1992	4,569
1993	5,827
1994	6,542
1995	7,532
1996	8,716
1997	8,692
1998	9,490
1999	9,735
2000	9,747
2001	9,974
2002	10,647
2003	10,891
2004	10,952
2005	11,922
2006	13,128

The average success rate for Donor Insemination treatment in the UK
(latest available data 2006)

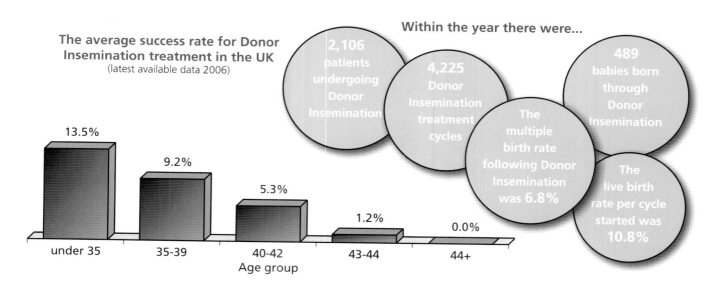

Age group	Success rate
under 35	13.5%
35-39	9.2%
40-42	5.3%
43-44	1.2%
44+	0.0%

Within the year there were...

2,106 patients undergoing Donor Insemination

4,225 Donor Insemination treatment cycles

489 babies born through Donor Insemination

The multiple birth rate following Donor Insemination was 6.8%

The live birth rate per cycle started was 10.8%

Zannah's thoughts on page 88 of *Essential Articles 12* is a personal account of a donor conceived child.

Source: © Human Fertilisation & Embryology Authority 2008

http://www.hfea.gov.uk

Creating families – one at a time

IVF can give couples an 'instant family' – but at a high risk

A multiple pregnancy ie twins, triplets or more, is **20 times** more likely following fertility treatment than by a natural conception.

A typical cycle of IVF treatment alone is around **£5,000** – and not always successful – so there is a strong incentive to transfer more than one embyro at a time. This obviously increases the chances of multiple births which also increases the risk of death around the time of birth – **3-6** times higher for twins and **9** times higher for triplets.

60% of transfers carried out in 1992 involved three embryos. Now a maximum of two embryos can be transferred to women under the age of 40, with no exceptions, and a maximum of three to women aged 40 and over.

This removes the possibility of someone becoming 'too pregnant' as in the case of 'Octomum' Nadya Suleman, who gave birth in 2009 to **eight** babies conceived by IVF in the US.

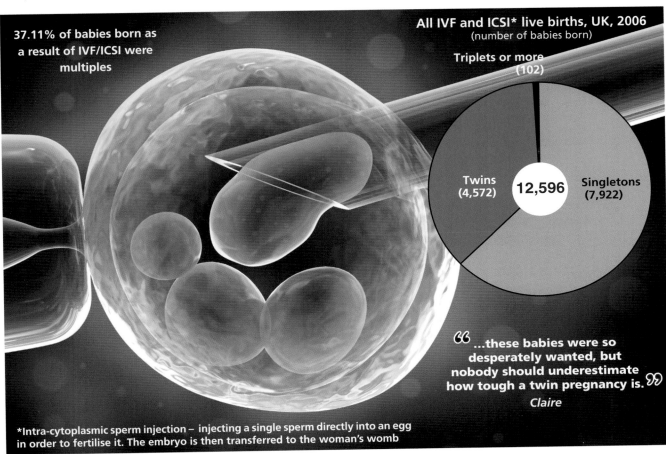

37.11% of babies born as a result of IVF/ICSI were multiples

All IVF and ICSI* live births, UK, 2006
(number of babies born)

Triplets or more (102)

Twins (4,572)

12,596

Singletons (7,922)

66 ...these babies were so desperately wanted, but nobody should underestimate how tough a twin pregnancy is. 99
Claire

*Intra-cytoplasmic sperm injection – injecting a single sperm directly into an egg in order to fertilise it. The embryo is then transferred to the woman's womb

A national strategy aims to reduce the rate of multiple births from the 2005 average of **24%** of all IVF births to **10%** over 3 years starting in January 2009.

Single embryo transfer (SET) is one strategy for reducing multiple pregnancies.

Sweden was the top country for using SET procedures at **67%** compared to the **UK** at only **9.4%**.

In countries where a single embryo transfer policy was introduced, the number of multiple births was significantly reduced.

An act of extreme, wilful fecundity? on page 80 of *Essential Articles 12*
tells why the birth of Nadya Suleman's octuplets turned into an environmental morality tale

Source: © Human Fertilisation & Embryology Authority 2009,
One at a time, European Society for Human Reproduction and Embryology (ESHRE) IVF report

http://www.hfea.gov.uk
http://www.oneatatime.org.uk/
http://www.eshre.com

Lifeline

Children who feel they can't talk to family and friends can become desperate

Children and young people who call *ChildLine* about feeling suicidal can be very lonely and often do not believe that there is anyone they can talk to about their problems. For many, *ChildLine* is literally a lifeline.

Problems mentioned by girls and boys counselled about suicide as a main problem, UK

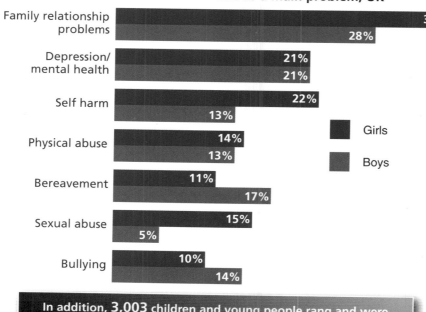

Problem	Girls	Boys
Family relationship problems	36%	28%
Depression/mental health	21%	21%
Self harm	22%	13%
Physical abuse	14%	13%
Bereavement	11%	17%
Sexual abuse	15%	5%
Bullying	10%	14%

In addition, 3,003 children and young people rang and were counselled about another problem but also talked about suicide during the course of the call.

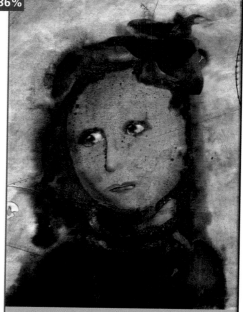

"I feel sad and tearful all the time but I don't know why. I don't think that anyone else has noticed. No one can help me anyway, nothing is going to change. I'm thinking about killing myself."
(Teenage girl)

Age breakdown of children and young people in the UK calling *ChildLine* in 2007/08 with suicide as a main problem

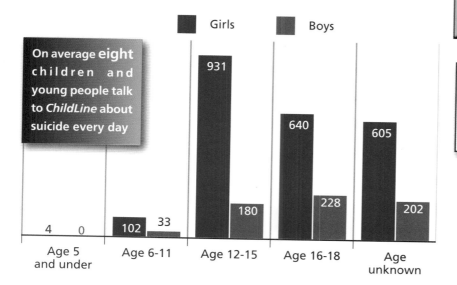

Age	Girls	Boys
Age 5 and under	4	0
Age 6-11	102	33
Age 12-15	931	180
Age 16-18	640	228
Age unknown	605	202

On average eight children and young people talk to *ChildLine* about suicide every day

In 2007/08 a total of **2,925** callers rang *ChildLine* and were counselled specifically about suicide. This is an increase of **221%**

☎ *ChildLine* 0800 1111

Source: NSPCC - Children talking to ChildLine about suicide report, March 2009
http://www.nspcc.org.uk

Boys' talk

The number of boys calling ChildLine has more than doubled

ChildLine counselled **58,311** boys in 2007/08 and over the past five years, the boy-to-girl ratio of callers to ChildLine has increased, changing from one boy for every four girl callers to one boy for every two girl callers

Main problems boys called about and percentage increase in calls from boys between 2002/03 and 2007/08, UK

Loneliness	444%
Sexuality	258%
Facts of life	206%
Bullying	148%
Sexual abuse	121%
Family relationship problems	128%
Physical abuse	61%
Boys calling overall	135%

22% of calls mentioned **family relationship problems** as a main or additional concern

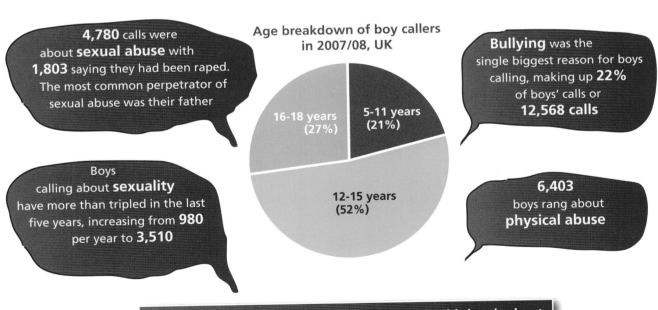

4,780 calls were about **sexual abuse** with **1,803** saying they had been raped. The most common perpetrator of sexual abuse was their father

Age breakdown of boy callers in 2007/08, UK

16-18 years (27%)
5-11 years (21%)
12-15 years (52%)

Bullying was the single biggest reason for boys calling, making up **22%** of boys' calls or **12,568 calls**

Boys calling about **sexuality** have more than tripled in the last five years, increasing from **980** per year to **3,510**

6,403 boys rang about **physical abuse**

Of the boys who gave this information, 46% said they had not told anyone about their problem before calling ChildLine

"When boys call it is the absolute last resort"
ChildLine Counsellor

Source: NSPCC – What Boys Talk About to ChildLine
http://www.nspcc.org.uk

Girl power?

A recent survey conducted by Women's Aid and Bliss Magazine reveals the reality of abuse within teenage relationships. It also shows some confusion. For example a massive **96%** of teenagers think it is **NEVER** ok for someone they are seeing to hit or physically hurt them,

94% think it is **NEVER** ok for someone they're seeing to force them to do something sexual, yet **59%** think it's **OK** for someone they're seeing to tell them what to do in certain circumstances.

Which of these has happened to you in a relationship?

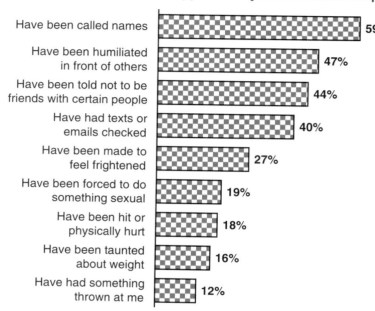

- Have been called names — **59%**
- Have been humiliated in front of others — **47%**
- Have been told not to be friends with certain people — **44%**
- Have had texts or emails checked — **40%**
- Have been made to feel frightened — **27%**
- Have been forced to do something sexual — **19%**
- Have been hit or physically hurt — **18%**
- Have been taunted about weight — **16%**
- Have had something thrown at me — **12%**

Getting physical

Younger girls were less likely to suffer sexual abuse, but **nearly a quarter** of 14 year old girls have been forced to have sex or do something sexual they didn't want to do.

One in six 15 year olds, and **one in four** 16 year olds have been hurt by someone they were dating.

More than words

Over half of 14 and 15 year old girls have been humiliated in front of others by someone they were dating and **45%** of all age groups know someone who has had their texts and emails checked, and/or been told not to go somewhere by someone they were dating.

National Domestic Violence Helpline:
0808 2000 24 7

Women's Aid & Refuge
http://www.womensaid.org.uk

Base: This survey is part of the Expect Respect campaign launched by Women's Aid and Bliss magazine.
Teenagers aged 11-17 who read Bliss were invited to take part in the online survey. 633 responded. Although these were self-selecting, and perhaps took part because they had an interest or concern in the issue, it does still reflect the existence of domestic abuse within teenage relationships.

Source: Expect Respect, Women's Aid and Bliss Survey Statistics, December 2008

It's good to talk

Emotions are discussed more freely nowadays

We are now relatively open to the idea that it is good to talk, but most people regularly rely on friends and relatives for emotional support rather than professionals

When asked about talking about their feelings, people said:
(Base: 2,102)

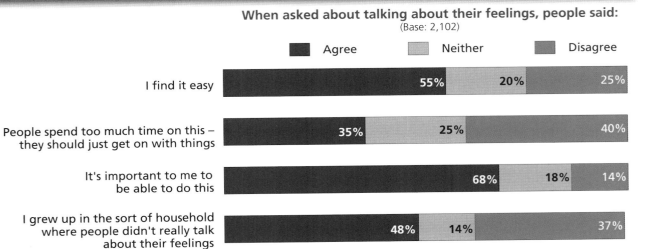

Legend: Agree | Neither | Disagree

Statement	Agree	Neither	Disagree
I find it easy	55%	20%	25%
People spend too much time on this – they should just get on with things	35%	25%	40%
It's important to me to be able to do this	68%	18%	14%
I grew up in the sort of household where people didn't really talk about their feelings	48%	14%	37%
People nowadays spend more time on this than in the past	66%	19%	12%

Some groups of people find it easier to talk about these things than others. Men, people aged 60 and over, and non-graduates are less talkative than women, the young and graduates.

47% of people had spoken to a friend or relative at least once a month in the past year when they felt worried, stressed or down

70% feel they have at least three people in their lives that they can talk to when they are feeling like this

Although people are generally comfortable with discussing emotions, they are less likely to seek formal support such as therapy and counselling.

Attitudes towards therapy and counselling
(Base: 1,025)

I would feel comfortable talking to...

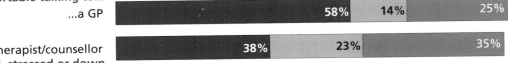

Statement	Agree	Neither	Disagree
...a GP	58%	14%	25%
...a therapist/counsellor ...if I was feeling worried, stressed or down	38%	23%	35%

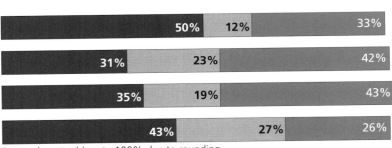

Statement	Agree	Neither	Disagree
I would know how to find counsellor/therapist if needed	50%	12%	33%
Counselling or therapy is only for people with really serious problems	31%	23%	42%
I don't really know anything about counselling or therapy	35%	19%	43%
I wouldn't want anyone to know if I had seen a counsellor therapist	43%	27%	26%

Figures do not add up to 100% due to rounding

Source: British Social Attitudes 25th Edition, 2008/09

http://www.natcen.ac.uk

Baby P's legacy

The horrific story of a toddler may have had some lasting effects

The case of Baby P:

A toddler – known at first only as Baby P – died, aged 17 months, on 3rd August 2007. He had been subjected to horrific cruelty throughout his short life but chances to save him had been missed by social workers, doctors and police.

In May 2009, Baby Peter's mother, her boyfriend and his brother, who lived with them, were all found guilty of causing or allowing a child's death.

Although the child was not saved, there are indications that the publicity surrounding the trial may have made both the public and the authorities more ready to intervene when they suspect a child is being abused.

Care cases

Cafcass stands for the Children and Family Court Support Service.

Amongst other roles, Cafcass works with families and local authorities when there is a possibility that a child may be taken into care.

In the final part of 2008-2009, following the Baby Peter trial, there was a significant increase in the number of care cases. March 2009 saw 743 cases, the highest ever for a single month, and an increase of 34.8% on the previous year.

The facts behind the stats:

Public Law Care Requests, England & Wales

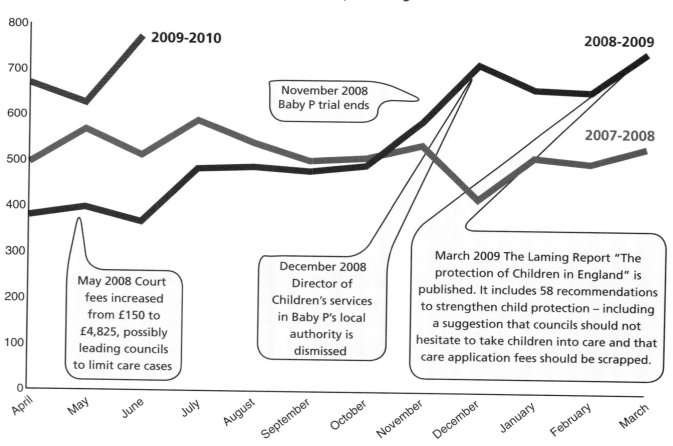

2009-2010

2008-2009

November 2008 Baby P trial ends

2007-2008

May 2008 Court fees increased from £150 to £4,825, possibly leading councils to limit care cases

December 2008 Director of Children's services in Baby P's local authority is dismissed

March 2009 The Laming Report "The protection of Children in England" is published. It includes 58 recommendations to strengthen child protection – including a suggestion that councils should not hesitate to take children into care and that care application fees should be scrapped.

Baby Peter died aged only 17 months in 2007. Photo: ITV News

Speaking out!

The NSPCC Helpline has received more calls about serious child abuse since the death of Baby Peter.

From Apr 2008 to March 2009, the 24-hour freephone service passed on **11,243** suspected child protection cases to police or social services - an increase of more than a third over two years.

In the year before Baby Peter's death, the NSPCC made **8,170** referrals; the following year the figure rose to **9,620.**

Many of the calls were about children being physically assaulted, sexually abused or badly neglected. Most came from neighbours, relatives and friends of the family.

"Fortunately people seem to be more aware of children who might be at risk of serious harm and are taking action to help them. The brutal torture and death of Baby Peter was terrible but we know it was a wake-up call for some people to look out for children. It only takes a few seconds to dial our number and it could be the difference between life and death for a child."
Christine Renouf, Director of Helpline Services

If you or anybody you know needs help then contact the NSPCC Helpline:
0808 800 5000

The lessons that need to be learnt from Baby P on page 94-95 of Essential Articles 12 tells a campaigner's response to the tragedy.

Sources: Cafcass, NSPCC
http://www.cafcass.gov.uk
http://www.nspcc.org.uk

Financial issues

Deep in debt

The average **owed** by every UK adult is **£30,190** (including mortgages).

This is **132%** of average earnings.

The average household debt in the UK is **£58,290** (including mortgages).

The average outstanding mortgage for the **11.1m** households who currently have mortgages now stands at **£110,600**.

Britain's interest repayments on personal debt were **£66.1bn** in the last 12months.

The average interest paid by each household on their total debt is approximately **£2,645** each year.

The average consumer borrowing via credit cards, motor and retail finance deals, overdrafts and unsecured personal loans **rose** to **£4,760** per average UK adult at the end of August 2009.

£2.96
Average saved by consumers every day

£181m
interest paid in UK daily

Every **11.5 minutes** a property is repossessed

Every **3.97 minutes** 1 person is declared bankrupt or insolvent

£5,454 a second
increase in Government national debt

21.9m plastic card purchase transactions per day

£1.05bn total value of transactions

Source Credit Action
http://www.creditaction.org.uk

No strings attached

The average weekly pocket money received by children aged between 5 and 15 is £3.30.

47% of the parents surveyed firmly believe that pocket money should be used to teach children the value of money, but for many, their actions don't support their attitudes.

88% of parents said they hadn't reduced their children's pocket money because of the recession.

One in five parents let their children spend their money on anything they want, without restriction, and only 16% of parents make their children save any of their pocket money.

Half of the parents in the survey said their children spent the pocket money on sweets, with pocket collectibles coming a close second (48%).

Just 15% of parents stopped their children spending their pocket money on sweets.

The items most parents were likely to place a restriction on were unsuitable clothing, (42%) and toy guns and swords (40%).

'Once children reach a certain age, pocket money can be an invaluable tool for parents to show children how to spend, save and appreciate money'
Dr Pat Spungin, parenting expert, Raisingkids.co.uk

Average weekly pocket money per age group

age 5	£ 1.80
age 6	£ 1.83
age 7	£ 2.03
age 8	£ 2.27
age 9	£ 2.59
age 10	£ 3.35
age 11	£ 3.47
age 12	£ 4.01
age 13	£ 4.42
age 14	£ 5.28
age 15	£ 5.52

Of the parents whose children were old enough to do a part-time job to boost their pocket money, newspaper delivery was still the most popular job for 45% of the children.

Base: 1,000 parents

Source: Raisingkids Pocket Money Survey 2009
http://www.raisingkids.co.uk

Expensive teens

Young people in the UK have an increasingly pricy lifestyle

A 17 year old today is **12 times** more expensive in real terms than 30 years ago.

Much of this extra cost comes from the fact that things which used to be luxuries are now essentials, eg mobile phones, dvds, Nintendo DS games, iPods and music downloads. They form a major part of teenage society.

In 1975 the yearly cost of being a teenager was **£700** in today's prices. By comparison, they now need **£9,000** to get by and this excludes the cost of luxuries such as a scooter or driving lessons.

How it adds up per year

iPod and downloads	£620
Hair extensions (female)	£500
Haircuts (male)	£240
Trainers	£300
Cigarettes	£700
Mobile phone	£420
Magazines	£75

How the real costs have increased

	Today's teen	1970s teen	1970s cost adjusted to today's prices
Pint of beer	£3	20p	£2.40
Hi-fi/stereo	£100	£96	£1,125
Electric guitar	£300	£25	£300
Cinema	£7	40p	£4.80
Adidas Gazelle trainers	£40	£7	£84
Mini	£13,000	£600	£7,200
Camcorder	£100	£43-£79	£516
Hair curlers/straighteners	£35	£8	£96
Dress - River Island	£45	£5	£60
Fish & chips	£5	45p	£5.40
Jeans	£70	£8	£96
Computer games console	Sony PS3 £200	Atari 2600 £100	£1,200

Source: Association of Accounting Technicians
http://www.aat.org.uk

Organic market

90% of UK households now buy organic products but what effect will the economic downturn have?

UK sales of organic products increased overall by 1.7% in 2008 to over £2.1 billion

% of organic consumers who ranked this issue as 'EXTREMELY important' when buying products

Issue	%
Quality & taste	31%
No GM ingredients	26%
High animal welfare standards	25%
Avoiding food grown with pesticides	25%
Avoiding artificial colouring or additives	23%
Wanting to know where my food comes from	22%
Fair prices & wages for farmers & workers	22%
Farming methods that encourage wildlife	20%
Impact made by producing & transporting food on greenhouse gas emissions & climate change	14%

Each of these nine motivations was rated as 'important' by more than 75% of respondents

FOOD

The effect of the economic downturn on the organic market

There seems to be an appetite for economising across the board, however, food is an area where people seem least likely to economise. Only **24%** of shoppers expect to spend less on their food bills. In contrast, more than **50%** expect to spend less on holidays, eating out, alcoholic drinks and leisure activities.

Although in general respondents were more likely to economise on organic food, a committed group of consumers were less put off by the economic downturn.

Are you expecting to spend less or more on organic food this year?

	Less		More
General consumers	33%		11%
Consumers who spend 40% or more of their food budget on organic food	15%		36%

FOOD

"It seems that while people may want to economise many still look for quality."
Dorothy McKenzie
Chairman, Dragon Rouge, a branding consultancy

CLOTHING

The current economic downturn is likely to cause a slowing of growth in organic clothing and textiles. However, it is forecast that sales will pick up again and that they will treble by 2012, reaching **£280 million**

MADE IN NATURE · MADE IN NATURE
ORGANIC

Base: 1,000 people surveyed on behalf of the Soil Association

Sales of organic cotton increased by **40%** in 2008 and the total UK sales of organic clothing and textiles reached **£100 million.**

The UK makes up about **8-10%** of the global organic cotton market

CLOTHING

The health and environmental concerns that have fuelled sales of organic food and drink are increasingly prompting consumers to consider the health implications of products absorbed through the skin and the environmental impact of intensive cotton production.

Mainstream clothing brands and retailers such as *Nike, Timberland, Marks & Spencer* and *New Look*

are sharply increasing the volumes of organic cotton they use.

Marks & Spencer sold 1.1million organic cotton items in 2008 – more than five times the volume sold in 2007.

New Look sold 2.3 million organic cotton items in 2008 – a 50% increase on 2007. Organic cotton now accounts for 4.2% of its womenswear.

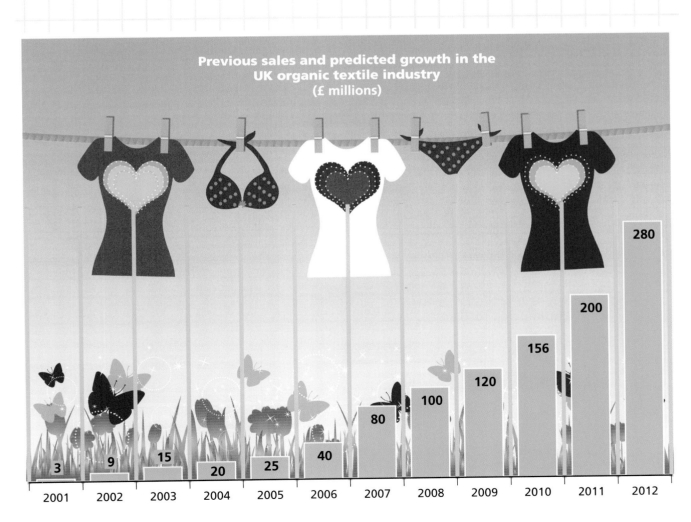

Previous sales and predicted growth in the UK organic textile industry (£ millions)

Year	Value
2001	3
2002	9
2003	15
2004	20
2005	25
2006	40
2007	80
2008	100
2009	120
2010	156
2011	200
2012	280

Source: Soil Association Organic market report 2009
http://www.soilassociation.org

Take the money... & run

More than £450 million has been raised for hundreds of charitable causes by London Marathon runners since 1981

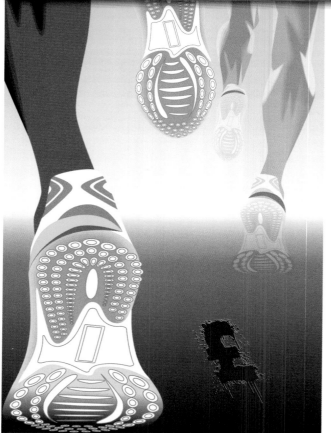

In 2008 the London Marathon became the largest single annual fundraising event in the world – raising **£46.7 million.**

JustGiving – the largest **online** giving site in the world – said that 2009 was its most successful fundraising year ever for the London Marathon. **15%** more runners raised funds online and over **half** of all runners had a fundraising page.

The total raised though *JustGiving* amounted to around **£25 million.**

20% more charities received funds compared to 2008.

At peak times, the *JustGiving* site was dealing with **2 donations** a second.

1,608
charities were supported in 2009 by London Marathon fundraisers

JustGiving London Marathon 2009 fundraising by charity category

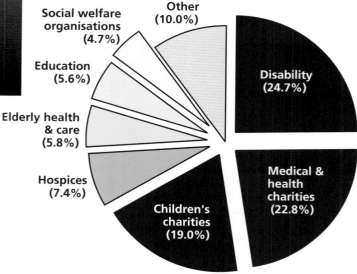

Social welfare organisations (4.7%)
Other (10.0%)
Education (5.6%)
Elderly health & care (5.8%)
Hospices (7.4%)
Disability (24.7%)
Medical & health charities (22.8%)
Children's charities (19.0%)

Other includes: sports, animal shelters, rescue, international aid agencies, homelessness and corporate social responsibility

Rising and falling fundraising share 2009 compared to 2008

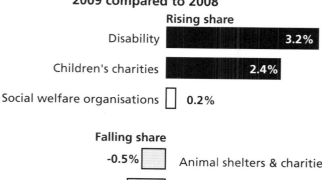

Rising share

Disability	3.2%
Children's charities	2.4%
Social welfare organisations	0.2%

Falling share

-0.5%	Animal shelters & charities
-0.8%	Elderly health & care
-3.9%	Medical and health charities

Not only were Disability and Children's charities major recipients of London Marathon fundraising in 2009, they also grew their overall share compared to 2008.

Medical and health charities retain their number 2 position overall but their share of the total has fallen by almost 4%.

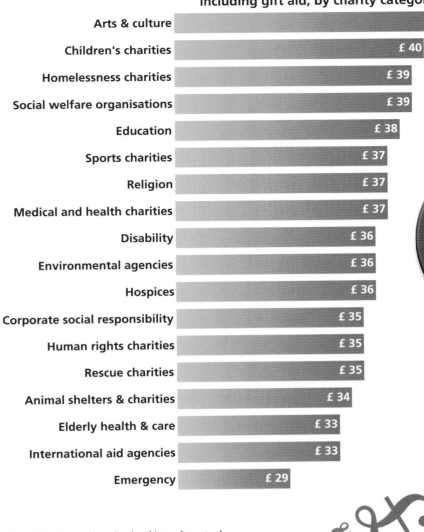

Average London Marathon donation, including gift aid, by charity category

Arts & culture	£ 43
Children's charities	£ 40
Homelessness charities	£ 39
Social welfare organisations	£ 39
Education	£ 38
Sports charities	£ 37
Religion	£ 37
Medical and health charities	£ 37
Disability	£ 36
Environmental agencies	£ 36
Hospices	£ 36
Corporate social responsibility	£ 35
Human rights charities	£ 35
Rescue charities	£ 35
Animal shelters & charities	£ 34
Elderly health & care	£ 33
International aid agencies	£ 33
Emergency	£ 29

The average value of single sponsorship donation in 2009 went down slightly compared to 2008 but the number of donations went up by 25%

Entrants to the 2009 London Marathon are expected to have raised more than **£45 million** for charity

Gift Aid is an easy way for charities to increase the value of gifts of money from UK taxpayers by claiming back the basic rate tax paid by the donor.

Gift Aid is now worth nearly **£1bn a year** to UK charities and their donors.

Over 2,000 people who had just donated on the *JustGiving* website were asked about their attitudes to giving:

56.1% said they had thought harder about how much they gave to charity. These people were asked if their attitude to giving had changed:

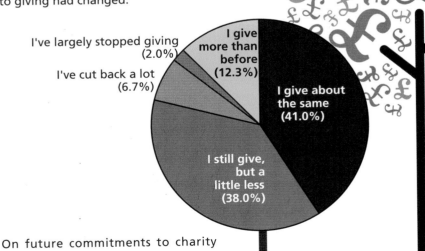

I've largely stopped giving (2.0%)

I've cut back a lot (6.7%)

I give more than before (12.3%)

I give about the same (41.0%)

I still give, but a little less (38.0%)

On future commitments to charity giving, **34.1%** said that they would consider giving less or stopping giving to charity.

Source: JustGiving – Flora London Marathon 2009. Online fundraising results, Donor attitudes to giving in the credit crunch September 2009

http://www.justgiving.com
http://www.direct.gov.uk

Dream home

Owning their own home now seems an impossible goal for many

Despite falling house prices and record low interest rates, **65%** of non-homeowners in the UK still believe that they will never have enough money to get on the property ladder.

Percentage of people who think they will never own a property by city

City	Percentage
Norwich	92%
Leeds	83%
Brighton	81%
Newcastle	75%
Bristol	71%
Glasgow	69%
Liverpool	68%
Cardiff	67%
Plymouth	65%
Manchester	63%
Edinburgh	63%
Birmingham	62%
London	62%
Nottingham	53%
Southampton	50%
Sheffield	47%

Of those still living in hope, one in 20 (**5%**) think they will have to wait more than five years to get a mortgage. One in 7 (**14%**) estimate they could be on the ladder in between two and five years' time, while one in 10 (**10%**) think it will be between one and two years; and one in 20 (**5%**) in between six months and a year.

Source: Propertylive.co.uk
http://www.propertylive.co.uk

Food & drink

Make a meal of it

Researchers have devised a simple guide to nutritional values of everyday foods - with some surprising results

We should eat healthy foods, but how do we know what food is healthy? Scientists from Yale University, USA, have come up with a guide to the nutritional quality of food.

The idea is simple – each food is given a score out of 100 based on how much good stuff and bad stuff is in it.

Overall Nutritional Quality Index (ONQI)

How does it work?

The quality and quantity of over 30 different nutrients are taken into account, as well as the strength of their association with specific health conditions, to calculate the ONQI score.

Nutrients that are generally **good** for you are added up. **The more good nutrients, the higher the final score.**

GOOD NUTRIENTS For example

FIBRE
Vitamins
OMEGA-3
Dietary minerals:
MAGNESIUM
IRON ETC

÷

Nutrients that are generally **bad** for you are added up. **The more bad nutrients, the lower the final score.**

BAD NUTRIENTS For example

SATURATED FAT
SODIUM
TRANSFAT
Sugar
Cholesterol

=

ONQI SCORE From 1-100.

How does this affect the food we eat?

Look at the meal below. Most people would think this was healthy food, and compared to many junk foods it definitely is. However, when you add up the ONQI score, the results are quite surprising:

Condensed cream of broccoli soup 21

Bagel 23 **Ham** 27
Swiss cheese 17

Apple chips 24

TOTAL 112

If you were to add lettuce to this meal, you increase the overall score dramatically. **The nutritional score of the lettuce alone is a massive 82.** That is more than all of the sandwich ingredients added together!

TOTAL with lettuce: 194

Small changes – big difference

The extras that go into our food, and the way we cook them can make a **BIG** difference to their nutritional value. For example, the broccoli in this pasta has the highest nutritional value of **100**, meaning there are only good nutrients in it. However, as an ingredient in the tinned soup, the value is only **21.** Apple chips were only worth **24**, whereas a plain uncooked apple is worth **96**. Ham, which has been cured and salted is only worth **27**, while a plain unprocessed salmon fillet is worth **87**.

Vegetarian split-pea soup 63

Pasta 50   **Salmon fillet** 87
Broccoli 100   **Tomato** 96

Apple 96

TOTAL 492

Fancy a drink with that?

Non-fat milk

91

Fizzy drinks

1

Because of the good nutrients in milk, the ONQI score in non-fat milk is very high. For **whole milk** however, because of its fat content, the ONQI score drops to **55**. Still, compared to fizzy drinks, which have little or no useful nutrients for our body, any plain unflavoured milk is a better option.

Hard to swallow?

When everything that goes into our food is taken into account we find many foods that we eat regularly have very little nutritional goodness in them at all. This means our body will work hard to digest them, and get very little in return.

A favourite breakfast treat we are all familiar with, the bacon butty, for example, is so much more than meat and carbohydrate. Once the pork has been cured and treated, and the flour to make white bread has been refined, there is very little left that is nutritionally good for us.

Non-streaky bacon 13

White bread 9

TOTAL 22

This has less nutritional value than sherbet **which has a score of:** 23

Source: Nuval Nutritional Scoring System, Yale University

Cost of 100 calories

Can you eat healthily on a budget?

Dr Tim Lobstein, Director of the Childhood Research Programme at the International Association for the Study of Obesity has calculated the cost of 100 calories of food energy from different types of food.

He discovered that the cheapest way to get 100 calories of energy is to eat fats, processed starches and sugars, all of which are most commonly used and most highly used in budget foods.

People on a low income buy the kind of food that will fill them most cheaply but the nutritional value is often poor. For example:

- A budget beef pie may contain only **18%** beef and an even higher percentage of gristle, collagen and fat.
- An apple pie – just **14%** apple.
- A budget beef and onion pie – only **7%** beef.

Cost of 100 calories from healthy options

Cost of 100 calories from budget options

Premium sausages v 'Value' sausages

The typical premium sausage has a 92% pork content while the value version has only 34%. The next ingredients in the value sausage are water, rusk and pork fat. A similar problem occurs with mince. 100 calories of lean mince costs 22.8p, while 'value' mince, containing more fat, costs 4.8p.

22p

4p

Fresh potatoes v Frozen chips

Some oven chips contain as little as 88% potato, the rest being made up of batter, vegetable oil, colourings and sodium. The processing of the potato also affects its nutritional value. If you prepare your own potatoes from fresh, you do at least have control over what goes into them.

7.6p

2p

Fresh orange juice v Orange squash

Fresh orange juice contains 100% orange juice whilst orange squash contains only 3%. The rest is made up of water, sweeteners and additives.

38p

5p

"Someone receiving benefit has about 13p to spend on food with 100 calorie value"
— Dr Tim Lobstein, speaking to the Royal Society of Medicine's Forum on Maternity and the Newborn

There is a big difference between the price and the nutritional value of two 'identical' meals from different supermarket ranges. We are encouraged to eat more fresh vegetables and yet if you were to add them to a meal, it would add to the cost too. The cost of 100 calories of carrots is 21.8p, while broccoli, one of the so called nutritional 'superfoods' costs 51p for 100 calories.

Calories and Class on page 107 of *Essential Articles 12* explains how class affects your diet and your health
Top stores call them budget food lines on page 108-110 discusses the soaring sales of 'value' products during the credit crunch

Source: The Cost of 100 Calories, Tim Lobstein, IASO 2009

http://www.iaso.org

Food for thought

Salt, sugar, fat and fruit: the truth about our diets!

The good news

A survey of UK adults showed a decline in the number of people eating too much fat, a reduction in the average salt intake and more people consuming at least three portions of fruit and veg per day.

What we know

A survey also revealed that more women (78%) than men (62%) knew that the recommended portions of fruit and vegetables per day was five.

71% of men and 72% of women believed their diet to be 'quite' healthy. Women (19%) were more likely than men (16%) to consider their diet 'very healthy'.

The bad news

A new analysis of the same information reveals a less rosy picture. **In fact just 8 people in every thousand in the UK are eating a healthy diet.** The new analysis looked at how many people were eating diets that met the recommended targets – not one at a time, but all of the targets at the same time.

Proportion of UK adults eating a healthy diet

	Recommended target (Proportion of daily energy intake)	Men	Women
Non Milk Extrinsic sugars*	less than 10%	32%	48%
Total fat	less than 30%	23%	28%
Saturated fat	less than 10%	17%	19%
Fruit & vegetables	more than 400g/day	10%	14%
Sodium	less than 2,000mg/day	8%	43%
All at once...		**0.4%**	**1.2%**

* Sugars which have been added to the food and are not found naturally within it

Sources: The Food Magazine, The Food Commission, 2008; The NHS Healthy Survey for England 2007
http://www.ic.nhs.uk/
http://www.foodmagazine.org.uk

Salty start

How one meal can tip you over your daily limit of salt

Breakfast is considered the 'most important meal of the day' yet a survey reveals that many foods commonly eaten for breakfast have large amounts of hidden salt, often more than the recommended daily amount of 6g (for an adult)

A traditional full English breakfast of:

- one sausage
- two rashers of bacon
- one fried egg
- baked beans
- two slices of buttered toast

contains 4.5g of salt

A slightly larger full English breakfast, as served in many cafés around the country (before any ketchup, brown sauce or extra salt is added) of:

- two rashers of bacon
- two sausages
- one fried egg
- mushrooms
- baked beans
- two slices of black pudding
- a tomato
- one slice of buttered toast

contains 6.1g of salt

But many who would not dream of eating a fry-up could find that their 'healthier options' breakfast is still very high in salt.

A healthy start at home of coffee, orange juice, small 30g serving of Kellogg's Cornflakes plus two slices of toast with butter and Marmite contains over **2.8g** of salt, nearly half the adult recommended salt limit for the day.

0.175g salt in one boiled egg

As a general rule:

Foods **high** in salt have more than **1.5g**/100g (or 0.6g sodium/100g)

Foods **low** in salt have less than **0.3g** salt/100g (or 0.1g sodium/100g)

Examples of some higher and lower salt breakfast options

Higher salt product	Salt per portion	Lower salt alternative	Salt per portion
Burger King Big Breakfast Butty with HP Sauce	5.6g	Caffe Nero All Day Breakfast Panini	2.0g
EAT Bacon Butty	2.3g	Pret A Manger Free-Range Egg Mayo & Bacon Breakfast Baguette	1.0g
Pret A Manger Egg and Bacon Croissant	2.4g	McDonalds Bacon & Egg McMuffin	1.4g
Costa Raspberry and White Choc Muffin	1.7g	Caffe Nero Raspberry and White Chocolate Muffin	0.6g
2 slices of Marmite on Toast	2.1g	2 slices of Jam/Marmalade on toast	1.1g
30g portion of Kellogg's Cornflakes with 125ml semi-skimmed milk	0.7g	45g portion of Shredded Wheat with 125ml semi-skimmed milk	0.2g
Large portion of baked beans on 2 toast and 2 butter	2.58g	2 portions of mushrooms on 2 toast and 2 butter	1.08g

We all need to be aware of the amount of salt in our diet. The amount we currently eat puts our blood pressure up which is the major cause of strokes and heart attacks in later life.

Reducing salt intake by around 2.5g a day can reduce this risk by a quarter.

Source: CASH – Consensus Action on Salt & Health, 2008

http://www.actiononsalt.org.uk

Added extras

The Food Standards Agency has to ensure that the additives in food do not compromise safety in any way.

Additives typically seen on food labels include: antioxidants, colours, emulsifiers, stabilisers, gelling agents and thickeners, flavour enhancers, preservatives and sweeteners.

Flavourings are **NOT** classed as additives.

3,000 people were questioned to find out what they considered to be additives – and how that was different to the legal position.

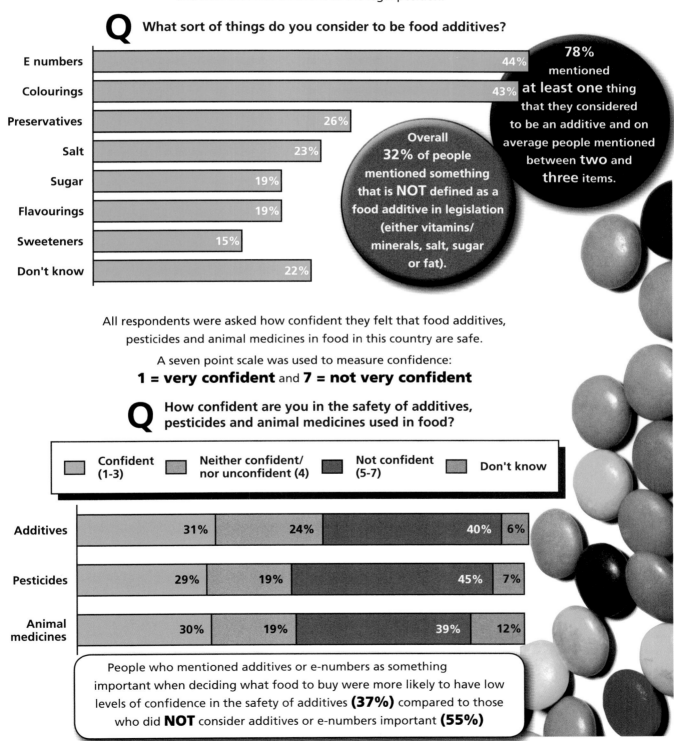

Q **What sort of things do you consider to be food additives?**

E numbers	44%
Colourings	43%
Preservatives	26%
Salt	23%
Sugar	19%
Flavourings	19%
Sweeteners	15%
Don't know	22%

78% mentioned **at least one** thing that they considered to be an additive and on average people mentioned between **two** and **three** items.

Overall **32%** of people mentioned something that is **NOT** defined as a food additive in legislation (either vitamins/minerals, salt, sugar or fat).

All respondents were asked how confident they felt that food additives, pesticides and animal medicines in food in this country are safe.

A seven point scale was used to measure confidence:
1 = very confident and **7 = not very confident**

Q **How confident are you in the safety of additives, pesticides and animal medicines used in food?**

- Confident (1-3)
- Neither confident/ nor unconfident (4)
- Not confident (5-7)
- Don't know

	Confident (1-3)	Neither (4)	Not confident (5-7)	Don't know
Additives	31%	24%	40%	6%
Pesticides	29%	19%	45%	7%
Animal medicines	30%	19%	39%	12%

People who mentioned additives or e-numbers as something important when deciding what food to buy were more likely to have low levels of confidence in the safety of additives **(37%)** compared to those who did **NOT** consider additives or e-numbers important **(55%)**

Source: Gfk NOP, Food Standards Agency

http://www.food.gov.uk

Pesticides on a plate

An average of 30-40% of food we eat contains pesticide residue

What are pesticides?

The word pesticide covers a wide range of chemicals used to control insect pests (insecticides), plant diseases (fungicides), weeds (herbicides), but also to control rats and mice, slugs and snails or other unwanted organisms.

These may be applied to food crops to prevent damage to crop quantity and quality.

Why do we use them?

Today's demand from supermarkets and consumers for cosmetically perfect fresh fruit and vegetables encourages the continued use of pesticides. People like to buy produce with no blemishes or variations in colour, size and shape – Grade 1 produce.

Grade II fruits and vegetables are equally good in terms of nutrition but may not look so good. If consumers want perfect-looking produce, supermarkets will supply it and producers will continue to use pesticides to make it.

- There are over 1,000 different pesticides used in the world today
- Over **31 million** kg of pesticides were applied to UK crops in 2005
- Equivalent to 0.5kg per person living in Britain

Who do they affect?

The workers:

There are regulations in place for the safe use of pesticides in developed countries, but much of our food is imported from developing countries.

Each year, 3 million workers in agriculture in the developing world experience severe poisoning from pesticides and about 18,000 die. According to one study, as many as 25 million workers in developing countries may suffer mild pesticide poisoning yearly.

The environment:

People are not the only potential victims of pesticide poisoning: wildlife, livestock and household pets are also at risk as pesticides spread beyond their target.

Over 98% of sprayed insecticides and 95% of herbicides reach a destination other than their target species, including non-target species. Pesticides suspended in the air as particles are carried by wind to other areas. They are one of the causes of water pollution, and some pesticides contribute to soil contamination.

The consumer:

On average, 30% of the food purchased by the British public contains pesticide residues, according to government data.

It is highly unlikely that UK consumers would suffer acute poisoning from the tiny concentrations of pesticides regularly found in food but the possible long-term consequences cause concern.

Current risk assessment is done on a single chemical basis, yet we are exposed to a daily diet of a mixture of pesticides, and scientists have very little understanding of how these 'cocktails' may act inside the human body.

The top five fruits, vegetables and other foods most frequently contaminated by pesticides

Product	Number of samples	% with residue
Fruit		
Soft citrus eg mandarins	167	100%
Citrus	512	91%
Pears	1066	73%
Bananas	205	71%
Strawberries	283	70%
Vegetables		
Speciality beans	70	76%
Salads	70	74%
Celery	137	69%
Herbs	51	53%
Potato chips	48	48%
Other food items		
Barley, pearl	4	100%
Bran	107	98%
Rye	34	91%
Oats	34	85%
Wheat grain	137	82%

Some suggestions from the Pesticides Action Network:

1. Don't stop eating your 5-a-day fruit and vegetables. You need them. However if they are not organic, make sure you wash them before you eat them.

2. If you cannot switch to a wholly organic diet, look at the things you eat most often, and replace them with organic versions.

3. Be prepared to buy groceries that are not cosmetically perfect. Only when consumers show that they are willing to buy blemished produce will supermarkets and growers have to stop hiding behind the argument that "it's what customers want".

4. Buy organic and fair-trade produce as much as you can. Remember that pesticides are not just used in food. Cotton, for example, is the most pesticide intensive crop in the world and many poor cotton farming families and workers in Africa, Asia and Latin America suffer poisonings and fatalities.

5. Grow your own fruit and veg. Even a window box can grow a crop of salad; a small patio can accommodate pots of tomatoes.

Sources: Pesticides on a plate, Pesticide Action Network
http://www.pan-uk.org/
http://www.click4carbon.com

Best before...

Over 3,000 people in the UK were asked
about their views on various food issues

**What date do you think is the best
indicator of whether food is safe to eat?**
(Correct answer below)

49%	32%	10%	5%	5%
Use by date	Best before end date (BBE)	Sell by date	Display until date	Don't know

NB Figures may not add up to 100% due to rounding

About of **quarter** of the people asked said they would not eat bread or cereals past their BBE dates, despite this being a guide to their **quality** rather than their **safety.** This suggests a significant amount of food may be **wasted** unnecessarily.

What time limit would you eat food past its use by/best before end date?

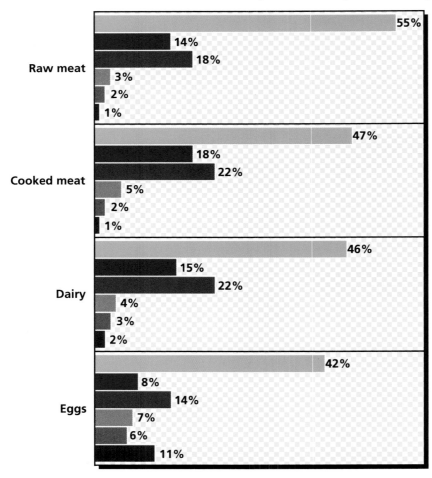

Raw meat
- 55%
- 14%
- 18%
- 3%
- 2%
- 1%

Cooked meat
- 47%
- 18%
- 22%
- 5%
- 2%
- 1%

Dairy
- 46%
- 15%
- 22%
- 4%
- 3%
- 2%

Eggs
- 42%
- 8%
- 14%
- 7%
- 6%
- 11%

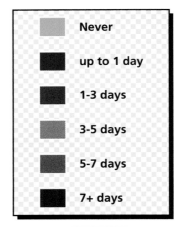

	Never
	up to 1 day
	1-3 days
	3-5 days
	5-7 days
	7+ days

Respondents aged 16-34 were the most likely to say that they would **NOT** eat any of the different food types if they were past their dates.

Overall respondents were more likely to take notice of the **use by dates** when using meat, dairy and egg products.

*Source: Food Standards Agency – Public Attitudes to Food Issues, 2009
http://www.food.gov.uk*

Answer: Use by date

Save your bacon?

A survey of UK adults about food issues showed that **36%** of people were concerned about the way the animals we raise for meat are treated during their lives, and **30%** were concerned about the way those animals were slaughtered.

What concerns you about the way food animals are raised? (%)

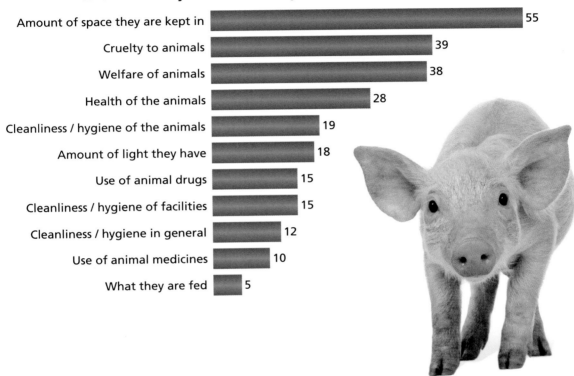

Amount of space they are kept in	55
Cruelty to animals	39
Welfare of animals	38
Health of the animals	28
Cleanliness / hygiene of the animals	19
Amount of light they have	18
Use of animal drugs	15
Cleanliness / hygiene of facilities	15
Cleanliness / hygiene in general	12
Use of animal medicines	10
What they are fed	5

What concerns you about the way food animals are slaughtered? (%)

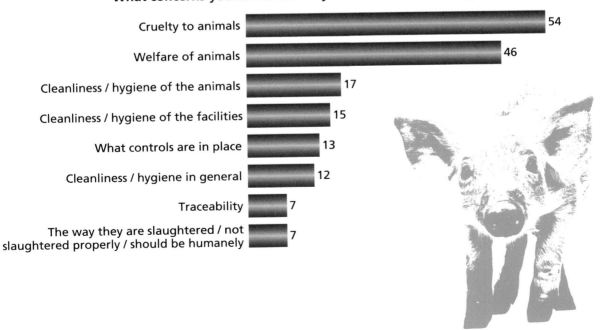

Cruelty to animals	54
Welfare of animals	46
Cleanliness / hygiene of the animals	17
Cleanliness / hygiene of the facilities	15
What controls are in place	13
Cleanliness / hygiene in general	12
Traceability	7
The way they are slaughtered / not slaughtered properly / should be humanely	7

Source: Food Standards Agency: Quarterly Public Tracker, September 2008
http://www.food.gov.uk

Cooking up a storm

Believe it or not meat & milk are destroying our environment

The problem with food

There are many major environmental and ethical problems affected by the way we produce and consume food. For example – **water use, biodiversity, various forms of air, soil and water pollution, animal welfare, international development** and **food security. One of these major issues is GHG (greenhouse gas) emissions.**

Emerging research suggests that the UK and other developed countries need to **reduce** their **emissions by at least 80% by 2050** if we are to keep the concentration of greenhouse gases below a critical 450 ppm (parts per million).

What percentage of the UK's total GHG emissions are from our food production and consumption?

- 7.5% Agriculture
- 0.7% Fertiliser manufacture
- 1.8% Food manufacture
- 2.5% Packaging & transport
- 5.5% Home, retail & catering
- 0.4% Waste disposal

What foods?

18.4% of all our GHG emissions are related to food. That means that all the other industries in the country account for just 81.6%. Of all the food related emissions, the meat and dairy sectors together account for just over half, fruit & vegetables account for 15%, drinks & other sugar products account for 15% and bread, pastry & flour for 13%.

As the population continues to increase not only in this country but all over the world, the likelihood of us reducing our food production and consumption is slim.

How much?

The way we eat now (average per person in the UK, per week)

1.6kg meat & 4.2 litres of milk. This is equivalent to:

6 Sausages (450g)

2 Chicken Breasts (350g)

4 Ham sandwiches (100g)

8 Slices of bacon (250g)

3 Burgers (450g)

3 Litres of milk

100g of cheese and a helping of cream

The solution?

Future recommended diet, based on recommended GHG reduction of 80% (average per person per week)

500g of meat and 1 litre of milk. This is equivalent to:

1 Quarter-pound beefburger

2 Sausages

3 Rashers of bacon

1 Chicken breast

1 Litre of milk or 100g of cheese

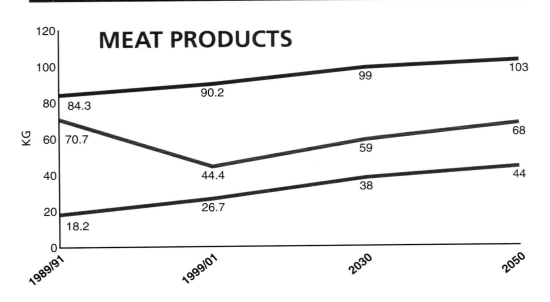

The problem is that there are far fewer people living in the developed and transition economies than there are in the developing world. And so, even if the 1.4 billion of us living in these wealthier countries were to reduce our consumption, the consequences would be only a 15% reduction in meat and 22% in milk production in 2050.

— Developed countries — Transition countries — Developing countries

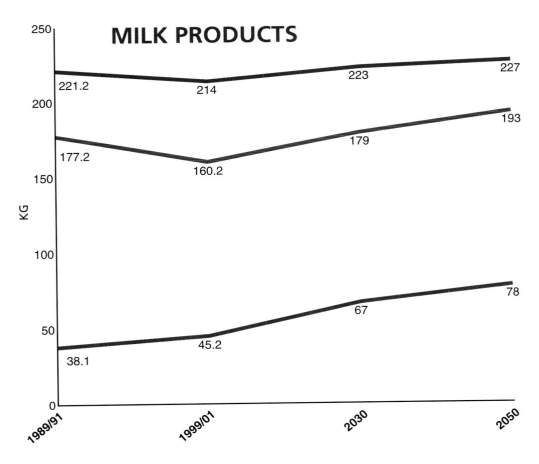

Meat and milk production is expected to double by 2050. So even with rich world reductions, global volumes for meat and milk would still be 70% and 45% higher in 2050 than today. All other things being equal, the consequences will be a very great increase in global livestock GHGs.

Source: Cooking up a storm,
Food Climate Research Network, September 2008
http://www.fcrn.org.uk/

Enough to eat

Where does our 5-a-day come from?

Food sufficiency

As a nation, we are encouraged to eat more fruit & veg, yet a large proportion of the fresh food we eat comes from abroad. This is a potential problem because it involves a complex mix of financial, environmental, ethical and political issues. For example, when we buy organic, fair trade green beans from Kenya, are we protecting our health and supporting a developing country or are we destroying the environment through a wasteful use of energy in food miles and stealing the water from a parched area?

Because population growth and climate change could also have an impact on UK food security – which for most people means their ability to feed themselves and their families with nutritious and affordable food – the government wants us to increase the amount of food which is 'home grown'.

Even though we can't grow all our own food, current supplies of food to the UK are likely to be secure because most food imports are from elsewhere in the EU and we also have good access to world markets.

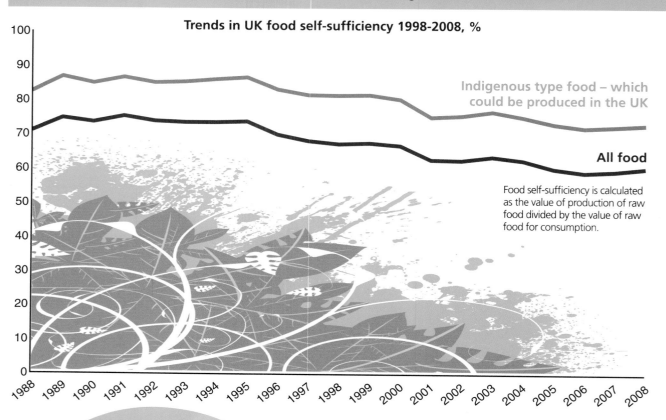

Trends in UK food self-sufficiency 1998-2008, %

Indigenous type food – which could be produced in the UK

All food

Food self-sufficiency is calculated as the value of production of raw food divided by the value of raw food for consumption.

What do we really want?

What we eat and our attitudes to food have changed markedly in recent years in the UK. People appear to want higher quality food and to eat more healthily. At the same time consumers have become more aware of what food production does to the environment.

On the other hand we also want food we can afford and which fits our lifestyles. We still like convenience food, takeaways and we eat outside of the home more often than in the past.

Can we grow what we want?

We are buying more fruit and vegetables yet between 1988 and 2007 UK "self-sufficiency" in fresh fruit roughly halved. Since then it has remained at just above **10%**. Self-sufficiency in fresh vegetable production has fallen by **20%** since 1988 and is still falling. It is now between **55%** and **60%**.

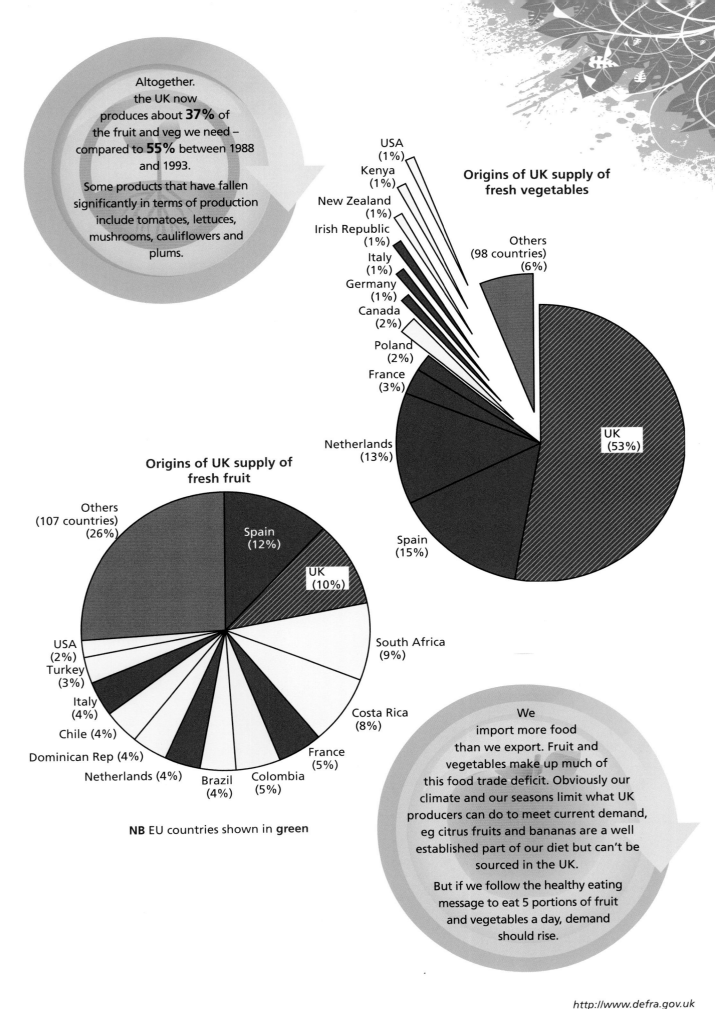

Altogether. the UK now produces about **37%** of the fruit and veg we need – compared to **55%** between 1988 and 1993.

Some products that have fallen significantly in terms of production include tomatoes, lettuces, mushrooms, cauliflowers and plums.

Origins of UK supply of fresh vegetables

USA (1%)
Kenya (1%)
New Zealand (1%)
Irish Republic (1%)
Italy (1%)
Germany (1%)
Canada (2%)
Poland (2%)
France (3%)
Netherlands (13%)
Spain (15%)
Others (98 countries) (6%)
UK (53%)

Origins of UK supply of fresh fruit

Others (107 countries) (26%)
Spain (12%)
UK (10%)
South Africa (9%)
Costa Rica (8%)
France (5%)
Colombia (5%)
Brazil (4%)
Netherlands (4%)
Dominican Rep (4%)
Chile (4%)
Italy (4%)
Turkey (3%)
USA (2%)

NB EU countries shown in **green**

We import more food than we export. Fruit and vegetables make up much of this food trade deficit. Obviously our climate and our seasons limit what UK producers can do to meet current demand, eg citrus fruits and bananas are a well established part of our diet but can't be sourced in the UK.

But if we follow the healthy eating message to eat 5 portions of fruit and vegetables a day, demand should rise.

Source: Defra, Cabinet Office – Food Matters © Crown copyright

http://www.defra.gov.uk
http://www.cabinetoffice.gov.uk

Hot...

Tea is the largest single drink choice and drunk each day by **59%** of people. It makes up **35%** of what we drink. Coffee makes up **19%**.

Advice from the Food Standards Agency is that people should consume approximately **1.2 litres** of fluid a day from drinks (excluding alcohol), on top of fluid obtained from foods.

The popularity of fruit juice and smoothies has been growing – a glass of fruit juice or a smoothie can count towards the recommended **five portions** of fruit and vegetables a day.

People consume **7-8 units per day** on average – a unit is classed as a serving of a product, regardless of the amount consumed (for example a **cup** of tea or **glass** of milk would equate to one unit each, regardless of whether 175ml of tea was consumed versus 330ml of milk).

What we are drinking
Base: all respondents

Drink	Percentage
Tea	58.8%
Instant coffee	34.0%
Juices/juice drinks	32.9%
Alcohol	26.7%
Fizzy drinks	26.1%
Squash	23.0%
Plain milk	16.7%
Bottled water	13.0%
Hot chocolate	6.2%
Fruit & herbal tea	5.1%
Speciality coffee	4.2%
Roasted & ground coffee	3.8%
Flavoured milk	2.4%
Drinking yoghurt	0.3%
Probiotics	0.3%

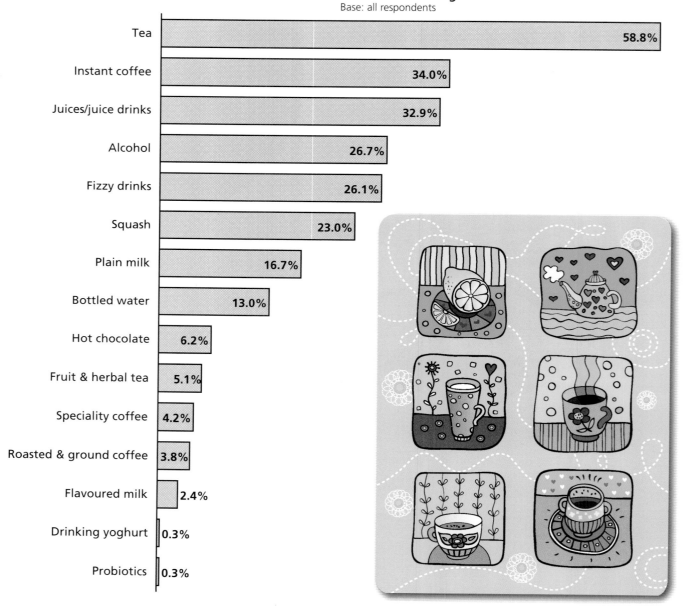

Base: Over 22,500 people including 3,500 children were surveyed in 2008

...or cold?

...but for young people, cold drinks are the most popular

If everything drunk by 13-15-year-olds was divided up, this is how it would look

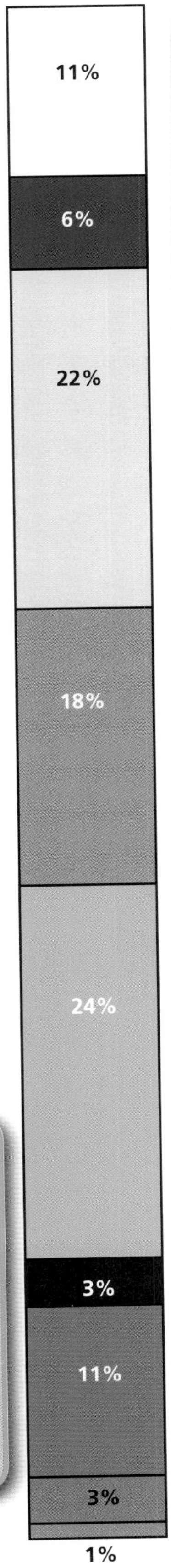

Milk
Bottled water
Squash
Juices/Juice drinks
Fizzy drinks
Coffee
Tea
Other hot
Alcohol
11%
6%
22%
18%
24%
3%
11%
3%
1%

Cold drinks make up a bigger proportion of children's diets than they do for adults.

For all ages, **squash** remains a very popular, low cost drink choice. Alongside squash, there is an increasing range of other cold drinks being consumed, while the largest decline overall can be seen in the consumption of tea and coffee – it is only in adulthood that tea and coffee make up a large part of daily drinks.

Drinks in school

71% of drinks are brought from home, **squash** is the main drink provided by parents, and **milk and tap water** make up over **50%** of drinks consumed in school.

When obtained elsewhere, **bottled water** is the most popular choice, accounting for **21%** of drinks choices, **fizzy drinks** make up **18%** and **fruit drinks 16%.**

ROBINSONS
orange
NO ADDED SUGAR

55% of soft drinks consumed by children now contain ***no added sugar*** compared to **46%** in 2004.

Children are now **20%** more likely to consume a drink with ***no added sugar*** than they were in 2004.

Out of home but not in school

Fizzy drinks are the most popular choice outside home and school and account for **21%** of drinks choices.

Squash and milk each account for **12%** of drinks choices, **tap water** for **13%** and **fruit drinks 11%.**

Source: British Soft Drinks Association 2008
http://www.britishsoftdrinks.com

Waiter – water!

Research commissioned by **WaterAid** reveals that tap water is the preferred choice for **63%** of people when they dine out

25% prefer to ask for **tap water**, but sometimes feel **pressure** to order **bottled water** in a restaurant

38% always ask for **tap water** in a restaurant

There's a steady upwards trend of people who order **tap water** ie from **34%** of the 25-34 age group, to **49%** of those aged 55-64

39% of women are more likely to choose **tap water** in a restaurant

Men are significantly more likely to order **bottled water** in a restaurant than women

37% of people always ask for **bottled water** in a restaurant

Those who order **bottled water** peak at **42%** for the 35-44 age group, falling steadily to **30%** for the 55-64s

The people most likely to order **bottled water** are in Greater London and Scotland **(44%)** and in the North West and East/West Midlands **(42%)**

The least likely were those in the South East/ East Anglia at **28%**

Why does it matter?
Whilst here in the UK we ponder which brand of 'lifestyle' water to choose, a staggering **884 million** people in the developing world are without any clean water

Base: 2,018 UK adults in March 2009

Source & photos: WaterAid
http://www.wateraid.org

Health

Stopping the spread

Measles is a leading cause of death among young children in low income countries...

Despite the availability of a safe and effective vaccine there were **280,771** reported cases worldwide and an estimated **197,000** deaths from measles in 2007 – that's **540** deaths every day or **22** deaths every hour.

Most of the deaths were children under the age of five.

Measles deaths have dropped by 74% since 2000. The African region was the largest contributor to this decline

The United Nations 2010 goal to reduce measles deaths by **90%** depends on ensuring that all children receive two doses of the measles vaccine.

Between 2000 and 2007, an intensified vaccination campaign has meant that the region which includes countries such as Afghanistan, Pakistan, Somalia and Sudan, has achieved this goal three years early, and reduced the deaths from **96,000** to **10,000**.

More than 95% of measles deaths occur in low-income countries with weak health infrastructure

Trend in global measles incidence and immunisation coverage

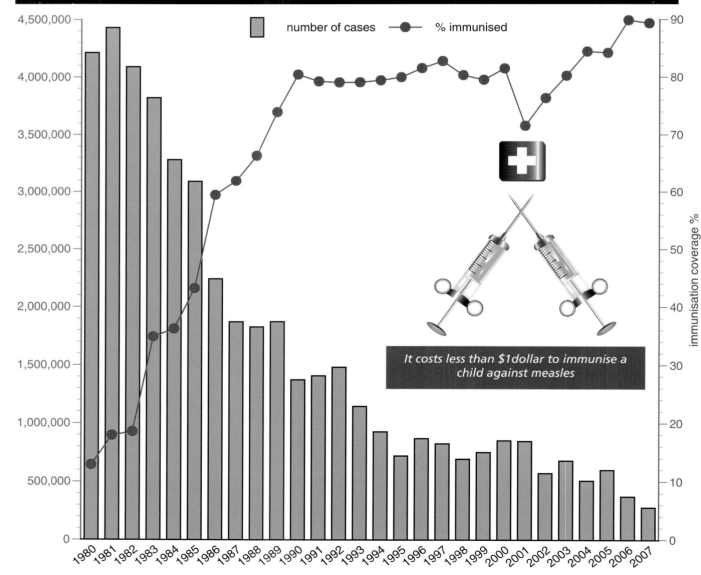

number of cases — % immunised

It costs less than $1dollar to immunise a child against measles

Source: World Heath Organization, UNICEF

http://www.who.int
http://www.unicef.org

...and is spreading quickly among unvaccinated children in the UK

Measles is highly infectious and cases have risen by over **36%** in the year from 2007 to 2008.

The majority of all measles cases could have been prevented as most were in children who were not fully protected with the MMR (measles, mumps & rubella) vaccine. Scare stories in 1998 that linked the vaccination to autism, caused a drop in the number of people allowing their children to be vaccinated.

However, public confidence in the vaccine is now high with more than 8 out of 10 children receiving one dose of MMR by their 2nd birthday.

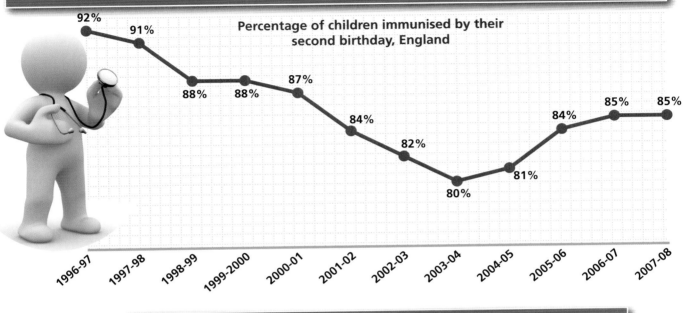

Percentage of children immunised by their second birthday, England

- 1996-97: 92%
- 1997-98: 91%
- 1998-99: 88%
- 1999-2000: 88%
- 2000-01: 87%
- 2001-02: 84%
- 2002-03: 82%
- 2003-04: 80%
- 2004-05: 81%
- 2005-06: 84%
- 2006-07: 85%
- 2007-08: 85%

A single dose of the MMR vaccine gives about 90% protection against measles and mumps and 95-99% protection against rubella.

A second dose of MMR was introduced in 1996. The number of pre-school children in the UK receiving both doses of MMR by their 5th birthday is **77.9%**.

Two doses of the vaccine are needed to achieve the greatest immunity and prevent any further outbreaks.

Children who weren't vaccinated many years ago are still at risk.

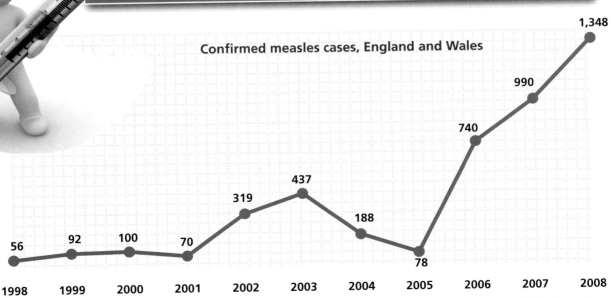

Confirmed measles cases, England and Wales

- 1998: 56
- 1999: 92
- 2000: 100
- 2001: 70
- 2002: 319
- 2003: 437
- 2004: 188
- 2005: 78
- 2006: 740
- 2007: 990
- 2008: 1,348

Source: Health Protection Agency; Centre for Public Health

http://www.hpa.org.uk
http://www.cph.org.uk

Diabetes – the silent assassin

80% of people with diabetes live in low and middle income countries

The total number of people worldwide with diabetes is projected to rise from **171 million** in 2000 to **366 million in 2030**

The number of people with diabetes is increasing due to population growth, ageing, urbanisation and the increase in obesity and physical inactivity

The prevalence of diabetes for all age groups worldwide was estimated to be **2.8%** in 2000 and **4.4%** in 2030

By 2030 it is estimated that the number of people aged over 64 with diabetes will be more than **82 million** in developing countries and **48 million** in developed countries

Estimated cases 2000 and 2030
Countries ranked in the top 10 in each year
(ranking shown in brackets)

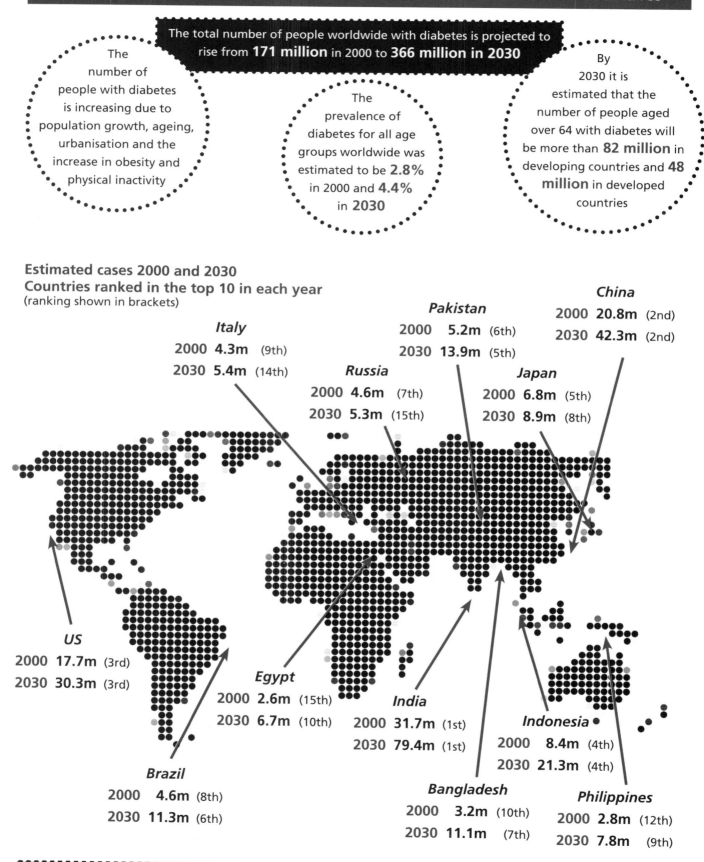

China
2000 **20.8m** (2nd)
2030 **42.3m** (2nd)

Pakistan
2000 **5.2m** (6th)
2030 **13.9m** (5th)

Italy
2000 **4.3m** (9th)
2030 **5.4m** (14th)

Russia
2000 **4.6m** (7th)
2030 **5.3m** (15th)

Japan
2000 **6.8m** (5th)
2030 **8.9m** (8th)

US
2000 **17.7m** (3rd)
2030 **30.3m** (3rd)

Egypt
2000 **2.6m** (15th)
2030 **6.7m** (10th)

India
2000 **31.7m** (1st)
2030 **79.4m** (1st)

Indonesia
2000 **8.4m** (4th)
2030 **21.3m** (4th)

Brazil
2000 **4.6m** (8th)
2030 **11.3m** (6th)

Bangladesh
2000 **3.2m** (10th)
2030 **11.1m** (7th)

Philippines
2000 **2.8m** (12th)
2030 **7.8m** (9th)

Bearing in mind all the factors that contribute to diabetes, especially obesity, it is likely that these figures are an underestimate

Source: World Health Organization
http://www.who.int/diabetes/en/

Type 1 diabetes develops when the body is unable to produce any insulin. It usually appears before the age of 40 and accounts for between 5-15% of people with diabetes.

Most cases of diabetes will be **Type 2** – this occurs when the body cannot use insulin properly and produces less than the body needs. It is often linked with being overweight and with an ageing population.

An increasingly unhealthy lifestyle is a major factor in this **preventable** disease now being diagnosed in a growing number of younger people and even children.

There are currently **2.3 million** people in the UK diagnosed with diabetes – approximately **2 million** of them have Type 2.

In addition, there are more than **500,000** who have Type 2 but are **NOT** aware of it.

Number of people diagnosed with diabetes, UK
(latest figures for each country)

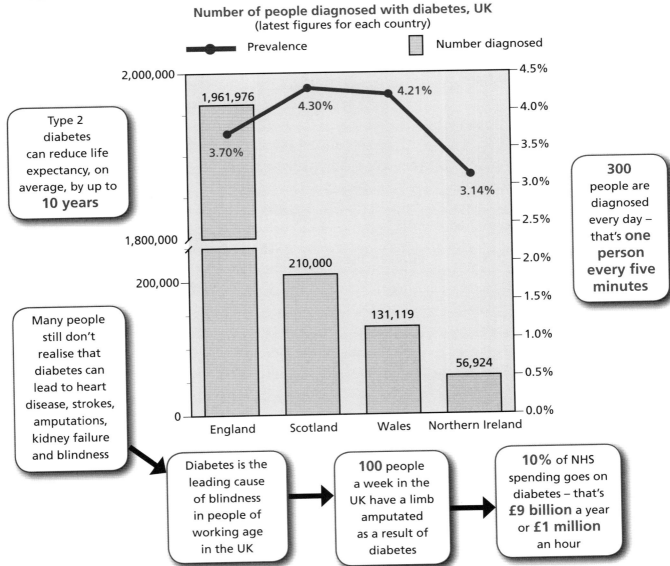

Prevalence — **Number diagnosed**

Type 2 diabetes can reduce life expectancy, on average, by up to **10 years**

England 1,961,976 — 3.70%
Scotland 210,000 — 4.30%
Wales 131,119 — 4.21%
Northern Ireland 56,924 — 3.14%

300 people are diagnosed every day – that's **one person every five minutes**

Many people still don't realise that diabetes can lead to heart disease, strokes, amputations, kidney failure and blindness

Diabetes is the leading cause of blindness in people of working age in the UK

100 people a week in the UK have a limb amputated as a result of diabetes

10% of NHS spending goes on diabetes – that's **£9 billion** a year or **£1 million** an hour

Source: Diabetes. Beware the silent assassin, October 2008, Diabetes UK

http://www.diabetes.org.uk/SilentAssassin

Whose problem?

Around 1 in 4 people will suffer from mental health problems in their lifetime

Mental illness can affect people of all ages and walks of life and can be triggered by **physical**, **social**, **environmental** or/and **genetic factors**.

About **10%** of children and young people have a mental health problem. Experiences during childhood such as trauma or abuse can increase the risk of mental illness by changing someone's behaviour and thinking patterns.

1,751 adults aged 16+ in England were asked about their attitudes to mental illness

58% of respondents said that someone close to them, ie family or friends or themselves, has had some kind of mental illness.

16% said it was their immediate family/live-in partner.

5% said they themselves had experienced some kind of mental illness.

20% of respondents currently lived or ever have lived with someone with a mental health problem, **27%** work with someone, **53%** have a neighbour and **35%** have a close friend with a mental health problem.

82% agreed that in the future they would be willing to continue a relationship with a friend who developed a mental health problem but only **57%** would be willing to live with someone.

Respondents aged between **45 and 64** were most likely to say that they knew someone who had experienced mental illness.

66% of respondents said they would feel comfortable talking to a friend or family member about their mental health

> **"** As I have become well and rebuilt my life I have found how very lonely mental illness can be. Friends never refer to it. They never ask how I am or tell me how well I am doing now. If I was recovering from a physical illness such as cancer I believe their attitude would be totally different. Nowadays I can count the number of friends I have on the fingers of one hand. **"**
>
> *Alison*

Source: TNS – Attitudes to Mental Illness 2009, Rethink

http://www.tnsglobal.com
http://www.rethink.org

Anorexia admissions

Girls admitted to hospital for treatment for anorexia (first episodes), England

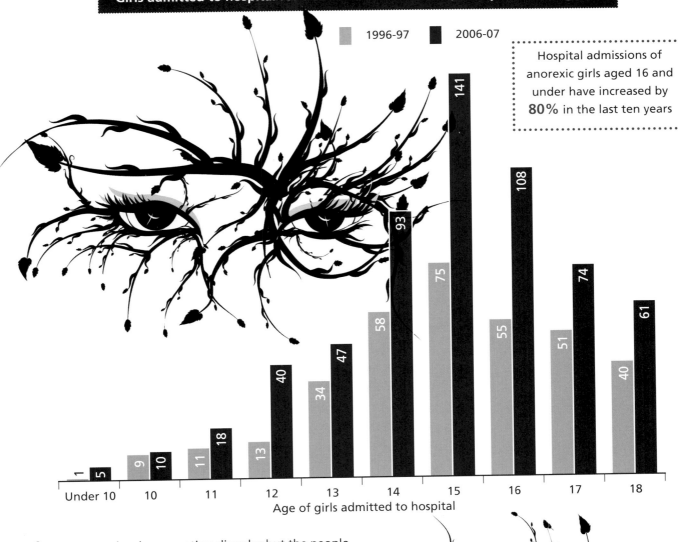

1996-97 ■ 2006-07

Hospital admissions of anorexic girls aged 16 and under have increased by **80%** in the last ten years

Age	1996-97	2006-07
Under 10	1	5
10	9	10
11	11	18
12	13	40
13	34	47
14	58	93
15	75	141
16	55	108
17	51	74
18	40	61

Age of girls admitted to hospital

Anyone can develop an eating disorder but the people most likely to be affected tend to be young women, particularly between the ages of 15-25.

In 2006-07 there were **597 girls** admitted to hospital for treatment and **55 boys**.

Your genetic make-up may have a small impact upon whether or not you develop an eating disorder.

In situations where there are:

- high academic expectations
- family issues or
- social pressures

you may focus on food and eating as a way of coping with these stresses.

beat
Youthline
0845 634 7650

In January 2009, the UK charity **beat** spoke to 1,500 people affected by eating disorders. They found that only **15%** felt their GP understood and knew how to help.

Source: Hospital Episode Statistics (HES), The Information Centre for Health and Social Care; Choice or chance? beat – beating eating disorders

www.hesonline.nhs.uk
http://www.b-eat.co.uk

NHS v US

When President Obama introduced his plans for health care reform, critics in the US cited Britain's NHS as an example of 'socialist' health care. There were claims that the NHS had 'death panels' which decided who 'deserved' treatment and even, in one American newspaper "People such as scientist Stephen Hawking wouldn't have a chance in the UK, where the NHS would say the life of this brilliant man, because of his physical handicaps, is essentially worthless". Stephen Hawking, who is in fact British, responded by saying "I wouldn't be here today if it weren't for the NHS".

How do they compare?

The NHS provides healthcare to anyone normally resident in the UK. Most services are free for the patient though there are charges for eye tests, dental care and prescriptions.

In the United States, doctors and hospitals are generally funded by payments from patients and insurance plans. If you can't pay you won't receive treatment. It's estimated that around 29% of the US population does not have the insurance cover which would guarantee their healthcare.

NHS		US
8.2%	HEALTH EXPENDITURE (% OF GDP)	15.3%
87.3%	GOVERNMENT EXPENDITURE ON HEALTH AS % OF TOTAL EXPENDITURE ON HEALTH	45.8%
12.7%	PRIVATE EXPENDITURE ON HEALTH AS % OF TOTAL EXPENDITURE ON HEALTH	54.2%
23	DOCTORS PER 10,000 POPULATION	26
128	NURSES & MIDWIVES PER 10,000	94
39	HOSPITAL BEDS PER 10,000	31
80	LIFE EXPECTANCY AT BIRTH	78
147	CANCER MORTALITY RATES PER 10,000	133

Source: WHO World Health Statistics 2009

http://www.who.int

All you need is blood

Blood stocks are low, and yet only 4% of us donate

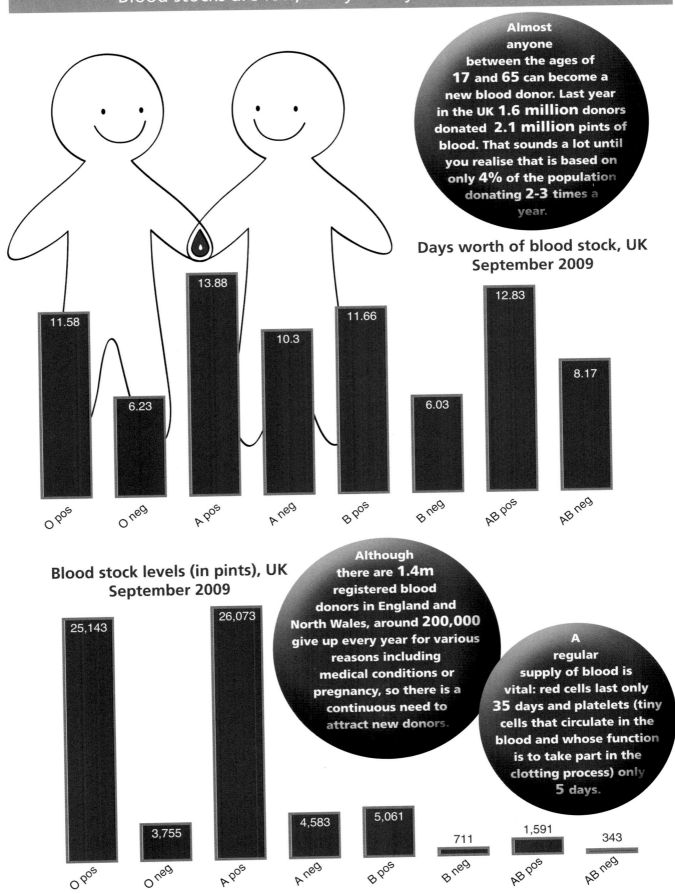

Almost anyone between the ages of **17** and **65** can become a new blood donor. Last year in the UK **1.6 million** donors donated **2.1 million** pints of blood. That sounds a lot until you realise that is based on only **4% of the population** donating **2-3 times a year.**

Days worth of blood stock, UK September 2009

O pos	O neg	A pos	A neg	B pos	B neg	AB pos	AB neg
11.58	6.23	13.88	10.3	11.66	6.03	12.83	8.17

Blood stock levels (in pints), UK September 2009

O pos	O neg	A pos	A neg	B pos	B neg	AB pos	AB neg
25,143	3,755	26,073	4,583	5,061	711	1,591	343

Although there are **1.4m** registered blood donors in England and North Wales, around **200,000** give up every year for various reasons including medical conditions or pregnancy, so there is a continuous need to attract new donors.

A regular supply of blood is vital: red cells last only **35 days** and platelets (tiny cells that circulate in the blood and whose function is to take part in the clotting process) only **5 days.**

Source: The National Blood Service 2009

http://www.blood.co.uk

Sexfactor

Young people's attitudes and awareness of STIs

2,042 UK respondents aged 16 to 24 completed a survey conducted by YouthNet which explored young people's attitudes towards sexual health, including awareness and knowledge of sexually transmitted infections (STIs)

Frequency of using contraception or protection

Always	Mostly	Sometimes	Not very often	Never

| 53% | 29% | 12% | 4% | 2% |

Base: All sexually active respondents – 1,887

A significant proportion of respondents had heard of some STIs in name only and knew nothing about the infections.

Awareness and knowledge of STIs

Heard of   **Any knowledge of**

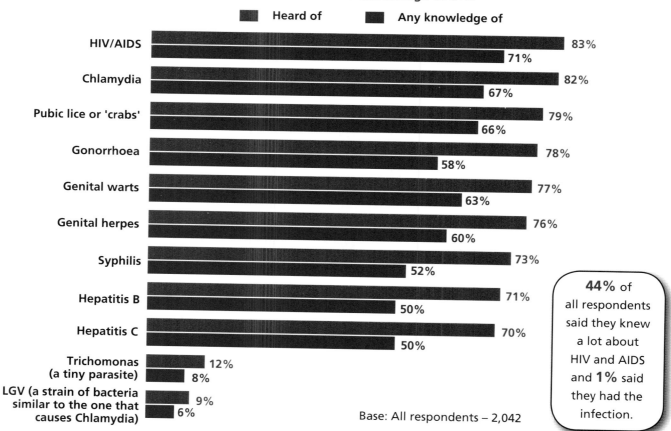

STI	Heard of	Any knowledge of
HIV/AIDS	83%	71%
Chlamydia	82%	67%
Pubic lice or 'crabs'	79%	66%
Gonorrhoea	78%	58%
Genital warts	77%	63%
Genital herpes	76%	60%
Syphilis	73%	52%
Hepatitis B	71%	50%
Hepatitis C	70%	50%
Trichomonas (a tiny parasite)	12%	8%
LGV (a strain of bacteria similar to the one that causes Chlamydia)	9%	6%

Base: All respondents – 2,042

44% of all respondents said they knew a lot about HIV and AIDS and **1%** said they had the infection.

Sex and sexual health are subjects some young people find it difficult to discuss openly.
52% said they wouldn't feel comfortable speaking to their parents about STIs.

All respondents (regardless of whether sexually active) were asked if they had ever sought advice about, or treatment for STIs from any of these sources

- Internet — 22%
- Friends — 16%
- GP — 16%
- *GUM clinic — 10%
- Family planning clinic — 10%
- Magazines or newspapers — 10%
- Parents — 8%
- School, college or university — 8%
- TV programmes — 8%
- Chemist — 4%
- Hospital — 3%

55% of respondents worry about contracting an STI.

80% said they would go for treatment straight away if they suspected they had contracted an infection, despite **56%** saying they would be embarrassed to do so.

53% of the young people who completed the survey had **NEVER** sought advice or information about STIs.

To keep young people safe and to avoid the spread of sexually transmitted infections, information must be available and accessible.

*GUM – Genito-urinary Medicine

16-24 year olds who completed the Sex Factor survey may not be representative of all young people in the UK. However, the results shown in this report imply that while the majority of young people are sexually active, awareness and knowledge of STIs is low. This is worrying especially in light of other findings that showed many young people engage in unprotected sex on a regular basis, and have many sexual partners.

Source: Sex Factor – Young people and sexual health, 2009
http://www.thesite.org

HIV UK

New cases and how they were acquired

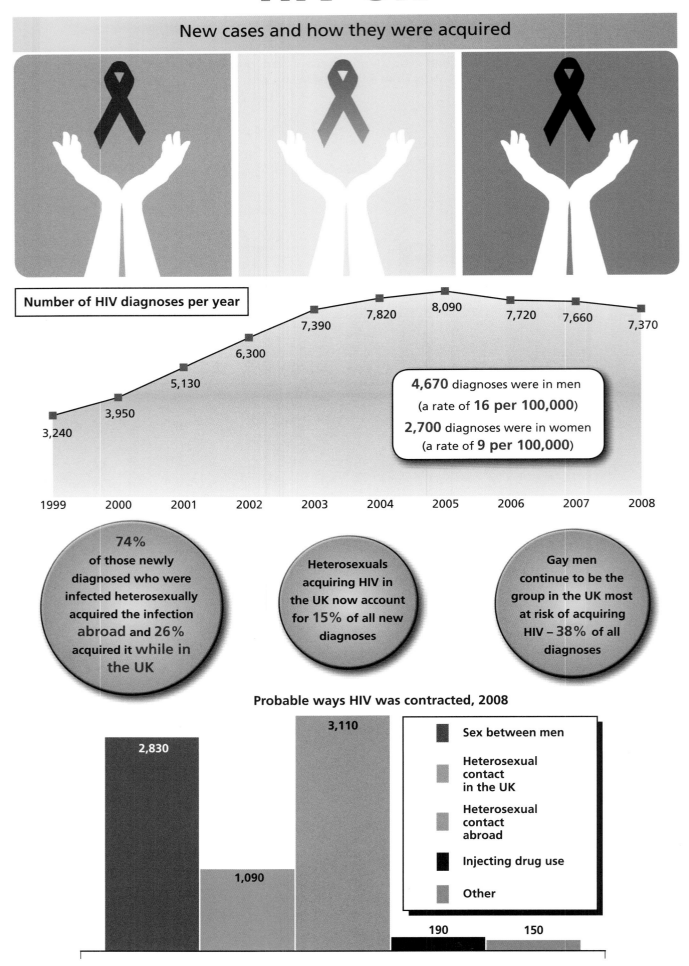

Number of HIV diagnoses per year

3,240 — 1999
3,950 — 2000
5,130 — 2001
6,300 — 2002
7,390 — 2003
7,820 — 2004
8,090 — 2005
7,720 — 2006
7,660 — 2007
7,370 — 2008

4,670 diagnoses were in men
(a rate of **16 per 100,000**)
2,700 diagnoses were in women
(a rate of **9 per 100,000**)

74% of those newly diagnosed who were infected heterosexually acquired the infection abroad and 26% acquired it while in the UK

Heterosexuals acquiring HIV in the UK now account for 15% of all new diagnoses

Gay men continue to be the group in the UK most at risk of acquiring HIV – 38% of all diagnoses

Probable ways HIV was contracted, 2008

2,830
1,090
3,110
190
150

- Sex between men
- Heterosexual contact in the UK
- Heterosexual contact abroad
- Injecting drug use
- Other

❝ People need to know that testing for HIV... is both free and confidential at sexual health clinics across the UK. If you have had unprotected sex with a new or casual partner you should go and get tested ❞

Professor Maria Zambon, Director of the Health Protection Agency's Centre for Infections

66% of those newly diagnosed who were infected heterosexually were of black-African ethnicity

31% of individuals are being diagnosed with HIV late – which means they are missing out on the benefits of early diagnosis including the chance of living longer

In 2008 there were **484 deaths** among HIV infected persons. This number is likely to rise as further reports are received

Individuals infected through heterosexual contact
Age at diagnosis, 2008

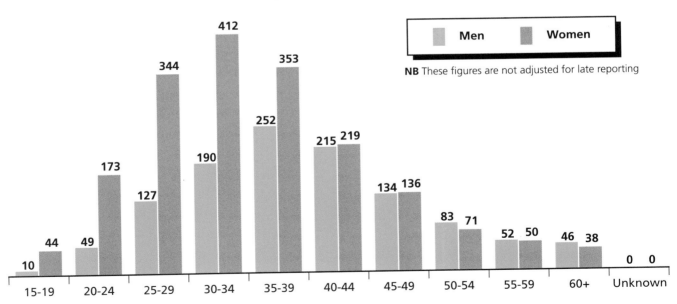

Legend: Men | Women

NB These figures are not adjusted for late reporting

Age	Men	Women
15-19	10	44
20-24	49	173
25-29	127	344
30-34	190	412
35-39	252	353
40-44	215	219
45-49	134	136
50-54	83	71
55-59	52	50
60+	46	38
Unknown	0	0

**❝ Safe sex is the best way to protect against HIV infection.
Using a condom with all new or casual partners is the surest way to ensure you do not become infected ❞**

Dr Barry Evans, Sexual Health Expert, Health Protection Agency

http://www.hpa.org.uk

Source: Health Protection Agency Centre for Infections

The big question

A change in the law to legalise euthanasia is supported by 82% of the public but only 34% of doctors

The British Social Attitudes (BSA) survey put questions about euthanasia to the general public in 2007. A 2009 study of more than **3,700** doctors mirrored the questions. The answers show that the majority of British doctors DON'T support legalising assisted dying – but it is even more true for palliative medicine doctors, who might be described as doctors who specialise in the care of dying patients.

First, a person with an incurable and painful illness, from which they will die – for example, someone dying of cancer.

☐ General public (BSA survey)

☐ Doctors

Q Do you think that, if they ask for it, a doctor should ever be allowed by law to end their life, or not?

	Definitely should be allowed	Probably should be allowed	Probably should NOT be allowed	Definitely should NOT be allowed	Don't know/ Not answered
General public	51.5%	30.3%	6.2%	9.9%	2.2%
Doctors	8.6%	25.4%	29.6%	34.8%	1.6%

Figures may not add up to 100% due to rounding

Q And do you think that, if this person asks for it, a doctor should ever be allowed by law to give them lethal medication that will allow the person to take their own life?

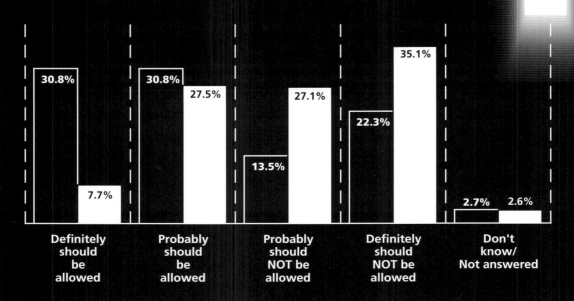

	Definitely should be allowed	Probably should be allowed	Probably should NOT be allowed	Definitely should NOT be allowed	Don't know/ Not answered
General public	30.8%	30.8%	13.5%	22.3%	2.7%
Doctors	7.7%	27.5%	27.1%	35.1%	2.6%

Now, how about a person with an incurable and painful illness, from which they will not die.

Q Do you think that, if they ask for it, a doctor should ever be allowed by law to end their life, or not?

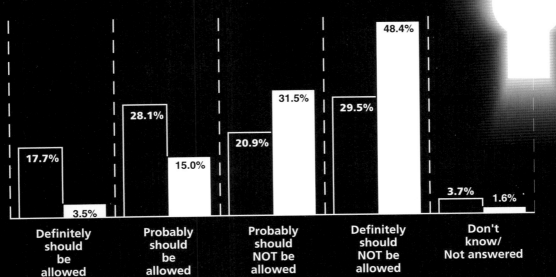

- **Definitely should be allowed** — 17.7% / 3.5%
- **Probably should be allowed** — 28.1% / 15.0%
- **Probably should NOT be allowed** — 20.9% / 31.5%
- **Definitely should NOT be allowed** — 29.5% / 48.4%
- **Don't know/ Not answered** — 3.7% / 1.6%

Q And do you think that, if this person asks for it, a doctor should ever be allowed by law to give them lethal medication that will allow the person to take their own life?

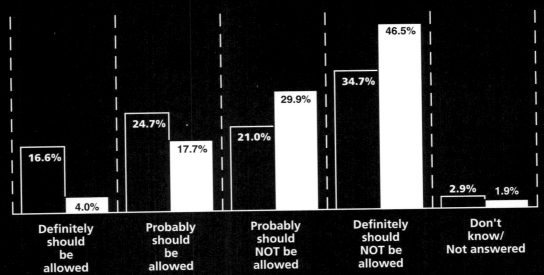

- **Definitely should be allowed** — 16.6% / 4.0%
- **Probably should be allowed** — 24.7% / 17.7%
- **Probably should NOT be allowed** — 21.0% / 29.9%
- **Definitely should NOT be allowed** — 34.7% / 46.5%
- **Don't know/ Not answered** — 2.9% / 1.9%

"Cases of euthanasia in the UK are very rare. Instead, end of life treatment decisions are often taken with input from patients and family, and it is rare for such decisions to have shortened life by more than a day."

Professor Clive Seale, Study Author

Source: Centre for Health Sciences, Queen Mary
University of London
http://www.ihse.qmul.ac.uk/

Big impact

The 20 worst places for obesity in the UK

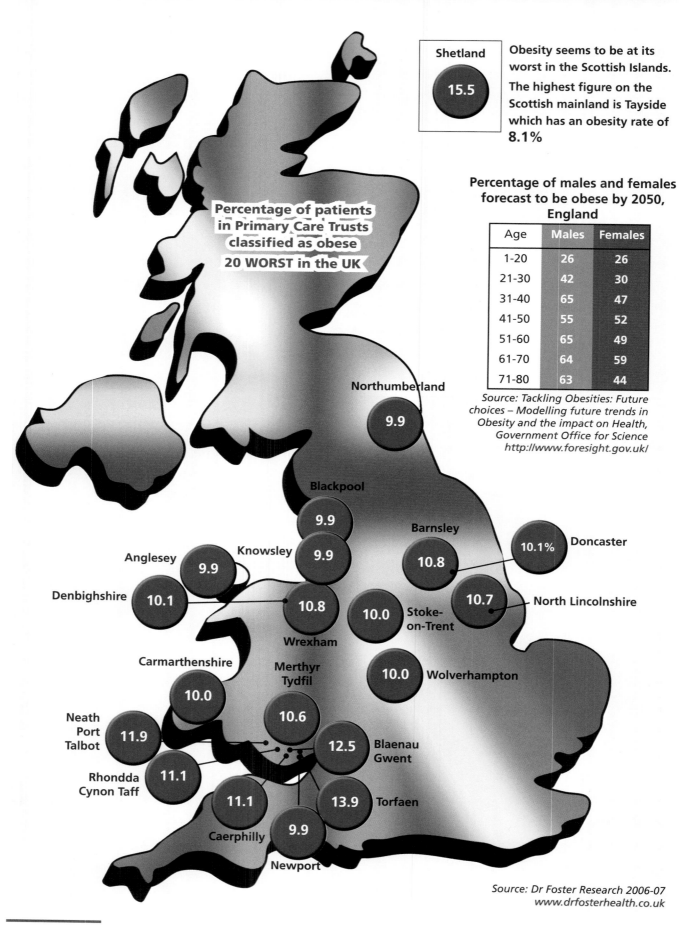

Shetland

15.5

Obesity seems to be at its worst in the Scottish Islands.

The highest figure on the Scottish mainland is Tayside which has an obesity rate of 8.1%

Percentage of patients in Primary Care Trusts classified as obese
20 WORST in the UK

Percentage of males and females forecast to be obese by 2050, England

Age	Males	Females
1-20	26	26
21-30	42	30
31-40	65	47
41-50	55	52
51-60	65	49
61-70	64	59
71-80	63	44

Source: Tackling Obesities: Future choices – Modelling future trends in Obesity and the impact on Health, Government Office for Science http://www.foresight.gov.uk/

Northumberland 9.9

Blackpool 9.9

Barnsley 10.8

Doncaster 10.1%

Knowsley 9.9

North Lincolnshire 10.7

Anglesey 9.9

Denbighshire 10.1

Wrexham 10.8

Stoke-on-Trent 10.0

Carmarthenshire 10.0

Merthyr Tydfil 10.6

Wolverhampton 10.0

Neath Port Talbot 11.9

Blaenau Gwent 12.5

Rhondda Cynon Taff 11.1

Caerphilly 11.1

Torfaen 13.9

Newport 9.9

Source: Dr Foster Research 2006-07
www.drfosterhealth.co.uk

Law & order

Protection & prevention

Knives

More than **one in six** young people **believe** knife crime is a problem in their area and this more than doubles to **36%** of young people from London.

Only **2%** of those aged 12 to 17 **actually** carry a knife illegally – **fear** or **self-protection** is the most common reason given.

Only **4%** of 12-17 year olds admitted to carrying a knife either now or in the past and most of them did not do this often.

The majority of current or former knife carriers were aged between 15 and 17, white and male.

Young people from black and minority ethnic backgrounds are twice as likely to state that knife crime is a problem compared with young white people.

...because they THINK other people are carrying them

If a child or young person was caught

■ with a gun

▨ with a knife

which THREE of the following do you think would be the BEST ways to stop them carrying it again?

Base: 12-17 year olds (1,005)

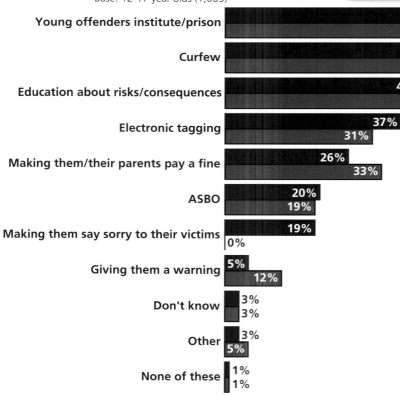

	with a gun	with a knife
Young offenders institute/prison	68%	49%
Curfew	45%	57%
Education about risks/consequences	42%	52%
Electronic tagging	37%	31%
Making them/their parents pay a fine	26%	33%
ASBO	20%	19%
Making them say sorry to their victims	19%	0%
Giving them a warning	5%	12%
Don't know	3%	3%
Other	3%	5%
None of these	1%	1%

Guns

The perception of gun crime as a problem is lower than knife crime. Only **7%** saw it as a big or fairly big problem, but this rose to **16%** in high risk areas.

Only **4** young people aged 12-17 said they carry a gun or had ever carried one.

Staying safe from gun and knife crime

When asked who they would listen to most on how to stay safe, **74%** said they would listen to their parents, **67%** said they would listen to the police. Teachers were also seen to be a good source of advice at **46%**

Young people favoured a mixture of solutions to tackle gun and knife crime. The most popular measures were focused on prevention, rehabilitation and harsher prison sentences.

There is a sharp difference between the high risk areas (Birmingham, Essex, Leeds, Liverpool, London, Manchester and Nottingham) and the rest of the country in relation to how safe young people feel. **13%** of young people overall felt fairly or very unsafe in their area, but this rose to **21%** in high risk areas.

There was also a difference by age, with older children more likely to say that they feel unsafe. Just under **one in five** 16 and 17 year olds consider their local area to be unsafe. This is double the figure for eight and nine year olds.

Which of these do you think would be most effective in stopping children and young people committing gun and knife crime?

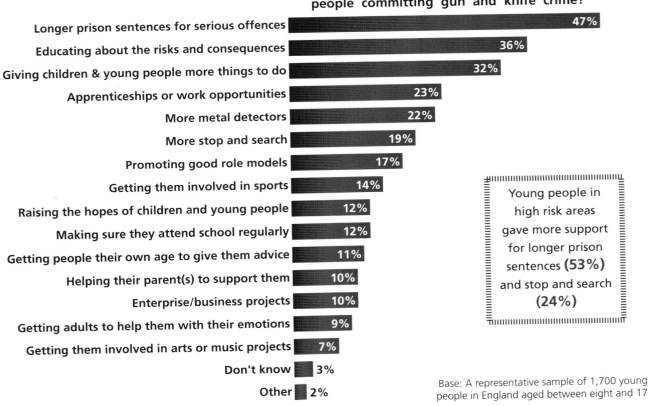

Longer prison sentences for serious offences	47%
Educating about the risks and consequences	36%
Giving children & young people more things to do	32%
Apprenticeships or work opportunities	23%
More metal detectors	22%
More stop and search	19%
Promoting good role models	17%
Getting them involved in sports	14%
Raising the hopes of children and young people	12%
Making sure they attend school regularly	12%
Getting people their own age to give them advice	11%
Helping their parent(s) to support them	10%
Enterprise/business projects	10%
Getting adults to help them with their emotions	9%
Getting them involved in arts or music projects	7%
Don't know	3%
Other	2%

Young people in high risk areas gave more support for longer prison sentences **(53%)** and stop and search **(24%)**

Source: Solutions to Gun and Knife crime, 2009 YouGov survey for 11 Million

Base: A representative sample of 1,700 young people in England aged between eight and 17

http://www.11million.org.uk

Fear factor

We believe crime is increasing and yet the likelihood of being affected is small

Perception of changing crime levels 1998-2008/09

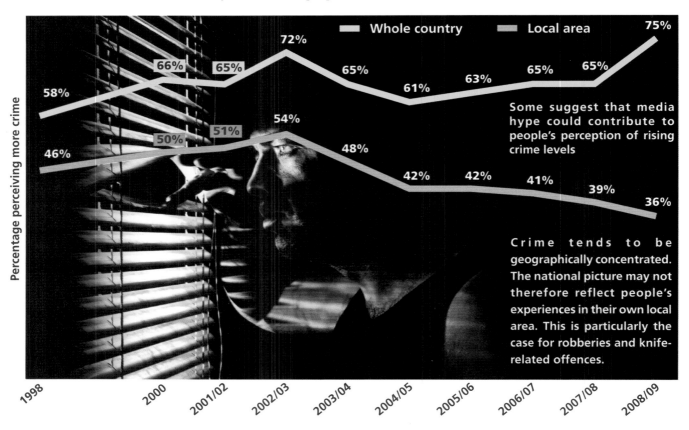

Whole country   **Local area**

58%   66%   65%   72%   65%   61%   63%   65%   65%   75%

46%   50%   51%   54%   48%   42%   42%   41%   39%   36%

Percentage perceiving more crime

Some suggest that media hype could contribute to people's perception of rising crime levels

Crime tends to be geographically concentrated. The national picture may not therefore reflect people's experiences in their own local area. This is particularly the case for robberies and knife-related offences.

1998   2000   2001/02   2002/03   2003/04   2004/05   2005/06   2006/07   2007/08   2008/09

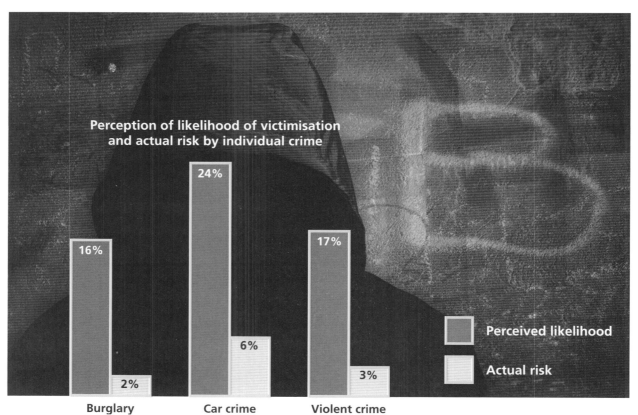

Perception of likelihood of victimisation and actual risk by individual crime

16%   2%   24%   6%   17%   3%

Perceived likelihood

Actual risk

Burglary   Car crime   Violent crime

Risk of being a victim of violent crime, 2008/09

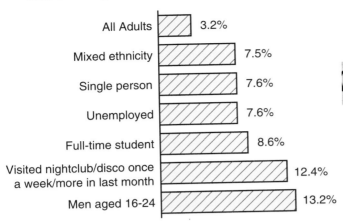

All Adults	3.2%
Mixed ethnicity	7.5%
Single person	7.6%
Unemployed	7.6%
Full-time student	8.6%
Visited nightclub/disco once a week/more in last month	12.4%
Men aged 16-24	13.2%

Overall, 2.5% of households had experienced a burglary in the last year. For both burglary and vehicle-related thefts, security measures make a difference.

For example: Households with less than 'basic' home security measures were much more likely to have been victims of burglary (3.4%) than households with 'basic' (1.4%) or 'enhanced' (0.7%) home security measures.

REPEATED VICTIMISATION

Levels of repeat victimisation (being a victim of the same crime type more than once) vary by offence type. Victims of domestic violence and vandalism are most likely to experience repeat victimisation.

Proportion of victims who were victimised more than once by crime type, 2008/09

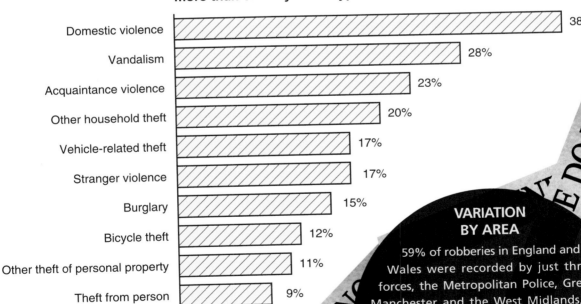

Domestic violence	38%
Vandalism	28%
Acquaintance violence	23%
Other household theft	20%
Vehicle-related theft	17%
Stranger violence	17%
Burglary	15%
Bicycle theft	12%
Other theft of personal property	11%
Theft from person	9%

VARIATION BY AREA

59% of robberies in England and Wales were recorded by just three forces, the Metropolitan Police, Greater Manchester and the West Midlands, that represent 24% of the population.

In the case of vandalism, vehicle related crime and burglary, rural households are less at risk of crime than urban ones: 13% compared with 19%. In the least deprived areas the risk is 16% compared with 22% in the most deprived areas.

Source: Crime in England & Wales 2008/09
http://www.homeoffice.gov.uk/

Safe trip?

Most people feel safe on public transport but 43% of users have felt intimidated

3,108 adults in Great Britain were asked about their experiences and perceptions of anti-social behaviour and crime such as intimidating, insulting or disruptive behaviour, vandalism or littering on public transport

How safe do you feel?

How safe from crime or threatening behaviour do you feel/would you feel travelling on public transport?

% of respondents
(including those who don't travel on public transport very often or at all)

Fairly or very SAFE   Fairly or very UNSAFE

84% 15%

Figures do not add up to 100% due to rounding

20% of respondents who had NOT used public transport in the last year felt UNSAFE. This might because they don't know about the safety of public transport or alternatively it might be this group had been put off using public transport by previous experiences of crime or threatening behaviour.

Asked about safety after dark, those who had actually used a bus or train after 9pm felt safer generally than those who had NOT travelled after 9pm.

What makes you feel unsafe?

All respondents who said that they would feel unsafe travelling by bus or train, either during the day or after dark, were asked why. Their responses were grouped into the most frequent answers

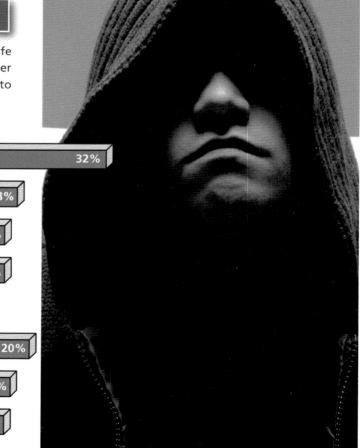

Feeling unsafe on buses

Anti-social/aggressive behaviour of young people — **32%**

Drunk people/people under the influence of drugs — **18%**

Anti-social/aggressive behaviour of people in general — **16%**

Violence/stabbings/muggings/crime — **16%**

Feeling unsafe on trains

Anti-social/aggressive behaviour of young people — **20%**

Dangerous/unsafe/different after dark — **17%**

Drunk people/people under the influence of drugs — **16%**

Bad people/unstable people characters in general — **14%**

Have you felt intimidated – more than once – by the
behaviour of other passengers?
% of respondents who had felt personally intimidated

Men   Women

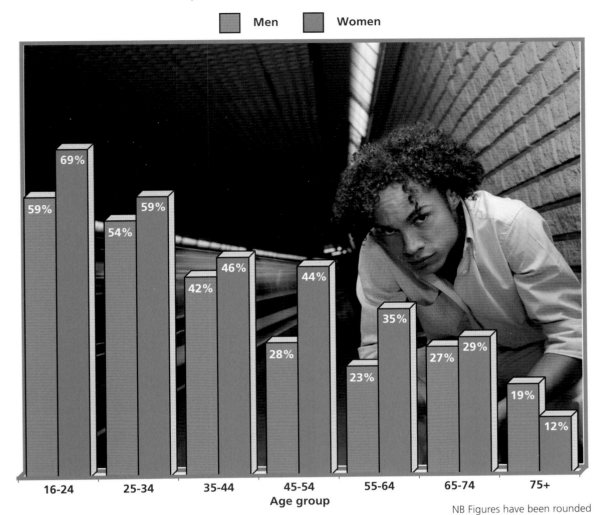

Age group

NB Figures have been rounded

22% of respondents said they had been a victim of one or more incidents of anti-social behaviour or crime while on public transport in the preceding year, while 76% had witnessed incidents.

Public transport users who travelled regularly and after 9pm were more likely to have experienced or witnessed anti-social behaviour or crime, as were younger, non-white and London respondents.

Women were more likely to say that they had felt intimidated than men and younger public transport users were much more likely to have felt intimidated than older users perhaps because they are more likely to travel after 9pm.

Witnessing certain behaviours even if not directly targeted at the individual, can lead to feelings of intimidation

Safety measures

Respondents thought that a policy of refusing to carry drunk or rowdy people, the presence of staff other than the driver, and CCTV would be particularly effective safety measures.

Source: Department for Transport – Experiences and perceptions of anti-social behaviour and crime on public transport, 2008
http://www.dft.gov.uk

Another bad night

A & E Only

...but there were **90,000 fewer violence-related A&E attendances in 2008 compared with 2001**

Overall in England and Wales, an estimated **351,468** people attended Emergency Departments for treatment following violence in 2008, **21,000 more** than in 2007.

In a sample of **49** Emergency Departments, Minor Injury Units and Walk-in Centres in 2008, **57,259** people were treated for injuries caused by violence – **41,883** were **male** and **15,376** were **female**.

Number of patients who attended for treatment following violence-related injury

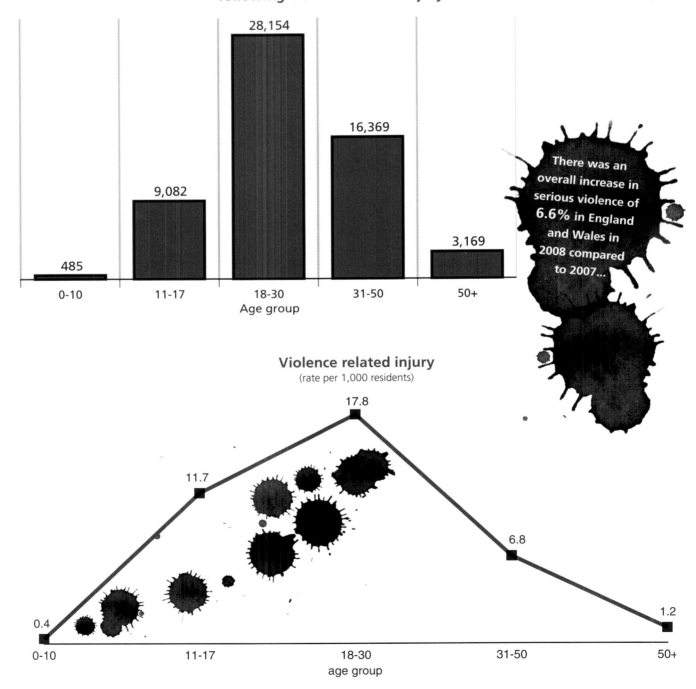

Age group	Number
0-10	485
11-17	9,082
18-30	28,154
31-50	16,369
50+	3,169

There was an overall increase in serious violence of **6.6%** in England and Wales in 2008 compared to 2007...

Violence related injury
(rate per 1,000 residents)

age group	rate
0-10	0.4
11-17	11.7
18-30	17.8
31-50	6.8
50+	1.2

According to Professor Jonathan Shepherd,
Director of the Violence Research Group,
Cardiff University:

"Alcohol misuse is a major cause of injury in violence. Intoxication increases vulnerability – drinkers can reduce their risk of being a victim substantially by drinking sensibly"

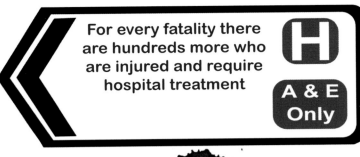

For every fatality there are hundreds more who are injured and require hospital treatment

H

A & E Only

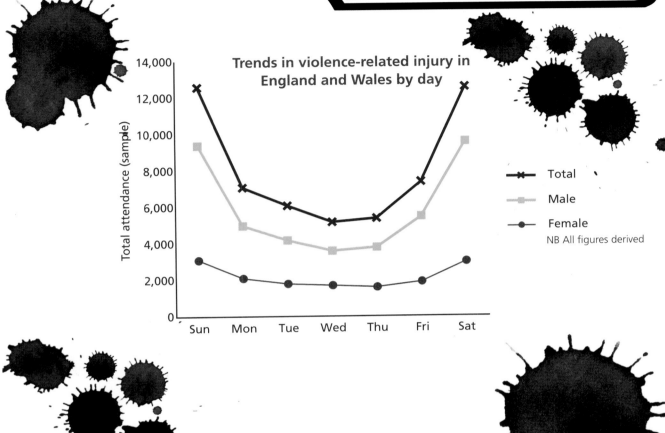

Trends in violence-related injury in England and Wales by day

Total
Male
Female
NB All figures derived

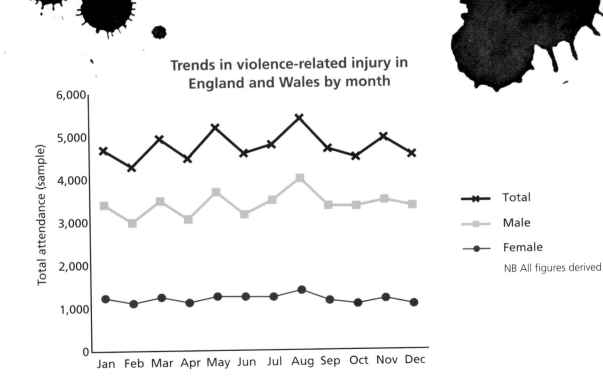

Trends in violence-related injury in England and Wales by month

Total
Male
Female
NB All figures derived

Source: Violence and Society Research Group, Cardiff University

http://www.vrg.cf.ac.uk

School shootings

Easy access to guns has had devastating effects

On 11th March 2009 in Stuttgart, Germany, a 17-year-old gunman used a semi-automatic pistol from his father's collection to kill **3** teachers and **9** students at Albertville Secondary School – **8** of the students were girls. The gunman also killed three passers-by, then committed suicide after a shoot-out with the police.

The minimum age for handgun ownership in Germany is 25. However, legal owners are allowed to store their handguns at home. Effectively this makes the weapons accessible to other family members, as well as to burglars or intruders.

2008
22 DEATHS

11 of these, including the gunman, occurred in Seinäjoki University, Finland.

A 22 year old gunman shot the victims with a semi-automatic pistol before shooting himself

2007
44 DEATHS

33 of these, including the gunman, occurred in Blacksburg, Virginia, US. The gunman opened fire in a classroom and a dormitory.

This was the largest shooting massacre by a civilian in US history

2006
18 DEATHS

6 of these including the gunman occurred in Paradise, Pennsylvania, US.

The gunman took young girls hostage in an Amish schoolhouse

2005
11 DEATHS

10 of these including the gunman occurred in Red Lake High School, US.

The gunman was a 16-year-old boy

2004
344 DEATHS

331 of these occurred in Beslan School, Russia and included **186 children**.

An armed group took children and teachers hostage

2003
5 DEATHS

all in the US

2002

31 DEATHS

18 of these, including the gunman who was an expelled former pupil, were in Erfurt, Germany.

Both guns used were obtained legally

2001

6 DEATHS

5 of these occurred in the US

2000

6 DEATHS

4 in the US and the other **2** in one incident in Germany

1999

17 DEATHS

15 of these, including the 2 gunmen, occurred in Columbine High School, Colorado, US.

The weapons were obtained at gun shows, where there was no requirement of ID or background checks

1998

11 DEATHS

All in the US – **5** of these were in Jonesboro, Arkansas.

2 boys aged 13 and 11 stole 3 rifles and 4 handguns from their grandfather's house. The boys started the fire alarm and then shot at the students as they emerged from the school

1997

17 DEATHS

9 of which were in the US and **8** deaths occurred in Sana'a, Yemen.

1996

25 DEATHS

7 of these were in the US.

18 deaths, including the gunman, were in Dunblane primary school, Scotland. **16** children and their teacher were shot dead and another **12** children and **2** teachers wounded by a licensed handgun owner who then shot himself.

This tragedy led to handguns being banned in the UK

Laws on civilian ownership of handguns in selected countries

	Banned for civilians	Minimum age	Total gun death rate per 100,000 people	Minimum wait before possession
Japan	Yes	n/a	0.1	n/a
UK	Yes	n/a	0.3	n/a
Germany	No	25	1.2	1-12 months
Brazil	No	25	18.0	up to 1 month
South Africa	No	21	32.0	up to 3 months
USA (varies according to state)	No	17 (worst) 18 (best)	10.2	No wait at worst and 40 days at best
Switzerland	No	18	6.2	None
Finland	No	15 with parental permission	4.6	1 year

Source: International Action Network on Small Arms

http://www.iansa.org

Park life

What are young people doing with their time?

Nearly 150,000 children and young people aged 10-15, across England, were asked which of the following places or activities they **HAD BEEN TO** in the last 4 weeks (not including things as part of school lessons) and which, if any, they would **LIKE TO GO TO** that they didn't at the moment

■ Have been to in the last 4 weeks

■ Would like to go to

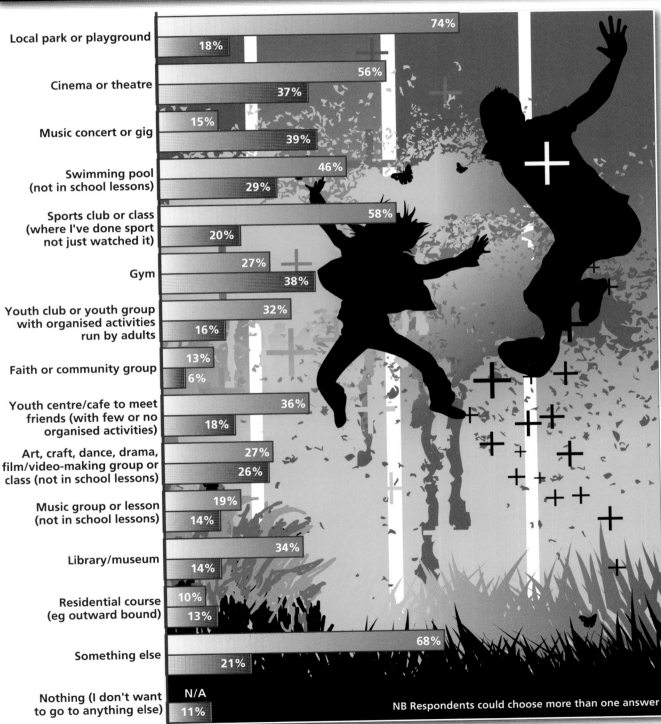

Activity	Have been to in the last 4 weeks	Would like to go to
Local park or playground	18%	74%
Cinema or theatre	37%	56%
Music concert or gig	15%	39%
Swimming pool (not in school lessons)	29%	46%
Sports club or class (where I've done sport not just watched it)	58%	20%
Gym	27%	38%
Youth club or youth group with organised activities run by adults	16%	32%
Faith or community group	13%	6%
Youth centre/cafe to meet friends (with few or no organised activities)	36%	18%
Art, craft, dance, drama, film/video-making group or class (not in school lessons)	27%	26%
Music group or lesson (not in school lessons)	19%	14%
Library/museum	34%	14%
Residential course (eg outward bound)	10%	13%
Something else	68%	21%
Nothing (I don't want to go to anything else)	N/A	11%

NB Respondents could choose more than one answer

Source: Ofsted TellUs3 National Report © Crown copyright 2008
http://www.ofsted.gov.uk

Fanzone

Watching football remains a popular activity

29.9 million spectators watched football matches in the
top 4 English football leagues 2008/09 season

AVERAGE ATTENDANCE
Top 10 English football clubs, 2008/09 season

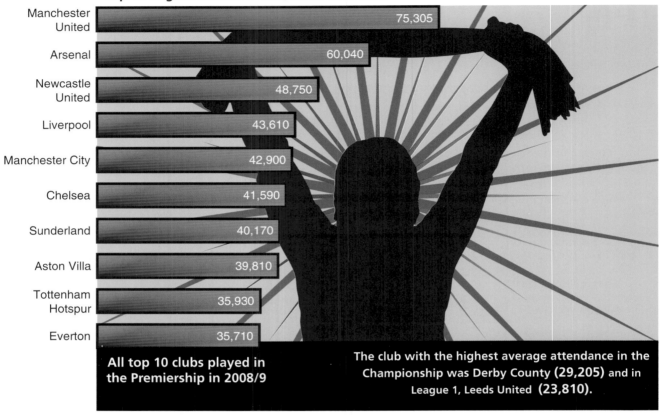

Club	Attendance
Manchester United	75,305
Arsenal	60,040
Newcastle United	48,750
Liverpool	43,610
Manchester City	42,900
Chelsea	41,590
Sunderland	40,170
Aston Villa	39,810
Tottenham Hotspur	35,930
Everton	35,710

All top 10 clubs played in the Premiership in 2008/9

The club with the highest average attendance in the Championship was Derby County **(29,205)** and in League 1, Leeds United **(23,810).**

TOTAL ATTENDANCE
Top 4 English football leagues, 1998/99-2008/09
(millions)

Figures from domestic league matches only

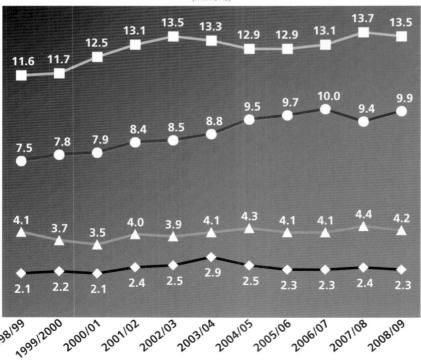

- ■ Premier League
- ● Championship
- ▲ League 1
- ◆ League 2

Premier League: 11.6, 11.7, 12.5, 13.1, 13.5, 13.3, 12.9, 12.9, 13.1, 13.7, 13.5

Championship: 7.5, 7.8, 7.9, 8.4, 8.5, 8.8, 9.5, 9.7, 10.0, 9.4, 9.9

League 1: 4.1, 3.7, 3.5, 4.0, 3.9, 4.1, 4.3, 4.1, 4.1, 4.4, 4.2

League 2: 2.1, 2.2, 2.1, 2.4, 2.5, 2.9, 2.5, 2.3, 2.3, 2.4, 2.3

1998/99, 1999/2000, 2000/01, 2001/02, 2002/03, 2003/04, 2004/05, 2005/06, 2006/07, 2007/08, 2008/09

Source: The Political Economy of Football

http://www.footballeconomy.com

Fact File 2010 • www.carelpress.com

Our day out

Top 20 UK visitor attractions and number of visitors, 2008 and percentage change since 2007

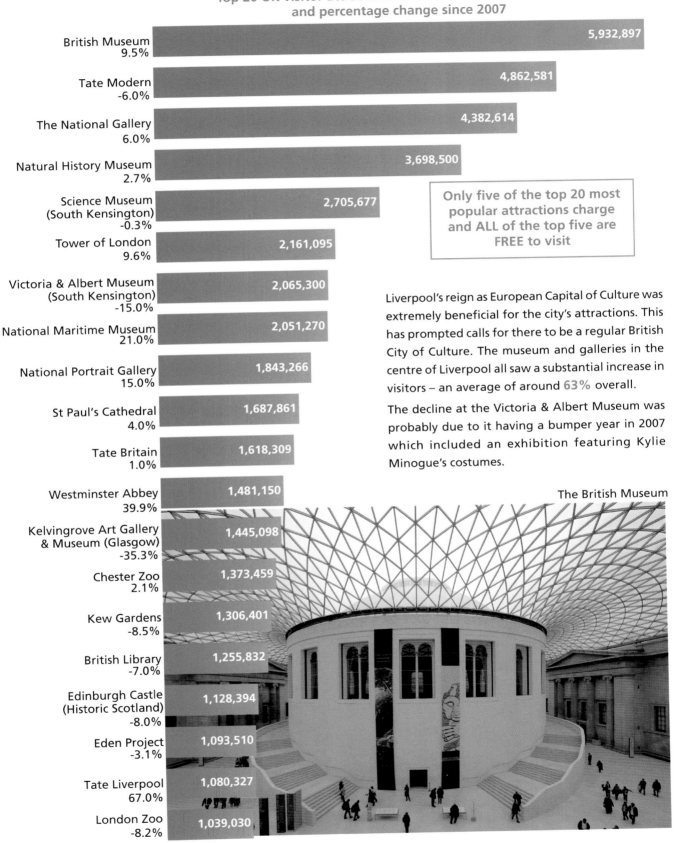

British Museum — 9.5%	5,932,897
Tate Modern — -6.0%	4,862,581
The National Gallery — 6.0%	4,382,614
Natural History Museum — 2.7%	3,698,500
Science Museum (South Kensington) — -0.3%	2,705,677
Tower of London — 9.6%	2,161,095
Victoria & Albert Museum (South Kensington) — -15.0%	2,065,300
National Maritime Museum — 21.0%	2,051,270
National Portrait Gallery — 15.0%	1,843,266
St Paul's Cathedral — 4.0%	1,687,861
Tate Britain — 1.0%	1,618,309
Westminster Abbey — 39.9%	1,481,150
Kelvingrove Art Gallery & Museum (Glasgow) — -35.3%	1,445,098
Chester Zoo — 2.1%	1,373,459
Kew Gardens — -8.5%	1,306,401
British Library — -7.0%	1,255,832
Edinburgh Castle (Historic Scotland) — -8.0%	1,128,394
Eden Project — -3.1%	1,093,510
Tate Liverpool — 67.0%	1,080,327
London Zoo — -8.2%	1,039,030

Only five of the top 20 most popular attractions charge and ALL of the top five are FREE to visit

Liverpool's reign as European Capital of Culture was extremely beneficial for the city's attractions. This has prompted calls for there to be a regular British City of Culture. The museum and galleries in the centre of Liverpool all saw a substantial increase in visitors – an average of around **63%** overall.

The decline at the Victoria & Albert Museum was probably due to it having a bumper year in 2007 which included an exhibition featuring Kylie Minogue's costumes.

The British Museum

Source: ALVA – Association of Leading Visitor Attractions

http://www.alva.org.uk

Bookworms

How young people feel about reading and readers

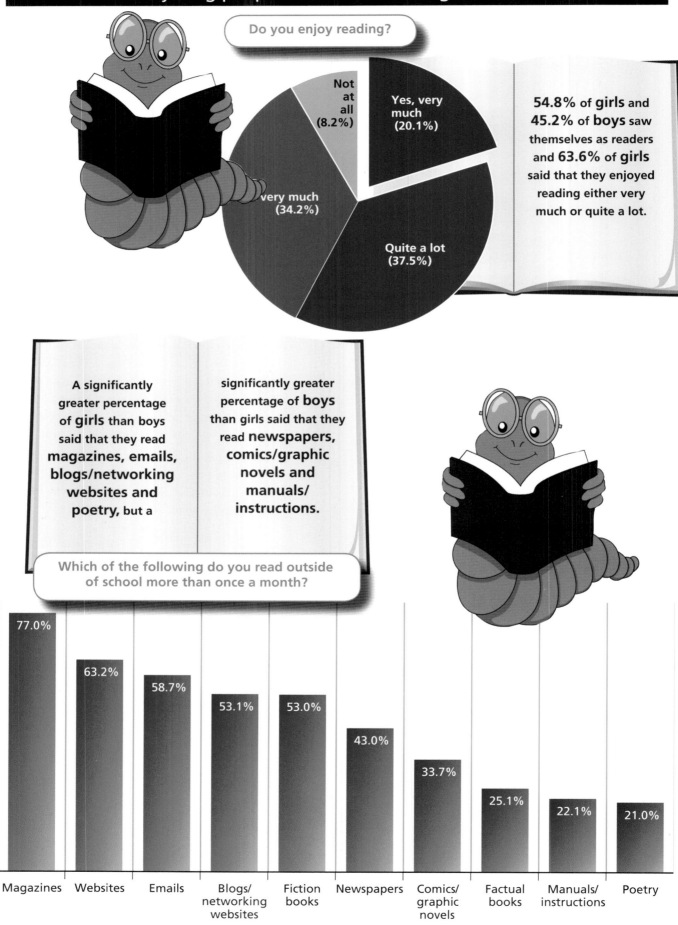

Do you enjoy reading?

Not at all (8.2%)

Yes, very much (20.1%)

...very much (34.2%)

Quite a lot (37.5%)

54.8% of **girls** and **45.2%** of **boys** saw themselves as readers and **63.6%** of **girls** said that they enjoyed reading either very much or quite a lot.

A significantly greater percentage of **girls** than boys said that they read **magazines, emails, blogs/networking websites and poetry,** but a significantly greater percentage of **boys** than girls said that they read **newspapers, comics/graphic novels and manuals/instructions.**

Which of the following do you read outside of school more than once a month?

Magazines	77.0%
Websites	63.2%
Emails	58.7%
Blogs/networking websites	53.1%
Fiction books	53.0%
Newspapers	43.0%
Comics/graphic novels	33.7%
Factual books	25.1%
Manuals/instructions	22.1%
Poetry	21.0%

How does reading make you feel?

- Calm — 68.2%
- Happy — 38.8%
- Bored — 33.7%
- Curious — 31.0%
- Clever/intelligent — 26.3%
- Sad — 12.3%
- Stressed — 8.8%
- Nervous — 6.8%

Pupils generally associated reading with **positive feelings** but a significantly greater percentage of **girls** than boys said that reading made them feel **calm** and **happy**.

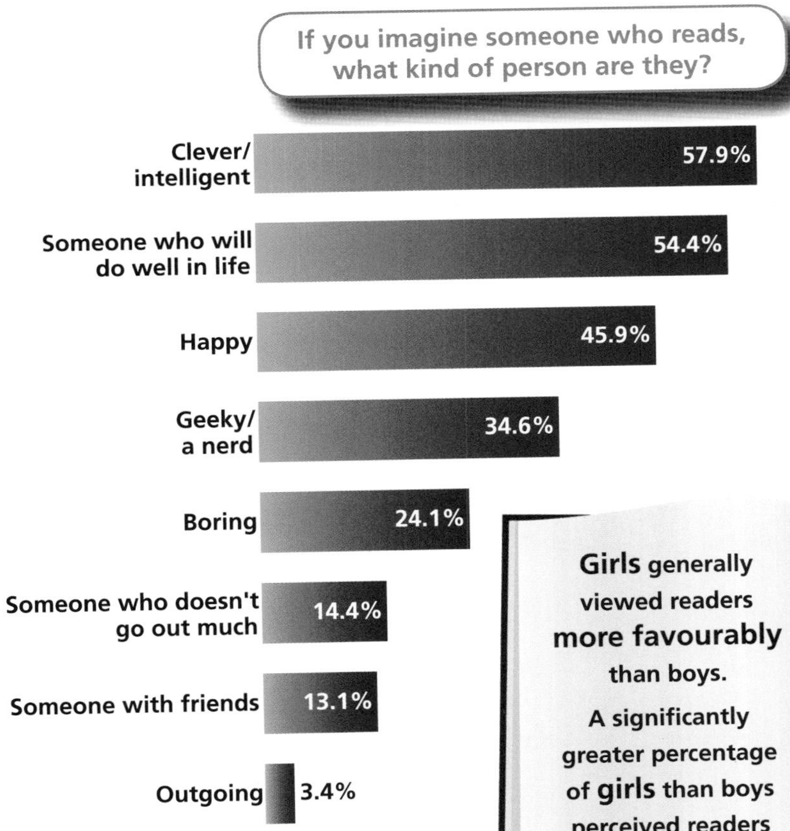

If you imagine someone who reads, what kind of person are they?

- Clever/intelligent — 57.9%
- Someone who will do well in life — 54.4%
- Happy — 45.9%
- Geeky/a nerd — 34.6%
- Boring — 24.1%
- Someone who doesn't go out much — 14.4%
- Someone with friends — 13.1%
- Outgoing — 3.4%

Girls generally viewed readers **more favourably** than boys.

A significantly greater percentage of **girls** than boys perceived readers to be **clever/intelligent** and someone who will **do well in life**.

By contrast, a significantly greater percentage of **boys** than girls believed a reader to be **geeky/a nerd**.

Base: over 1,600 KS2 and KS3 pupils in England

Source: Young people's self-perceptions as readers: An investigation including family, peer and school influences © National Literacy Trust, January 2008
http://www.literacytrust.org.uk

Big screen

...and the UK box office grew to a record **£850 million.** UK films took **31%** of the UK box office and internationally, UK films accounted for **15%** of the global box office. There were **527 new releases**, more than **one in five** of them UK films.

The recent development of digital screens and digital 3D technology may bring new audiences to the cinemas as it has allowed a wider range of content to be screened, including live events via streaming, eg operas, ballet and pop music concerts.

THE UK HAS 3,610 CINEMAS AND THE HIGHEST NUMBER OF DIGITAL SCREENS IN EUROPE

Cinemas provide the best environment for people to enjoy films as they are intended – on the big screen, with a large audience.

Age distribution of cinema-goers

The proportion of people aged 35+ going to the cinema has increased gradually but the number of younger cinema-goers has fallen. This coincided with a rapid rise in online entertainment and multi-channel TV, both of which may be substitutes for cinema.

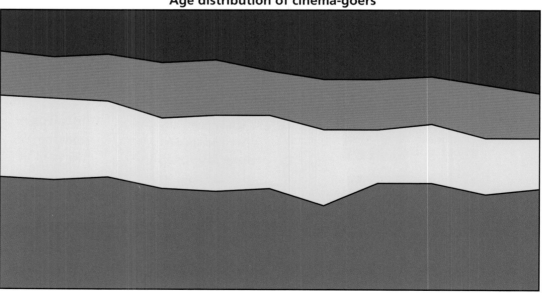

		1998	1999	2000	2001	2002	2003	2004	2005	2006	2007	2008
	15-24	40%	39%	40%	36%	35%	36%	30%	38%	38%	34%	36%
	25-34	29%	29%	27%	25%	27%	26%	27%	19%	21%	20%	18%
	35-44	16%	15%	17%	20%	20%	16%	18%	18%	17%	19%	16%
	45+	15%	17%	16%	19%	18%	22%	25%	25%	24%	27%	30%

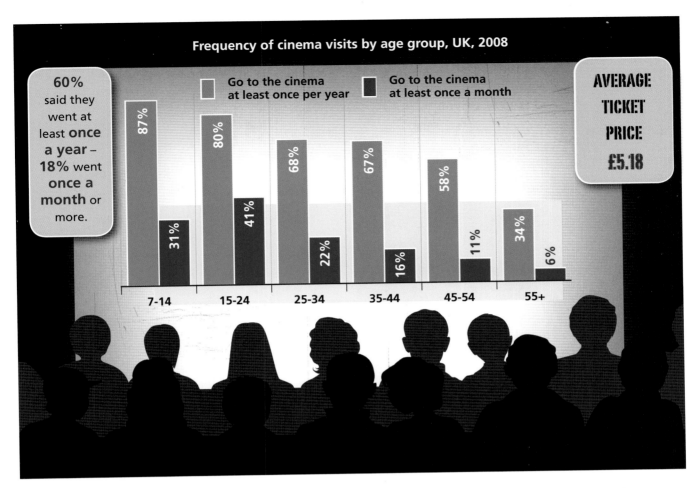

Frequency of cinema visits by age group, UK, 2008

60% said they went at least once a year – 18% went once a month or more.

Go to the cinema at least once per year
Go to the cinema at least once a month

Age group	At least once per year	At least once a month
7-14	87%	31%
15-24	80%	41%
25-34	68%	22%
35-44	67%	16%
45-54	58%	11%
55+	34%	6%

AVERAGE TICKET PRICE £5.18

The cinema audience for the top 20 films in 2008 was predominantly young, with the 7-34 age group (**40%** of the population) making up **64%** of the audience.

Cinema audience, by gender and age group, 2008

	7-14	15-24	25-34	35-44	45-54	55+
Male	8%	17%	11%	8%	4%	4%
Female	8%	15%	8%	8%	5%	6%

More films were released with a '15' classification than any other category (**37%** of all releases) but '12A' films took the largest share of the box office (**45%** of total box office).

There was a decrease in the number of screens in rural locations in 2008 – **97%** of all screens in the UK in 2008, were in town or city centres, edge of centre, 'out of town' or suburban locations.

The North West had the largest number of multiplex screens **(387)**, 20 more than London, and the highest proportion of multiplex screens **(89%)**.

The lowest proportion of multiplex screens was found in the South West **(59%)**, which had a particularly high number of traditional and mixed-use screens. The proportion of multiplex screens for **England** was **74%.**

A standard way to gauge the level of cinema provision is by **'screen density'**, that is the number of screens per unit population. In 2008 the UK figure was **6.0 screens per 100,000 people** – fewer than other major countries

The UK saw more admissions per person than Spain and Italy despite having a lower screen density than either of them.

	Screen Density per 100,000	Admissions per person
USA	12.7	4.1
Australia	9.4	4.2
Spain	9.1	2.4
France	8.8	3.0
Italy	7.1	1.7
UK	6.0	2.7
Germany	5.8	1.6

Source: UK Film Council Statistical Yearbook 2009
http://www.ukfilmcouncil.org.uk

Small screen

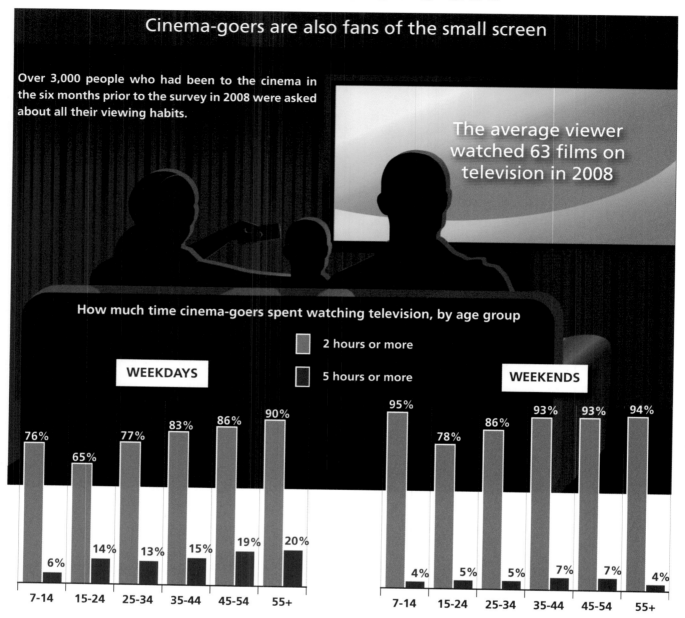

Cinema-goers are also fans of the small screen

Over 3,000 people who had been to the cinema in the six months prior to the survey in 2008 were asked about all their viewing habits.

The average viewer watched 63 films on television in 2008

How much time cinema-goers spent watching television, by age group

- 2 hours or more
- 5 hours or more

WEEKDAYS

	7-14	15-24	25-34	35-44	45-54	55+
2 hours or more	76%	65%	77%	83%	86%	90%
5 hours or more	6%	14%	13%	15%	19%	20%

WEEKENDS

	7-14	15-24	25-34	35-44	45-54	55+
2 hours or more	95%	78%	86%	93%	93%	94%
5 hours or more	4%	5%	5%	7%	7%	4%

How often cinema-goers watched DVDs, by age group

- Once a month or more
- Once a week or more

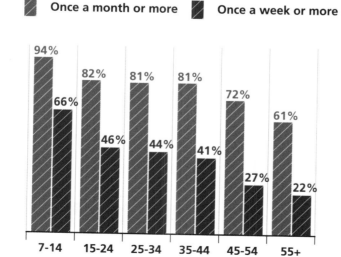

	7-14	15-24	25-34	35-44	45-54	55+
Once a month or more	94%	82%	81%	81%	72%	61%
Once a week or more	66%	46%	44%	41%	27%	22%

How often they bought a DVD

Age group	Once a month	Once a week
7-14	42%	4%
15-24	40%	7%
25-34	34%	5%
35-44	39%	4%
45-54	29%	1%
55+	16%	1%

Source: UK Film Council Statistical Yearbook 2009, Digital Cinema Media - Film Audience Measurement and Evaluation (FAME) survey

http://www.ukfilmcouncil.org.uk
http://www.dcm.co.uk

Science & technology

Digital life

Our leisure time is precious – that's why we spend almost a third of it using the internet

27,522 adults aged 18-55 in **16 countries** were surveyed about how the internet fits into their lives.

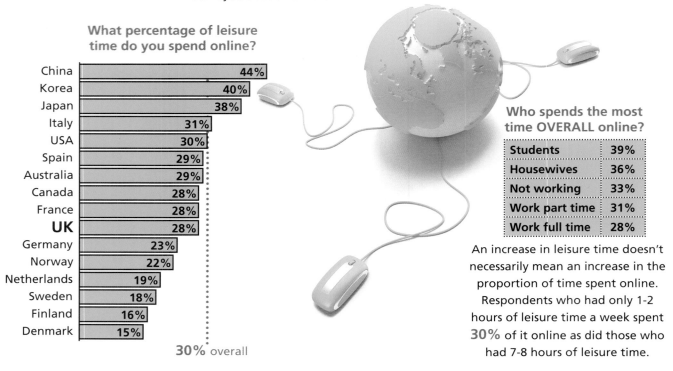

What percentage of leisure time do you spend online?

Country	%
China	44%
Korea	40%
Japan	38%
Italy	31%
USA	30%
Spain	29%
Australia	29%
Canada	28%
France	28%
UK	28%
Germany	23%
Norway	22%
Netherlands	19%
Sweden	18%
Finland	16%
Denmark	15%

30% overall

Who spends the most time OVERALL online?

Students	39%
Housewives	36%
Not working	33%
Work part time	31%
Work full time	28%

An increase in leisure time doesn't necessarily mean an increase in the proportion of time spent online. Respondents who had only 1-2 hours of leisure time a week spent **30%** of it online as did those who had 7-8 hours of leisure time.

In countries where the proportion of leisure time spent online is highest, the internet is also seen as being more important in personal life

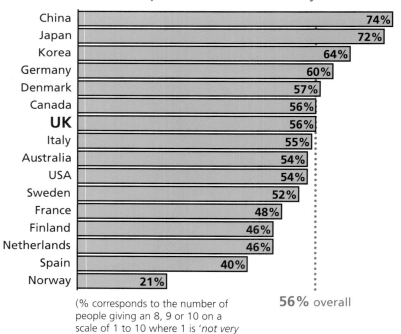

How important is the internet in your life?

Country	%
China	74%
Japan	72%
Korea	64%
Germany	60%
Denmark	57%
Canada	56%
UK	56%
Italy	55%
Australia	54%
USA	54%
Sweden	52%
France	48%
Finland	46%
Netherlands	46%
Spain	40%
Norway	21%

56% overall

(% corresponds to the number of people giving an 8, 9 or 10 on a scale of 1 to 10 where 1 is 'not very important' and 10 is 'very important')

How much would not having the internet affect your daily routine and personal activities?

Almost **25%** of respondents rated the internet at **10 out of 10** for importance in their personal life and **56%** of people rated it as 8 or higher (a score of 1 means 'having no impact at all' and 10 means 'a huge impact').

62% of people in China feel **NOT** having the internet would have a substantial impact on their personal activities compared to only **15%** of people in Finland.

In Germany, Italy and Korea **over 50%** of the respondents think **NOT** having the internet would have a substantial impact.

Percentage who have bought or ordered goods or services on the internet in the past month

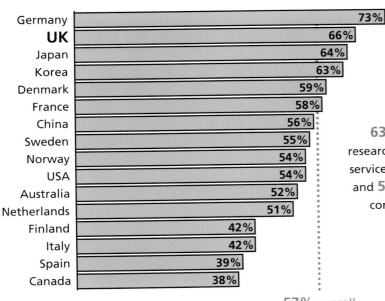

Germany	73%
UK	66%
Japan	64%
Korea	63%
Denmark	59%
France	58%
China	56%
Sweden	55%
Norway	54%
USA	54%
Australia	52%
Netherlands	51%
Finland	42%
Italy	42%
Spain	39%
Canada	38%

57% overall

Our leisure time is enriched through the ability to shop online and find information that makes shopping offline, in the real world, easier.

63% of people researched a product or service before buying it and **50%** used a price comparison site.

Is a digital life the same as a social life... or does a social life today require a complementary digital life?

Method of communicating with family & friends

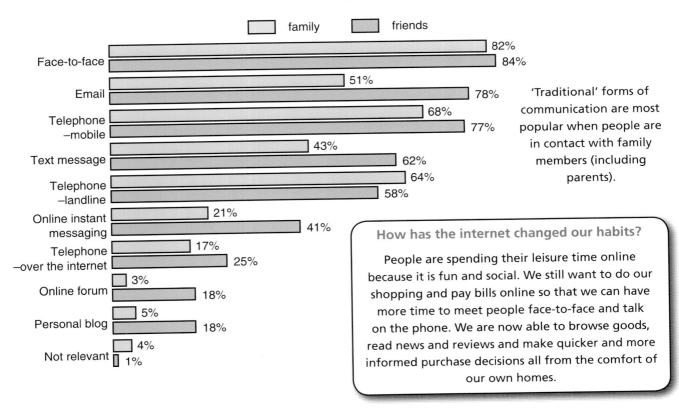

☐ family　　☐ friends

	family	friends
Face-to-face	82%	84%
Email	51%	78%
Telephone –mobile	68%	77%
Text message	43%	62%
Telephone –landline	64%	58%
Online instant messaging	21%	41%
Telephone –over the internet	17%	25%
Online forum	3%	18%
Personal blog	5%	18%
Not relevant	4%	1%

'Traditional' forms of communication are most popular when people are in contact with family members (including parents).

How has the internet changed our habits?

People are spending their leisure time online because it is fun and social. We still want to do our shopping and pay bills online so that we can have more time to meet people face-to-face and talk on the phone. We are now able to browse goods, read news and reviews and make quicker and more informed purchase decisions all from the comfort of our own homes.

Source: TNS digital world digital life survey, December 2008
http:// www.tnsglobal.com

Music collection

Despite digital downloading, people still want the hard copies

A comprehensive survey profiling the music consumption habits of 1,808 14-24 year olds across the UK was commissioned by UK Music and conducted by the University of Hertfordshire. The respondents for the survey were sourced via youth groups, secondary schools and universities across the UK as well as through media and social network and music partners such as the NME, Bebo, We7, Facebook and MySpace.

Which of the following do you use to listen to music every day?

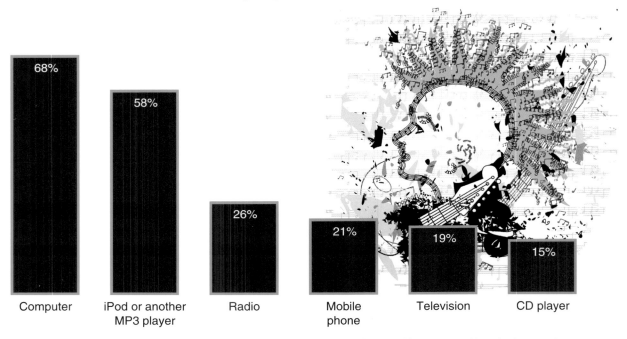

68%	58%	26%	21%	19%	15%
Computer	iPod or another MP3 player	Radio	Mobile phone	Television	CD player

'If I'm at home I listen to music either on the radio or on the internet from YouTube or iTunes. It depends where I am"

The average digital music collection – ie all the music on a respondent's computer or hard drive – was **8,159 tracks**. If we equate a single track as being 3 minutes in length, that's approximately 17 days' worth of continuous music.

Compared to their MP3 players, the volume of music loaded onto respondents' mobile phones was comparatively modest, at an average of 32 tracks. Indeed, **55%** of respondents had fewer than 50 tracks on their mobile handset. Only **3%** claimed to have more than 1,000 tracks on their mobiles.

What's the average number of tracks on your MP3 player?

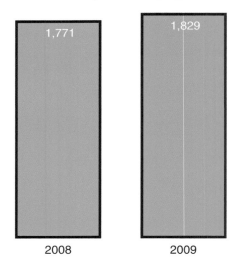

1,771	1,829
2008	2009

"I've got about 5gb of music on my iPod"

What is the average size of your CD collection - originals and copies?

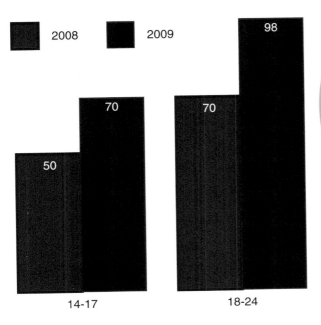

2008   2009

"I download a lot, to be honest, but if it's an artist that I really love, then I'm buying the CD."

Respondents still exhibit a strong desire to "own" music and most still purchase CDs. **51%** have fewer than **100** CDs (both original and copied) while only **4%** say they do not use CDs at all and **48%** of respondents claim that "most" of their CD collection consists of original discs. **25%** of **14-17 year-olds** claim that "all" their CD collection consists of original discs.

Almost all respondents want to copy music. **87%** agreed that being able to copy music onto different devices (eg MP3 player, mobile phone) is very important to them. **56%** of respondents believed that manufacturers of MP3 players, mobile phones and other recordable devices should pay a fee to artists whose music they enable to be copied.

"You feel like they're doing the service, the artists, the people in the recording studio and all the people involved should be getting paid for what they do."

Source: Music Experience and Behaviour in Young People Summer 2009
http://www.ukmusic.org/

Scientific interest

Two-thirds of young Europeans are interested in scientific developments

A survey about young people and science and technology interviewed 25,000 15-25 year olds, across all 27 EU member states, in September 2008.

Interest in news topics (% interested)

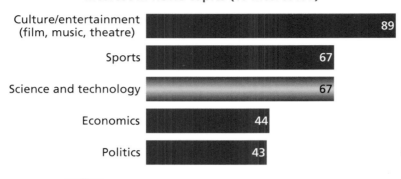

Topic	%
Culture/entertainment (film, music, theatre)	89
Sports	67
Science and technology	67
Economics	44
Politics	43

Of all the EU27 countries, the UK ranked in the bottom 5 for interest in news related to science and technology with 62%, compared to Portugal which ranked highest with 86%.

Within the EU27 there was a gender difference with 59% of young women showing an interest compared to 75% of young men.

Young men had a more positive view about science, with 4 out of 10 men compared to 3 out of 10 women thinking that science makes lives healthier and easier.

Interest in science and technology topics (%)

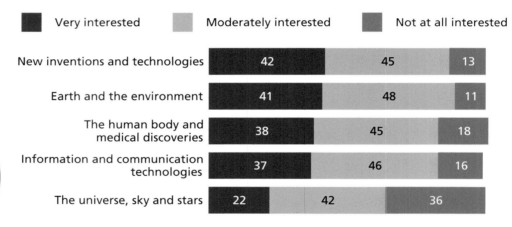

■ Very interested   ▨ Moderately interested   ■ Not at all interested

Topic	Very interested	Moderately interested	Not at all interested
New inventions and technologies	42	45	13
Earth and the environment	41	48	11
The human body and medical discoveries	38	45	18
Information and communication technologies	37	46	16
The universe, sky and stars	22	42	36

Optimistic and pessimistic views about science and technology (%)

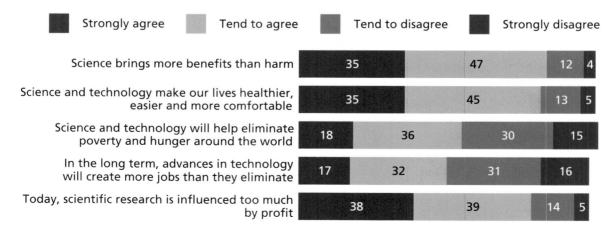

■ Strongly agree   ▨ Tend to agree   ▨ Tend to disagree   ■ Strongly disagree

Statement	Strongly agree	Tend to agree	Tend to disagree	Strongly disagree
Science brings more benefits than harm	35	47	12	4
Science and technology make our lives healthier, easier and more comfortable	35	45	13	5
Science and technology will help eliminate poverty and hunger around the world	18	36	30	15
In the long term, advances in technology will create more jobs than they eliminate	17	32	31	16
Today, scientific research is influenced too much by profit	38	39	14	5

Figures do not add up to 100% due to rounding.
Figures for Don't know/Not Applicable are not always shown.

Awareness and interest in innovations in different fields (% of respondents)

Heard about innovations and...

- ...not really interested in it
- ...interested in it

Not heard about innovations and...

- ...interested in it
- ...not really interested in it

	Heard – not interested	Heard – interested	Not heard – interested	Not heard – not interested
Mobile phones	22	75	1	2
Nuclear energy	44	44	4	7
Computer and video surveillance techniques	34	49	6	10
Human embryo research	35	46	7	11
Genetically modified food	47	35	5	12
Brain research	25	51	11	12
Nanotechnology	28	33	10	24

> In general UK attitudes were more negative about the risks involved with science and technology. For example, only 52% in the UK saw human embryo research as an advantage to society compared to 71% of those from Finland.

Perception of risks and advantages to society of scientific and technical innovations (%)

- Present more advantages than risks to society
- Same amount of risks and advantages
- More risks than advantages
- Don't know / N/A

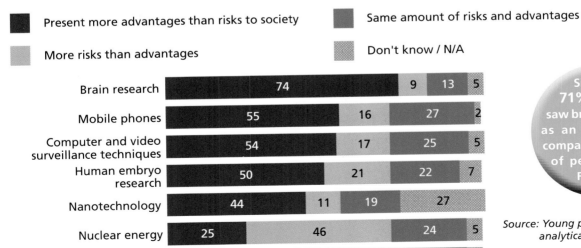

	Present more advantages than risks	More risks than advantages	Same amount of risks and advantages	Don't know / N/A
Brain research	74	9	13	5
Mobile phones	55	16	27	2
Computer and video surveillance techniques	54	17	25	5
Human embryo research	50	21	22	7
Nanotechnology	44	11	19	27
Nuclear energy	25	46	24	5
Genetically modified foods	17	49	29	5

> Similarly 71% in the UK saw brain research as an advantage, compared to 85% of people from Finland.

Source: Young people and science: analytical report. European Commission, 2008
http://ec.europa.eu/public_opinion

Amazed & confused

In the UK, eight out of ten people find science 'amazing'

The Public Attitudes to Science 2008 survey found that **79%** of the public thought that science was such a big part of our lives that we should all take an interest.

21% said school put them off science

62% thought it was important to know about science in their daily lives

56% thought science and technology was too specialised for most people to understand it

Keeping up to date with science
% of respondents who had done any of the following in the last 12 months

Watched a science documentary eg Horizon	68%
Asked friends or family about a scientific/medical topic	52%
Discussed science with a friend or member of your family	50%
Searched for information about a scientific topic using the internet	35%
Listened to a science programme on the radio	17%
Read a science magazine eg New Scientist	15%
Watched or listened to a broadcast about a scientific topic on your computer	15%
Read a blog about science	9%
Used interactive TV while watching a science programme	8%
Downloaded a podcast on a scientific topic	3%

43% thought that finding out about new scientific developments was easy these days

42% couldn't follow developments in science and technology because the speed of development is too fast

35% thought they were not clever enough to understand science and technology

60% thought there was so much conflicting information about science it was difficult to know what to do

27% didn't understand the point of all the science being done today

There has been a positive shift in public opinion over the past few years with levels of worry about science and scientific research decreasing significantly and greater recognition of the benefits. **46%** agreed that the benefits of science are greater than any harmful effect

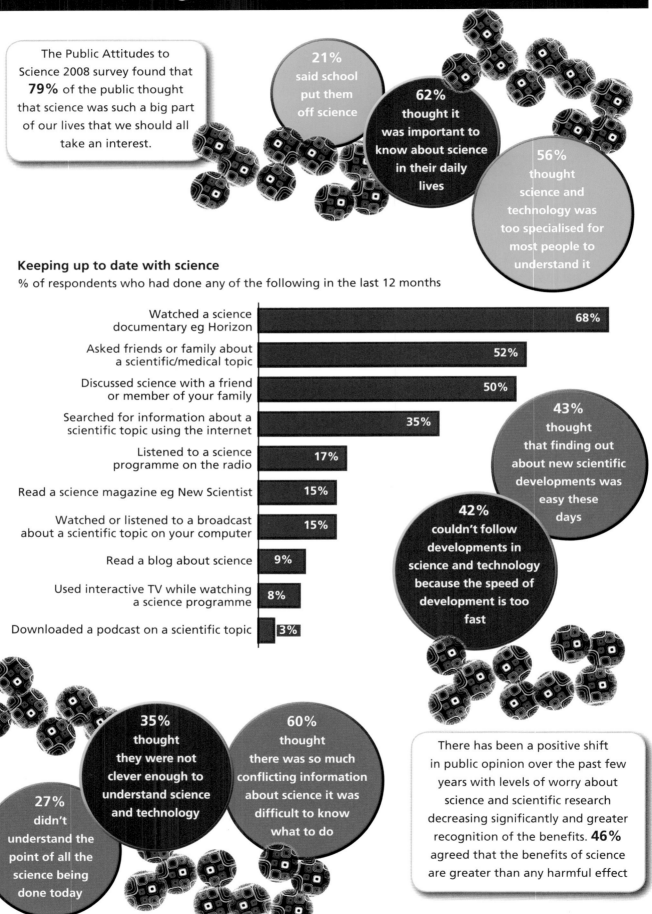

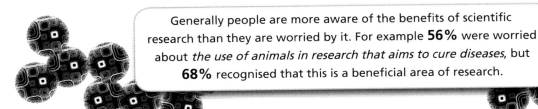

Generally people are more aware of the benefits of scientific research than they are worried by it. For example **56%** were worried about *the use of animals in research that aims to cure diseases*, but **68%** recognised that this is a beneficial area of research.

% who thought that research in specific areas was beneficial or worrying

Key

- 1 The use of technology for surveillance (eg CCTV)
- 2 Understanding more about space, planets and stars
- 3 Understanding the causes of climate change
- 4 Research into new drugs to cure human diseases
- 5 Understanding the causes of obesity
- 6 Research into new sources of energy
- 7 Research into storing radioactive waste
- 8 The development of robots that can think for themselves
- 9 The use of animals in research that aims to cure diseases

- 10 Research using stem cells, as a way of curing diseases
- 11 Understanding how people learn*
- 12 The impact of globalisation on developing countries*
- 13 The impact of immigration on the UK*
- 14 Developing faster methods of transport
- 15 Nanotechnology
- 16 Wi-fi networks

*social science questions – Relatively little is known about the UK population's attitudes towards and knowledge of social science and this study was seen as an opportunity to assess the situation.

% very or fairly beneficial (y-axis) vs *% very or fairly worried* (x-axis)

Younger women tended to be more interested than younger men in health and a range of social science issues, while younger men tended to be more interested than younger women in inventions and discoveries.

Base: 2,137 adults including a booster sample of young people aged 16-24

Source: Research Councils UK – Public Attitudes to Science 2008
http://www.rcuk.ac.uk/sis/pas.htm

Travel &
transport

Risk on the roads

Comparing death rates in different countries

Anyone who was killed outright in a road accident or died within
30 days as a result is included in these statistics

International comparisons of road deaths, selected OECD countries, per 100,000 population, 2007

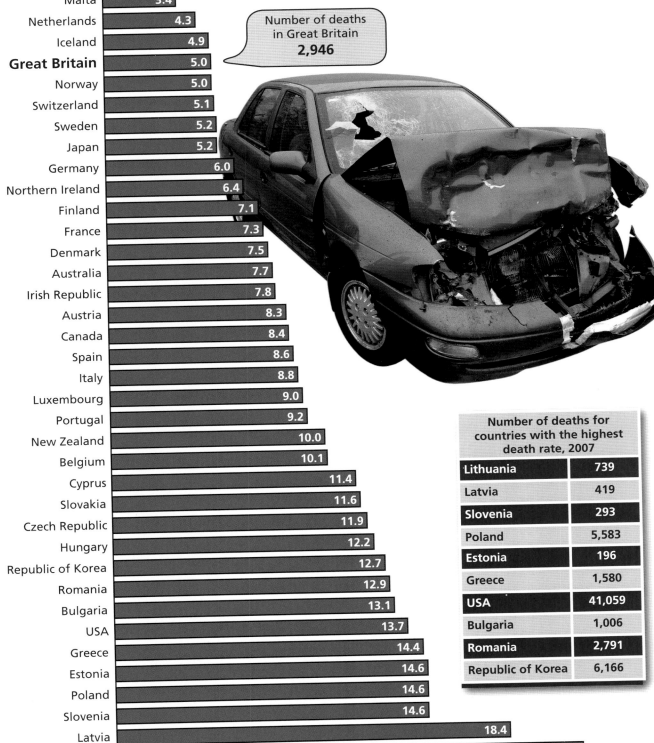

Malta	3.4
Netherlands	4.3
Iceland	4.9
Great Britain	5.0
Norway	5.0
Switzerland	5.1
Sweden	5.2
Japan	5.2
Germany	6.0
Northern Ireland	6.4
Finland	7.1
France	7.3
Denmark	7.5
Australia	7.7
Irish Republic	7.8
Austria	8.3
Canada	8.4
Spain	8.6
Italy	8.8
Luxembourg	9.0
Portugal	9.2
New Zealand	10.0
Belgium	10.1
Cyprus	11.4
Slovakia	11.6
Czech Republic	11.9
Hungary	12.2
Republic of Korea	12.7
Romania	12.9
Bulgaria	13.1
USA	13.7
Greece	14.4
Estonia	14.6
Poland	14.6
Slovenia	14.6
Latvia	18.4
Lithuania	21.8

Number of deaths
in Great Britain
2,946

NB Figures are provisional

Number of deaths for countries with the highest death rate, 2007	
Lithuania	739
Latvia	419
Slovenia	293
Poland	5,583
Estonia	196
Greece	1,580
USA	41,059
Bulgaria	1,006
Romania	2,791
Republic of Korea	6,166

Source: Department for Transport © Crown copyright 2008
http://www.dft.gov.uk

Some countries use different definitions but adjustments are
made for international comparability to a common 30 day basis.

Last breath

A drink drive **accident** is defined as being an incident on a public road in which someone is killed or injured and where one or more of the motor vehicle drivers or riders involved either refused to give a breath test or:

- failed a roadside breath test by registering over **35 micrograms** of alcohol per 100 millilitres of breath
- died and was subsequently found to have more than **80 milligrams** of alcohol per 100 millilitres of blood.

Number of reported ACCIDENTS involving at least one driver/rider over the legal alcohol limit for GB

Fatal accidents Serious Slight

Statistics refer to personal injury accidents on public roads (including footways) which became known to the police.
Figures for deaths refer to persons who sustained injuries which caused death less than 30 days after the accident
2008 figures are provisional

Drink drive **casualties** are defined as all road users killed or injured in a drink drive accident

Number of reported CASUALTIES involving at least one driver/rider over the legal alcohol limit for GB

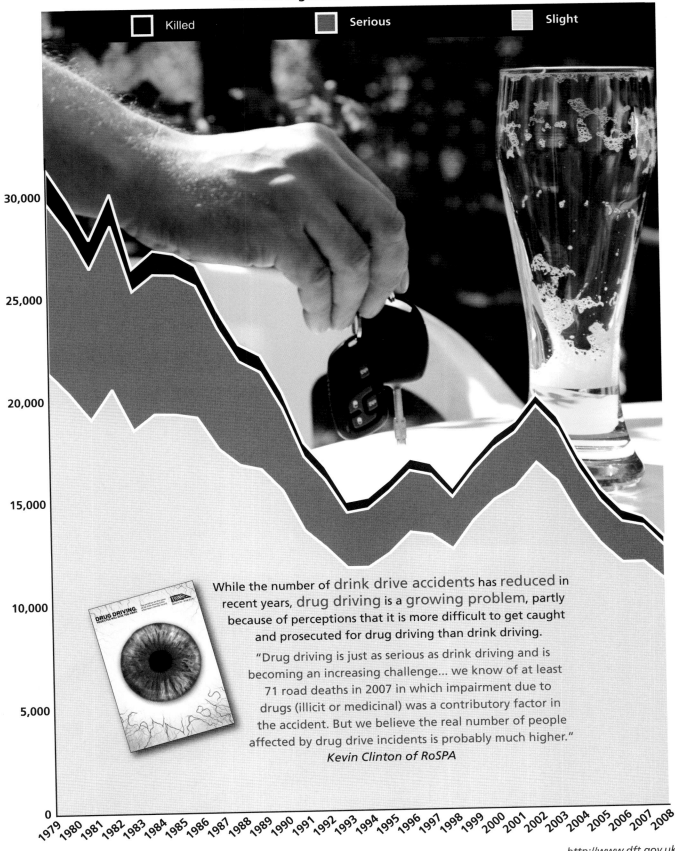

☐ Killed   ■ Serious   ☐ Slight

30,000

25,000

20,000

15,000

10,000

5,000

0

1979 1980 1981 1982 1983 1984 1985 1986 1987 1988 1989 1990 1991 1992 1993 1994 1995 1996 1997 1998 1999 2000 2001 2002 2003 2004 2005 2006 2007 2008

While the number of drink drive accidents has reduced in recent years, drug driving is a growing problem, partly because of perceptions that it is more difficult to get caught and prosecuted for drug driving than drink driving.

"Drug driving is just as serious as drink driving and is becoming an increasing challenge... we know of at least 71 road deaths in 2007 in which impairment due to drugs (illicit or medicinal) was a contributory factor in the accident. But we believe the real number of people affected by drug drive incidents is probably much higher."
Kevin Clinton of RoSPA

Source: Department for Transport © Crown copyright 2009,
The Royal Society for the Prevention of Accidents

http://www.dft.gov.uk
http://www.rospa.com
http://www.dft.gov.uk/think/drugdrive/

Traffic jam

Drivers would rather put up with congestion than change their habits

In a GB survey, the RAC found that over half of all motorists would rather take the chance of being stuck in a traffic jam than get on public transport.

Which, if any, of these modes of transport have you used in the last month? (%)

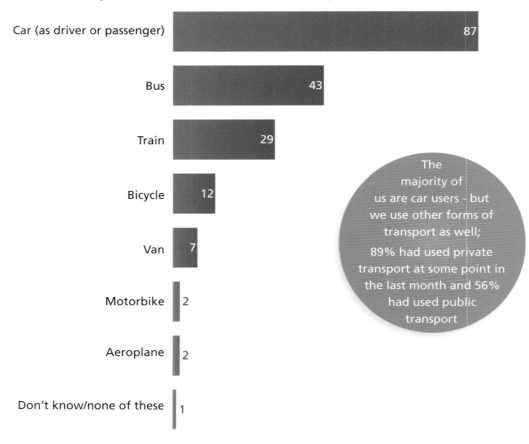

Mode	%
Car (as driver or passenger)	87
Bus	43
Train	29
Bicycle	12
Van	7
Motorbike	2
Aeroplane	2
Don't know/none of these	1

The majority of us are car users - but we use other forms of transport as well; 89% had used private transport at some point in the last month and 56% had used public transport

Many of us say that we would use public transport if services were better...

I would travel by car less if bus and train services around here were better (%)

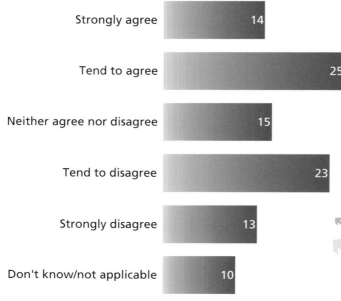

	%
Strongly agree	14
Tend to agree	25
Neither agree nor disagree	15
Tend to disagree	23
Strongly disagree	13
Don't know/not applicable	10

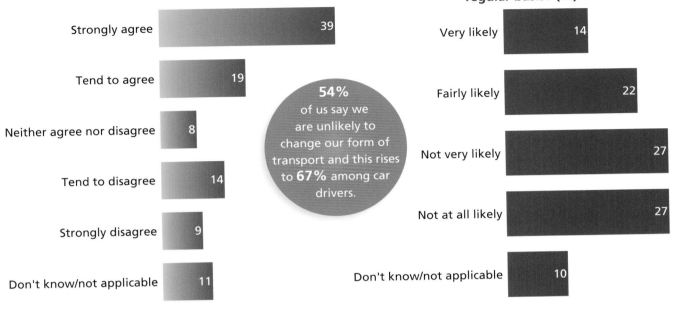

However most of us would struggle to give up our cars ...

I would find it difficult to adjust my lifestyle to being without a car (%)

- Strongly agree — 39
- Tend to agree — 19
- Neither agree nor disagree — 8
- Tend to disagree — 14
- Strongly disagree — 9
- Don't know/not applicable — 11

54% of us say we are unlikely to change our form of transport and this rises to **67%** among car drivers.

And not many of us would swap modes of transport...

Over the next twelve months or so, how likely or unlikely is it that you will use a bus, train or bicycle to make a journey you make by car on a regular basis? (%)

- Very likely — 14
- Fairly likely — 22
- Not very likely — 27
- Not at all likely — 27
- Don't know/not applicable — 10

In fact, we are so attached to our cars that many of us would rather be stuck in a traffic jam than take public transport - and this is especially true of car drivers...

I'd rather take the chance of being stuck in a traffic jam than get public transport (%)

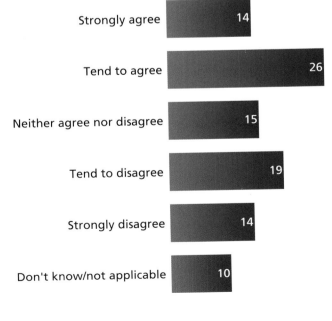

- Strongly agree — 14
- Tend to agree — 26
- Neither agree nor disagree — 15
- Tend to disagree — 19
- Strongly disagree — 14
- Don't know/not applicable — 10

Source: 'The Congestion Challenge', RAC/Ipsos-mori
http://www.capibus.co.uk

What price your life?

...although the true figure is thought to be much higher

Network Rail launched a poster campaign in 2009 to raise awareness of the dangers of trespassing on the railway.

Whilst the majority of incidents occur along the 20,000 miles of track between stations and at level crossings, platform to platform trespass at stations is a significant problem.

Many incidents are occurring after 9pm when, maybe after a night out, people's judgements aren't at their best.

The Dangers

Trains travel at up to **125mph** and can take the length of **20 football pitches to stop.**

It takes up to **25,000 volts** of electricity to power trains through the overhead lines. It's always switched on and can even jump through the air.

In some places, trains are powered by the third rail. It carries **750 volts** of electricity and is never switched off. Touching the rail will almost certainly result in death or serious injury.

The Penalties

Trespassing is a criminal offence which carries a fine of up to **£1,000.**

Anyone putting objects on the tracks (eg rocks or shopping trolleys) and endangering life can be prosecuted by the police, and the maximum penalty for causing a train accident is **life imprisonment.**

If a child is charged with causing a train accident, then a parent/guardian may be **prosecuted** too.

There were **227 trespass fatalities** and **119 casualties** requiring hospital treatment in 2008

What price your life?
A retrieved mobile? Making your train? Taking a short cut?
Stepping on the track isn't just illegal, it's a death sentence.

Trespasser fatalities involving young people, by age, GB 1991-2006

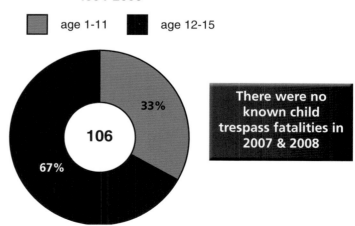

age 1-11   age 12-15

33%

106

67%

There were no known child trespass fatalities in 2007 & 2008

*Source: Office of Rail Regulation –
National Rail Trends Yearbook 2008/09 ©
Crown copyright 2009
Network Rail
http://www.rail-reg.gov.uk
http://www.networkrailmediacentre.co.uk*

Don't run the risk

On average, more than three motorists a week are involved in a near miss with a train

Network Rail's public safety awareness campaign on level crossings has been running since 2006, but in late 2008 they launched a new hard hitting tv and radio advertising campaign that illustrated in graphic detail the tragic consequences of both motorists and pedestrians misusing level crossings.

95% of accidents at level crossings are caused by misuse or error – ie drivers ignoring red signals, barriers or klaxons.

There were **20** collisions between trains and motor vehicles for those who didn't beat the lights.

Pedestrians were also putting themselves at risk with **more than five a week** involved in near misses.

15 people lost their lives at levels crossings in 2008.

Photos: Network Rail

Number of recorded level crossing incidents, 2008

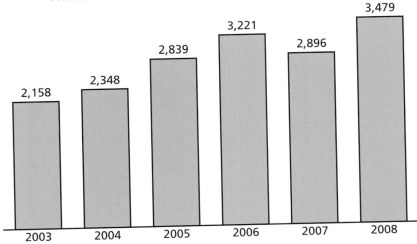

Year	Incidents
2003	2,158
2004	2,348
2005	2,839
2006	3,221
2007	2,896
2008	3,479

"Level crossings are safe, but tragically it is unsafe driver behaviour that causes accidents and deaths. Every week three motorists risk their lives and those of others by abusing level crossings... don't run the risk"
Iain Coucher, Network Rail Chief Executive

British deaths at level crossings are low by international standards – among the lowest in Europe and worldwide.

In Europe, at least **600** people fall victim of accidents at level crossings every year. **95 %** of these accidents are caused by road users. Level crossings account for **2%** of road deaths but a **third** of all rail fatalities.

Source: Office of Rail Regulation – National Rail Trends Yearbook 2008/09 © Crown copyright 2009
Network Rail, The Community of European Railway and Infrastructure
http://www.rail-reg.gov.uk
http://www.networkrailmediacentre.co.uk
http://www.cer.be

Capital advice

Travellers rate the top capital cities

TripAdvisor, the website which gives reviews and opinions from travellers, asked its users about Europe's capital cities. 2,376 travellers gave their views.

London

London was voted top for free attractions by **35%** of the travellers. Its nearest rival, Rome, polled only **9%**.

At the same time it came top for having the most tourist traps – in the opinion of **30%**.

23% also voted it the most expensive city – although Paris came close with **19%**.

It has the best public parks, in the opinion of a huge **50%** (only **7%** thought the Paris parks were best).

London also has the best nightlife – voted by **27%**, its nearest rivals being Amsterdam – **17%** and Barcelona **11%**.

However, London is also the dirtiest capital – **36%**, as well as having the worst cuisine – **10%**, just ahead of Moscow's **7%** – and the worst dressed people – **20%**.

No Mary, this is LITERALLY a tourist trap

Paris

Paris not surprisingly was rated top for best cuisine by **18%** of all travellers, though London, despite topping the worst cuisine category, scored **17%**. Perhaps it depends where you eat!

Parisians are also the best dressed – **26%** – but they are the least friendly – **36%** – and the city is the most over-rated (**25%** found this, as opposed to **12%** having this view of London).

Best of the rest?

For splendid buildings it's best to go to Barcelona – **15%**, Rome – **14%** or even London – **12%**.

If you want friendly locals then Dublin **15%**, Amsterdam **14%** and Edinburgh **8%** should be your choices.

If you are bothered by litter, head for the cleanest cities – Copenhagen **9%**, Zurich **8%** and Stockholm **7%**.

Lovers should travel to the most romantic cities – Venice **29%**, Paris **21%** or Rome **11%**.

Bargain hunters would be best to consider Prague **16%**, Amsterdam **9%** or Istanbul **8%** or the under-rated cities of Krakow **7%**, Bruges **6%** or Edinburgh **5%**.

And the worst?

Moscow features only in the lists for the least friendly, worst cuisine and worst dressed inhabitants.

We have appalling food, bad dress sense, are consistently rude – and yet still they come.

And TripAdvisor's correspondents are certainly not fans of Brussels, the Belgian capital features twice – it's third for ugly architecture and tops the list for most boring!

Source: TripAdvisor
http://www.tripadvisor.co.uk

War &
conflict

Conflicting countries

Over 75% of the world's wars take place in Africa and Asia

An armed conflict is defined as a political conflict in which combat involves the armed forces of at least one state (or armed factions seeking to gain control of the state). Part of the definition is that at least 1,000 people have been killed by the fighting during the course of the conflict.

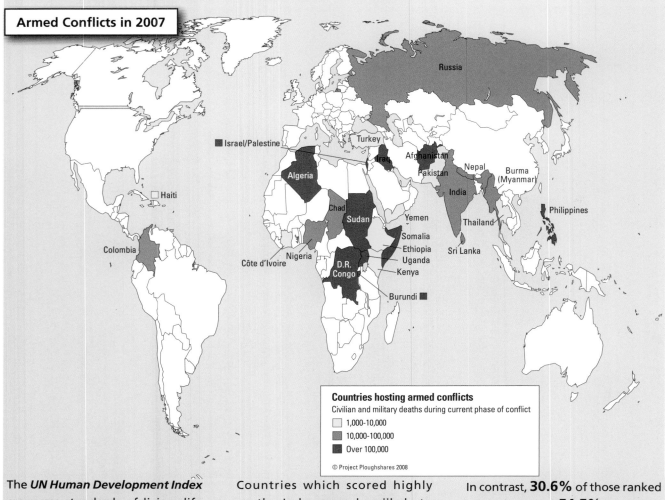

Armed Conflicts in 2007

Countries hosting armed conflicts
Civilian and military deaths during current phase of conflict

- 1,000-10,000
- 10,000-100,000
- Over 100,000

© Project Ploughshares 2008

The *UN Human Development Index* measures standards of living, life expectancy and education.

Countries which scored highly on the Index were less likely to experience conflict (only **2.9%** of these in the period 1998-2007).

In contrast, **30.6%** of those ranked as medium and **54.5%** ranked as low, experienced conflict in that same 10 year period.

Geographic distributions of armed conflicts in 2007

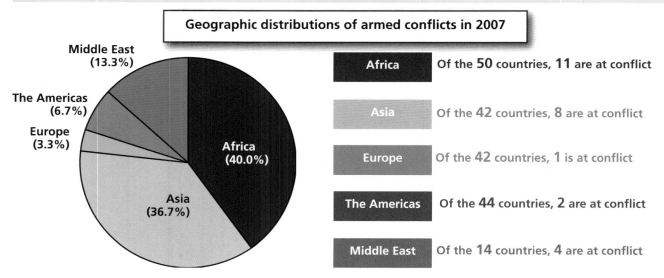

- Middle East (13.3%)
- The Americas (6.7%)
- Europe (3.3%)
- Africa (40.0%)
- Asia (36.7%)

Africa Of the **50** countries, **11** are at conflict

Asia Of the **42** countries, **8** are at conflict

Europe Of the **42** countries, **1** is at conflict

The Americas Of the **44** countries, **2** are at conflict

Middle East Of the **14** countries, **4** are at conflict

Source: Project Ploughshares – Armed Conflicts Report 2008

http://www.ploughshares.ca

Peacekeeping

The first UN peacekeeping mission was in 1948... since then there have been 63 operations around the world

UN peacekeeping operations monitor ceasefires, implement peace agreements and protect civilians.

Before 1990, the UN had mounted 15 peace operations. It mounted the same number in the next four years and the number keeps rising.

Peacekeepers now are administrators and economists, police officers and legal experts, de-miners and electoral observers, human rights monitors and specialists in civil affairs, gender, governance, humanitarian workers and experts in communications and public information. UN peacekeeping continues to evolve, rising to meet new challenges and political realities.

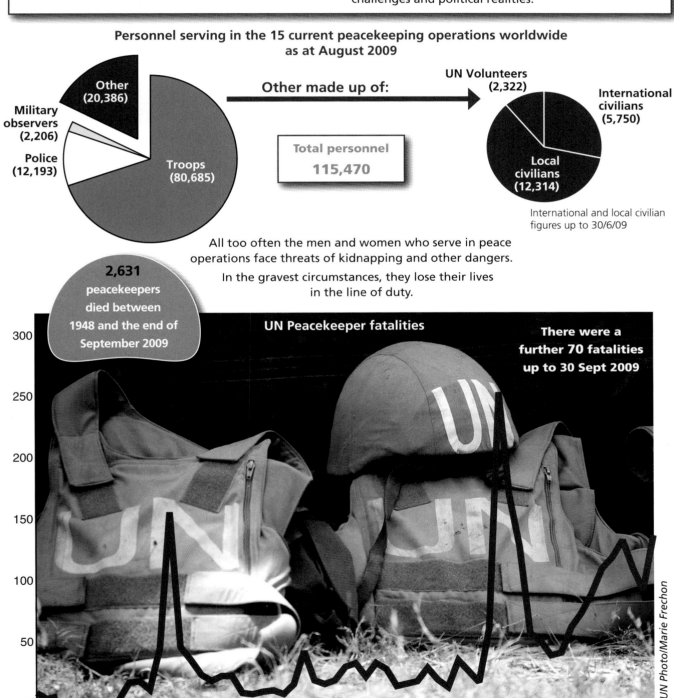

Personnel serving in the 15 current peacekeeping operations worldwide as at August 2009

Other (20,386)

Military observers (2,206)

Police (12,193)

Troops (80,685)

Total personnel
115,470

Other made up of:

UN Volunteers (2,322)

International civilians (5,750)

Local civilians (12,314)

International and local civilian figures up to 30/6/09

All too often the men and women who serve in peace operations face threats of kidnapping and other dangers.

In the gravest circumstances, they lose their lives in the line of duty.

2,631 peacekeepers died between 1948 and the end of September 2009

UN Peacekeeper fatalities

There were a further 70 fatalities up to 30 Sept 2009

300

250

200

150

100

50

0

1948   1958   1968   1978   1988   1998   2008

UN Photo/Marie Frechon

NB Figures unavailable for 1951, 1954 & 1955

Source: United Nations
http://www.un.org

The cost of war...

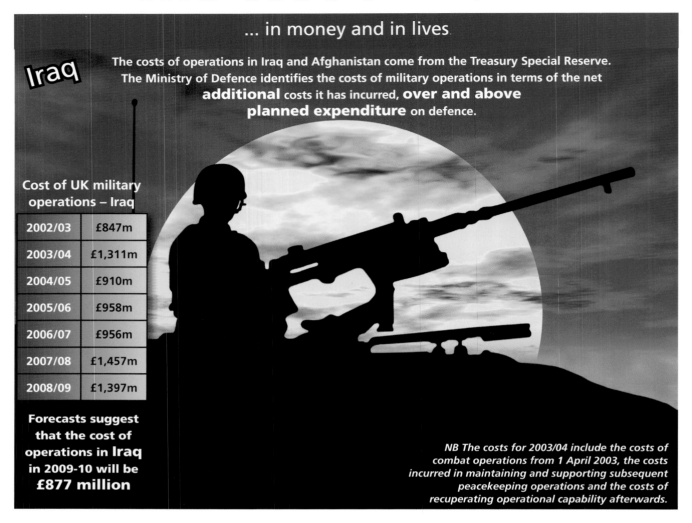

... in money and in lives

The costs of operations in Iraq and Afghanistan come from the Treasury Special Reserve. The Ministry of Defence identifies the costs of military operations in terms of the net **additional** costs it has incurred, **over and above planned expenditure** on defence.

Iraq

Cost of UK military operations – Iraq	
2002/03	£847m
2003/04	£1,311m
2004/05	£910m
2005/06	£958m
2006/07	£956m
2007/08	£1,457m
2008/09	£1,397m

Forecasts suggest that the cost of operations in Iraq in 2009-10 will be £877 million

NB The costs for 2003/04 include the costs of combat operations from 1 April 2003, the costs incurred in maintaining and supporting subsequent peacekeeping operations and the costs of recuperating operational capability afterwards.

Number of UK military and civilian casualties and fatalities - Iraq

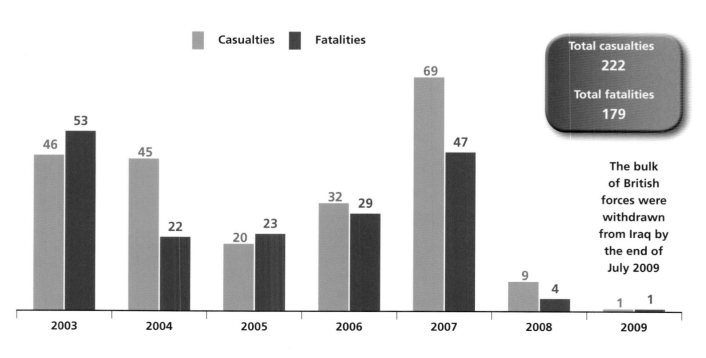

Casualties   Fatalities

Total casualties
222

Total fatalities
179

The bulk of British forces were withdrawn from Iraq by the end of July 2009

	2003	2004	2005	2006	2007	2008	2009
Casualties	46	45	20	32	69	9	1
Fatalities	53	22	23	29	47	4	1

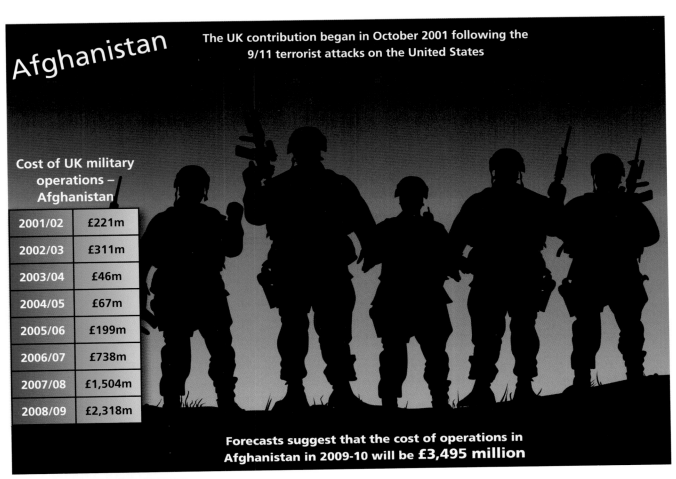

Afghanistan

The UK contribution began in October 2001 following the 9/11 terrorist attacks on the United States

Cost of UK military operations – Afghanistan

2001/02	£221m
2002/03	£311m
2003/04	£46m
2004/05	£67m
2005/06	£199m
2006/07	£738m
2007/08	£1,504m
2008/09	£2,318m

Forecasts suggest that the cost of operations in Afghanistan in 2009-10 will be **£3,495 million**

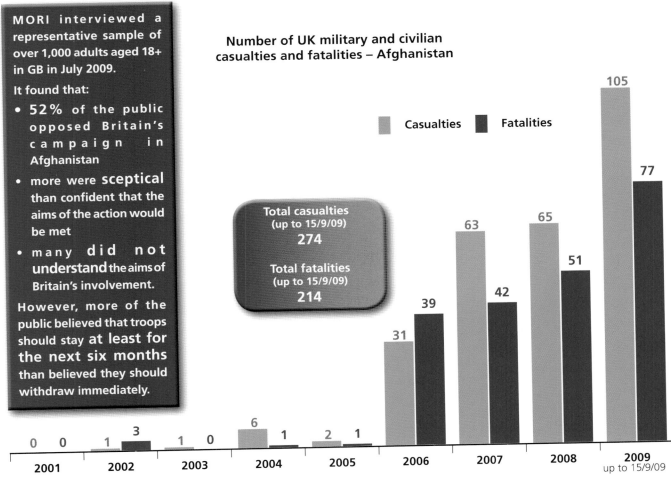

MORI interviewed a representative sample of over 1,000 adults aged 18+ in GB in July 2009.

It found that:

- **52%** of the public opposed Britain's campaign in Afghanistan
- more were **sceptical** than confident that the aims of the action would be met
- many **did not understand** the aims of Britain's involvement.

However, more of the public believed that troops should stay **at least for the next six months** than believed they should withdraw immediately.

Number of UK military and civilian casualties and fatalities – Afghanistan

Casualties ▪ Fatalities

Total casualties (up to 15/9/09) **274**

Total fatalities (up to 15/9/09) **214**

	2001	2002	2003	2004	2005	2006	2007	2008	2009 up to 15/9/09
Casualties	0	1	1	6	2	31	63	65	105
Fatalities	0	3	0	1	1	39	42	51	77

Source: MOD Main Estimates 2009-10 © Crown copyright 2009, Ipsos Mori

http://www.mod.gov.uk
http://www.ipsos-mori.com

Military mix

All the armed forces aim to have 8% of their personnel from ethnic minorities by 2013

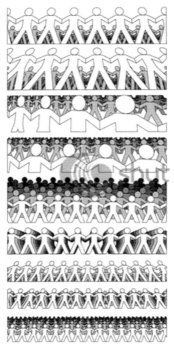

Although the number of people from ethnic minorities in the armed forces has risen from just over **1%** in 1994 to **6.1%** in 2008, a large number have come from the Commonwealth rather than the UK.

The long term goal is that the Armed Forces reflect the society they serve.

In the financial year 2008-09, 759 people from black and ethnic minority backgrounds applied to join the Royal Navy, **2,555** to join the Army and **657** to join the RAF.

In 2008, **1,810** out of a total of **21,801** successful applicants for the intake to UK regular forces were from ethnic minority backgrounds.

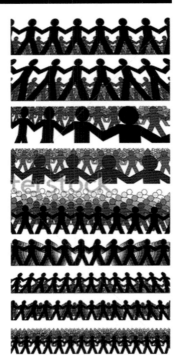

UK Armed Forces ethnic minority representation

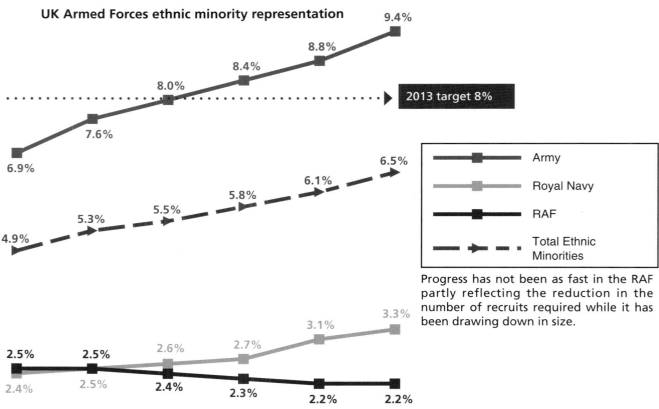

2013 target 8%

Army
Royal Navy
RAF
Total Ethnic Minorities

Progress has not been as fast in the RAF partly reflecting the reduction in the number of recruits required while it has been drawing down in size.

Army: 6.9% 7.6% 8.0% 8.4% 8.8% 9.4%

Total Ethnic Minorities: 4.9% 5.3% 5.5% 5.8% 6.1% 6.5%

Royal Navy: 2.4% 2.5% 2.6% 2.7% 3.1% 3.3%

RAF: 2.5% 2.5% 2.4% 2.3% 2.2% 2.2%

2004 2005 2006 2007 2008 2009

Ministry of Defence, Annual Report & Accounts © Crown copyright 2009
http://www.mod.uk

Wider world

Women & children first!

Each day around 1,500 women die from complications related to pregnancy and childbirth...

...**95%** of these are in sub-Saharan Africa and South Asia.

The global annual number of maternal deaths has exceeded 500,000 since 1990.

There are risks associated with all pregnancies, but these rise the more times a woman gives birth

Lifetime risk of maternal death
(cumulative across the reproductive years)

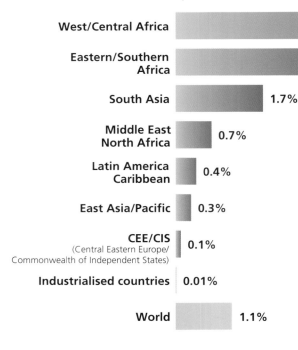

West/Central Africa	5.9%
Eastern/Southern Africa	3.4%
South Asia	1.7%
Middle East North Africa	0.7%
Latin America Caribbean	0.4%
East Asia/Pacific	0.3%
CEE/CIS (Central Eastern Europe/ Commonwealth of Independent States)	0.1%
Industrialised countries	0.01%
World	1.1%

The risk of a woman, in a least developed country, dying from complications in pregnancy or childbirth is more than **300** times greater than for a woman in an industrialised country.

NO OTHER MORTALITY RATE IS SO UNEQUAL

Percentage and number of maternal deaths in the world
(2005 – latest year for which figures are available)

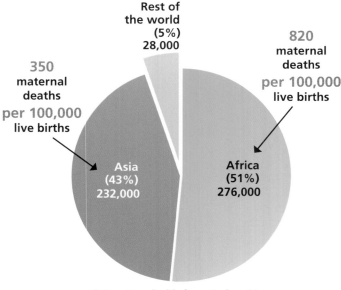

Rest of the world (5%) 28,000

820 maternal deaths **per 100,000 live births**

350 maternal deaths **per 100,000 live births**

Asia (43%) 232,000

Africa (51%) 276,000

Rate not applicable for rest of world
Figures do not add up to 100% due to rounding

The highest lifetime risk of maternal mortality is in Niger – **1 in 7**
For comparison, the risk for a mother in the UK is just **1 in 8,200**

© UNDP Brazil

Limited progress has been made worldwide towards the first target of **Millennium Development Goal 5** (MDG5) *which aims to reduce the 1990 maternal mortality ratio by three quarters by 2015.*

Progress on diminishing maternal mortality ratios has been virtually non-existent in sub-Saharan Africa.

© UNDP Brazil

MDG4

Improving reproductive and maternal health and services will directly contribute to attaining **MDG4**, *which seeks to reduce the under-five mortality rate by two thirds between 1990 and 2015.*

A child born in a least developed country is almost **14 times** more likely to die during the first 28 days of life than one born in an industrialised country.

In 2007, **9.2 million** children died before age five. Africa and Asia together accounted for **92%** of these deaths.

Half of the world's under five deaths occurred in Africa, which remains the most difficult place in the world for a child to survive until age five.

Many women in the developing world – and most women in the least developed countries – give birth at home without skilled attendants.

80% of maternal deaths could be averted if women had access to essential maternity and basic health-care services.

Lowering a mother's risk of death directly improves a child's prospects for survival.

In developing countries, babies whose mothers die during the first six weeks of their lives are far more likely to die in the first two years of life than babies whose mothers survive.

Percentage and number of Deaths of children under five

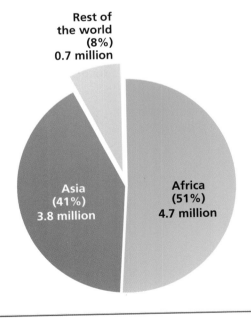

Rest of the world (8%) 0.7 million

Asia (41%) 3.8 million

Africa (51%) 4.7 million

Lost mothers, lost children on page 196 of *Essential Articles 12* looks at the personal tragedy of orphans in Sierra Leone – which has the highest maternal mortality rate in the world.

Source: The State of the World's Children 2009

http://www.unicef.org

Education inequality

Millions of children are denied education – and will be trapped in poverty as a result

School systems in many countries are chronically under-financed and under-resourced. In sub-Saharan Africa alone, **3.8 million** teachers will have to be recruited by 2015 if universal primary education is to be achieved.

Inequality among countries in public expenditure per primary school pupil
(latest available figures)

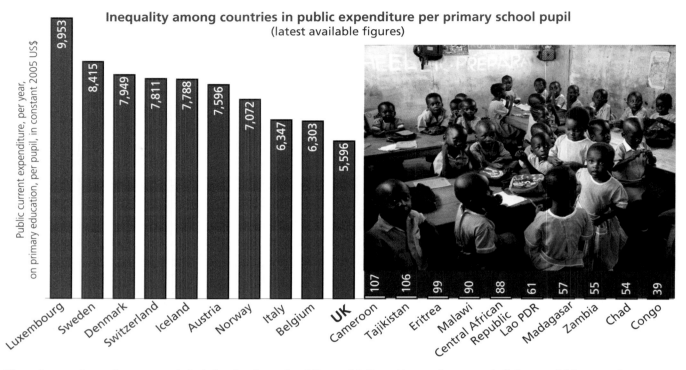

Public current expenditure, per year, on primary education, per pupil, in constant 2005 US$

Luxembourg	9,953
Sweden	8,415
Denmark	7,949
Switzerland	7,811
Iceland	7,788
Austria	7,596
Norway	7,072
Italy	6,347
Belgium	6,303
UK	5,596
Cameroon	107
Tajikistan	106
Eritrea	99
Malawi	90
Central African Republic	88
Lao PDR	61
Madagasar	57
Zambia	55
Chad	54
Congo	39

There is an extremely uneven global distribution of public expenditure on education – North America & Western Europe alone accounted for **55%** of the world's spending on education but only **10%** of the population aged 5 to 25.

At the other extreme, sub-Saharan Africa was home to **15%** of 5 to 25 year olds but accounted for just **2%** of global spending, and South & West Asia for **28%** of the age group but **7%** of the spending.

Even within countries there is a striking inequality

Average years of education for poorest and richest 20% of 17-22 year olds, selected countries
(latest available figures)

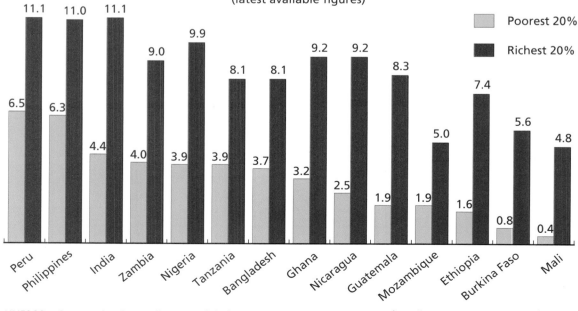

Country	Poorest 20%	Richest 20%
Peru	6.5	11.1
Philippines	6.3	11.0
India	4.4	11.1
Zambia	4.0	9.0
Nigeria	3.9	9.9
Tanzania	3.9	8.1
Bangladesh	3.7	8.1
Ghana	3.2	9.2
Nicaragua	2.5	9.2
Guatemala	1.9	8.3
Mozambique	1.9	5.0
Ethiopia	1.6	7.4
Burkina Faso	0.8	5.6
Mali	0.4	4.8

Source: UNESCO – Overcoming inequality, EFA Global Monitoring Report 2009

http:// www.unesco.org/en/education/efareport

101 million children of primary school age are out of school. This has declined in recent years from **115 million** in 2002 yet in some countries and regions the task remains enormous, for example in sub-Saharan Africa where **46 million** primary school-age children are out of school and in South Asia where **35 million** remain out of school.

❝ The circumstances into which children are born, their gender, the wealth of their parents, their language and the colour of their skin should not define their educational opportunities ❞
Unicef

BOYS
School attendance in developing regions, 2000-2007

Primary ■   Secondary ■

Region	Primary	Secondary
Sub-Saharan Africa	64%	26%
Eastern & Southern Africa	66%	20%
West and Central Africa	63%	31%
Middle East and North Africa	88%	54%
South Asia	81%	51%
East Asia & Pacific (excludes China)	92%	60%
Latin America & Caribbean	90%	
Central & Eastern Europe, CIS	93%	79%

Figures for Latin America & Caribbean secondary attendance not available

GIRLS
School attendance in developing regions, 2000-2007

Primary ■   Secondary ■

Region	Primary	Secondary
Sub-Saharan Africa	61%	22%
Eastern & Southern Africa	66%	18%
West & Central Africa	56%	26%
Middle East & North Africa	85%	52%
South Asia	77%	43%
East Asia & Pacific (excludes China)	92%	63%
Latin America & Caribbean	91%	
Central & Eastern Europe, CIS	91%	76%

Figures for Latin America & Caribbean secondary attendance not available

Educating a girl dramatically reduces the chance that her child will die before the age of five and improves her prospect of being able to support herself and have a say in her own welfare and in society.

Source: The State of the World's Children 2009, UNICEF
http://www.unicef.org/sowc/

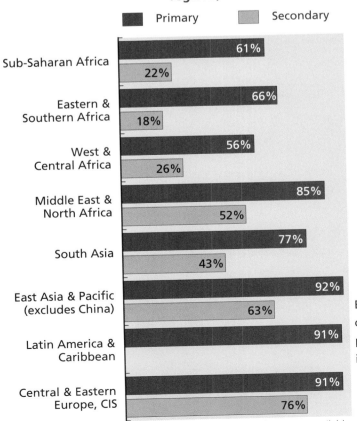

The challenge of hunger

923 million people in the world go hungry every day...

© World Food Programme (WFP)/Andrew Mambo

The **2008 Global Hunger Index** (GHI) measures hunger and malnutrition based on three indicators:

- the proportion of undernourished people as a percentage of the population
- the prevalence of underweight children under the age of five
- the mortality rate of children under the age of five

It ranks countries on a 100-point scale with 0 being the best score (no hunger) and 100 being the worst.

The GHI highlights which countries could be most vulnerable in a crisis

Worst and best scoring countries on the Global Hunger Index 2008

4.9 or less low hunger	5.0-9.9 moderate	10.0-19.9 serious	20.0-29.9 alarming	30.0 or more EXTREMELY alarming

Highest prevalence of hunger

Congo Dem. Rep.	42.7
Eritrea	39.0
Burundi	38.3
Niger	32.4
Sierra Leone	32.2

Lowest prevalence of hunger

Peru	5.6
Cuba	5.5
Moldova	5.4
Jamaica	5.1
Mauritius	5.0

Base: The GHI was originally calculated for 120 countries in Asia, Sub-Saharan Africa and Latin America and the Caribbean – 32 were excluded due to low levels of hunger, so figures are based on the remaining 88.

Industrialised countries were not included, as well as nations for which data was not available such as Iraq, Somalia and Afghanistan.

> **33 countries have levels of hunger that are alarming or extremely alarming**

Progress in reducing hunger since 1990
(percentage change in GHI 1990-2008)

Countries making the MOST progress		Countries making the LEAST progress	
Kuwait	-72.4	Congo Dem. Rep.	+67.6
Peru	-71.1	North Korea	+42.8
Syrian Arab Republic	-51.7	Swaziland	+32.3
Turkey	-51.0	Guinea-Bissau	+19.3
Mexico	-50.1	Zimbabwe	+18.0

The proportion of hungry people in the developing world is estimated at 17%, about the same level as a decade ago, and progress towards the The Millennium Development Goal hunger target has reversed.

In a year, the number of undernourished people increased by 75 million mostly as a result of soaring food prices

Hunger is closely tied to poverty, and countries with high levels of hunger are overwhelmingly low- or low-middle-income countries.

Most of the countries ranked in the Index are net importers of grains, and are therefore more likely to suffer because of rising food prices.

High prices also reduce the amount of food aid that donors can supply.

Woman at the UN World Food Programme food distribution point

© 2008 WFP/Marcus Prior

Impact of high food prices by region
(EXTRA numbers of undernourished in 2007)

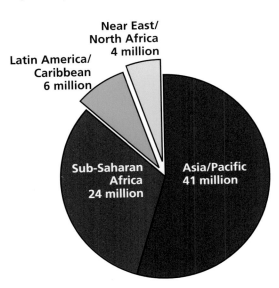

Near East/ North Africa
4 million

Latin America/ Caribbean
6 million

Sub-Saharan Africa
24 million

Asia/Pacific
41 million

The price of corn has increased threefold since 2003

The price of rice has increased fourfold since 2003

Prospects for improving food and nutrition security do not appear favourable. At least 800 million people were food insecure – living in hunger or fear of starvation – even before the food price crisis hit.

Source: The Challenge of Hunger – The 2008 Global Hunger Index, International Food Policy Research Institute; Food and Agriculture Organization of the United Nations, UN World Food Programme

http://www.ifpri.org
http://www.fao.org
http://www.wfp.org

Live long and prosper

A good life is possible without costing the earth

The Happy Planet Index

The Happy Planet Index measures what truly matters to us – our well-being in terms of long, happy and meaningful lives – and what matters to the planet – our rate of resource consumption.

Three components are measured for each country: Life expectancy in years, Life satisfaction by a score out of ten, Ecological footprint by planet's worth of consumption – the lower the better. 143 countries representing **99%** of

the world's population were given scores ranging from 0 to 100 – with high total HPI scores only achievable by meeting all three targets.

Surprisingly, nine out of the top ten countries are in South America – less surprisingly, the bottom ten are all in sub-Saharan Africa, with Zimbabwe at the very bottom.

The top 10

Rank	Country	Life expectancy	Life satisfaction	Footprint	HPI score
1	Costa Rica	78.5	8.5	2.3	76.1
2	Dominican Rep	71.5	7.6	1.5	71.8
3	Jamaica	72.2	6.7	1.1	70.1
4	Guatemala	69.7	7.4	1.5	68.4
5	Vietnam	73.7	6.5	1.3	66.5
6	Colombia	72.3	7.3	1.8	66.1
7	Cuba	77.7	6.7	1.8	65.7
8	El Salvador	71.3	6.7	1.6	61.5
9	Brazil	71.7	7.6	2.4	61.0
10	Honduras	69.4	7.0	1.8	61.0

HPI score colour key

All 3 components good
2 components good 1 middling
1 component good, 2 middling
3 components middling
Any with 1 component poor
2 components poor, or 'blood red' footprint

What makes a success?

Costa Rica has the fifth-lowest human poverty index in the developing world, and the proportion of people living on less than $2-a-day is lower than in Romania – an EU member.

It has taken very deliberate steps to reduce its environmental impact. A staggering **99%** of its energy comes from renewable sources. Deforestation has been reversed, and forests cover twice as much land as 20 years ago.

Costa Rica has no army, freeing up government money to spend on social programmes.

It combines solid social networks of friends, families and neighbourhoods, with strong political participation and equal treatment of women.

On the minus side, there are high levels of inequality, and almost **10%** of the population live on under $2-a-day. Clean water and adult literacy are almost universal, but not quite.

Costa Rica
A haven of democracy and peace in turbulent Central America

Zimbabwe

And a failure?

In contrast to Costa Rica, Zimbabwe has a life expectancy of around **41,** which actually represents a decline; life expectancy was **62** years in Zimbabwe in 1987 – only one year shorter than in Turkey. Nowadays, people in Turkey can expect to live more than **30** years longer than people living in Zimbabwe.

Less than half the population **(46%)** have access to decent sanitation.

The unemployment rate is over **80%** and so is the proportion of the population living below the poverty line.

Military service is compulsory.

The bottom 10

Rank	Country	Life expectancy	Life satisfaction	Footprint	HPI score	HPI score colour key
134	Benin	55.4	3.0	1.0	24.6	All 3 components good
135	Togo	57.8	2.6	0.8	23.3	2 components good 1 middling
136	Sierra Leone	41.8	3.6	0.8	23.1	
137	Central African Rep	43.7	4.0	1.6	22.9	1 component good, 2 middling
138	Burkina Faso	51.4	3.6	2.0	22.4	
139	Burundi	48.5	2.9	0.8	21.8	3 components middling
140	Namibia	51.6	4.5	3.7	21.1	
141	Botswana	48.1	4.7	3.6	20.9	Any with 1 component poor
142	Tanzania	51.0	2.4	1.1	17.8	2 components poor, or 'blood red' footprint
143	Zimbabwe	40.9	2.8	1.1	16.6	

In the middle

Rich developed nations fall somewhere in the middle. The highest-placed Western nation is the Netherlands – 43rd out of 143. The UK ranks midway down the table – 74th, behind Germany, Italy and France. The USA comes a long way back in 114th place.

No country successfully achieves the three goals of high life satisfaction, high life expectancy and consuming only their share of one-planet's worth of resources.

Source: The (Un)happy Planet Index 2.0, NEF
http://www.happyplanetindex.org

Age concern

The population of the world is changing: by 2050 one in every five people will be aged 60 or over

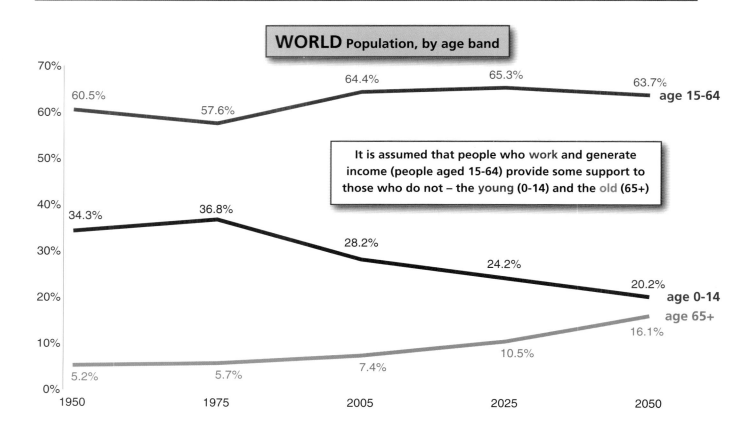

WORLD Population, by age band

60.5% · 57.6% · 64.4% · 65.3% · 63.7% **age 15-64**

It is assumed that people who work and generate income (people aged 15-64) provide some support to those who do not – the young (0-14) and the old (65+)

34.3% · 36.8% · 28.2% · 24.2% · 20.2% **age 0-14**

age 65+

5.2% · 5.7% · 7.4% · 10.5% · 16.1%

1950 · 1975 · 2005 · 2025 · 2050

The percentage of the population of working age is decreasing compared to the number of dependants – and this is mostly being driven by an increase in the proportion of older people.

Estimated percentage of population aged 65 and over

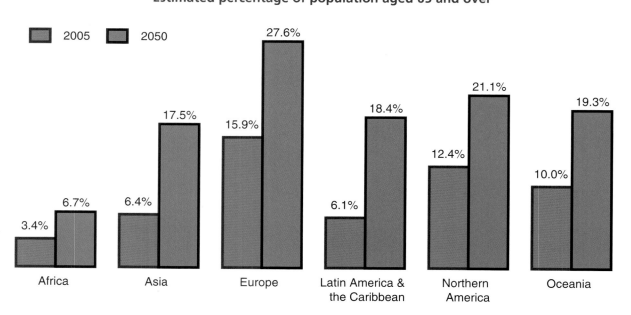

■ 2005 ■ 2050

Africa: 3.4%, 6.7%
Asia: 6.4%, 17.5%
Europe: 15.9%, 27.6%
Latin America & the Caribbean: 6.1%, 18.4%
Northern America: 12.4%, 21.1%
Oceania: 10.0%, 19.3%

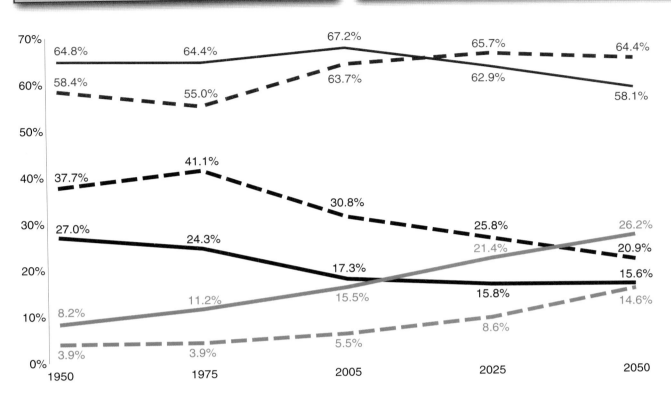

DEVELOPING WORLD population	DEVELOPED WORLD population
- - - age 0-14 - - - age 15-64 - - - age 65+	—— age 0-14 —— age 15-64 —— age 65+

Developing World values:
- 58.4% → 55.0% → 63.7% → 65.7% → 64.4% (age 15-64, dashed)
- 37.7% → 41.1% → 30.8% → 25.8% → 20.9% (age 0-14, dashed)
- 3.9% → 3.9% → 5.5% → 8.6% → 14.6% (age 65+, dashed)

Developed World values:
- 64.8% → 64.4% → 67.2% → 62.9% → 58.1% (age 15-64)
- 27.0% → 24.3% → 17.3% → 15.8% → 15.6% (age 0-14)
- 8.2% → 11.2% → 15.5% → 21.4% → 26.2% (age 65+)

Years: 1950, 1975, 2005, 2025, 2050

- In the **most developed** regions there were **47.7 dependants** per 100 people of working age in 2005. This will increase to **71.2** in 2050 as the large group currently of working age moves into old age. In the **least developed** regions the ratio will decline from **81.8 dependants** per 100 workers to **55.1** as the younger population moves into the working age group.

- Striking differences exist between regions. **One out of five Europeans**, but **one out of twenty Africans**, is 60 years or older.

- As the pace of ageing in developing countries is more rapid than in developed countries, developing countries will have less time to adapt to the consequences of population ageing.

- The older population itself is ageing. The **oldest old** (80+) is the fastest growing segment of the older population. They currently make up **13%** of the 60+ age group and will grow to **20%** by 2050. The number of people aged **100+** is projected to increase 14-fold and reach **3.7 million by 2050.**

Source: United Nations Programme on Ageing
http://www.un.org

Megacities

Within two decades, nearly 60% of the world's population will live in cities

Urban growth is most rapid in the developing world, where cities gain an average of 5 million residents every month. As cities grow in size and population, it is important that people, and the environment they live in, can exist in harmony.

This harmony depends on two key elements: **social balance** and **environmental sustainability**. If these things are not established and maintained, there is social unrest and the environment is harmed.

World's most populated cities

Population 2007

	City	Population
1	Tokyo - Japan	35.7m
2	Mexico City - Mexico	19.0m
3	New York - USA	19.0m
4	Mumbai - India	19.0m
5	Sao Paulo - Brazil	18.8m
6	Delhi - India	15.9m
7	Shanghai - China	15.0m
8	Kolkata - India	14.8m
9	Buenos Aires - Argentina	12.8m
10	Dhaka - Bangladesh	13.5m
11	LA Long Beach - USA	12.5m
12	Karachi - Pakistan	12.1m
13	Cairo - Egypt	11.9m
14	Rio de Janeiro - Brazil	11.7m
15	Osaka-Kobe - Japan	11.3m
16	Beijing - China	11.1m
17	Manila - Philippines	11.1m
18	Moscow - Russia	10.5m
19	Istanbul - Turkey	10.1m

Population 2025

36.4m	Tokyo - Japan	1
26.4m	Mumbai - India	2
22.5m	Delhi - India	3
22.0m	Dhaka - Bangladesh	4
21.4m	Sao Paulo - Brazil	5
21.0m	Mexico City - Mexico	6
20.6m	New York - USA	7
20.6m	Kolkata - India	8
19.4m	Shanghai - China	9
19.1m	Karachi - Pakistan	10
16.8m	Kinshasa - Dem Rep of Congo	11
15.8m	Lagos - Dem Rep of Congo	12
15.6m	Cairo - Egypt	13
14.8m	Manila - Philippines	14
14.5m	Beijing - China	15
13.8m	Buenos Aires - Argentina	16
13.7m	LA Long Beach - USA	17
13.4m	Rio de Janeiro - Brazil	18
12.4m	Jakarta - Indonesia	19
12.1m	Istanbul - Turkey	20
11.8m	Guangzhou - China	21
11.4m	Osaka-Kobe - Japan	22
10.5m	Moscow - Russia	23
10.5m	Lahore - Pakistan	24
10.2m	Shenzhen - China	25
10.1m	Chennai - India	26

Cities located near large water body (sea, river or delta)

New megacities

Megacities are cities with populations of more than **10 million**

Climate change

In the 20th century, sea levels rose by an estimated **17cm** and they are expected to rise a further **22cm-34cm** by 2080. The low elevation coastal zone – the continuous area along coastlines that is less than 10 metres above sea level – represents **2%** of the world's land area but contains **10%** of its total population and **13%** of its urban population.

Who is affected?

There are **3,351** cities in the low elevation coastal zones around the world. Of these cities, **64%** are in developing regions; Asia alone accounts for more than half of the most vulnerable cities, followed by Latin America and the Caribbean **(27%)** and Africa **(15%)**. Almost one-fifth of all cities in North America are in low elevation coastal zones.

Number of cities worldwide with 500,000+ inhabitants

■ 500,000 to 1 million inhabitants □ 1 million to 5 million inhabitants ▨ 5 million+ inhabitants

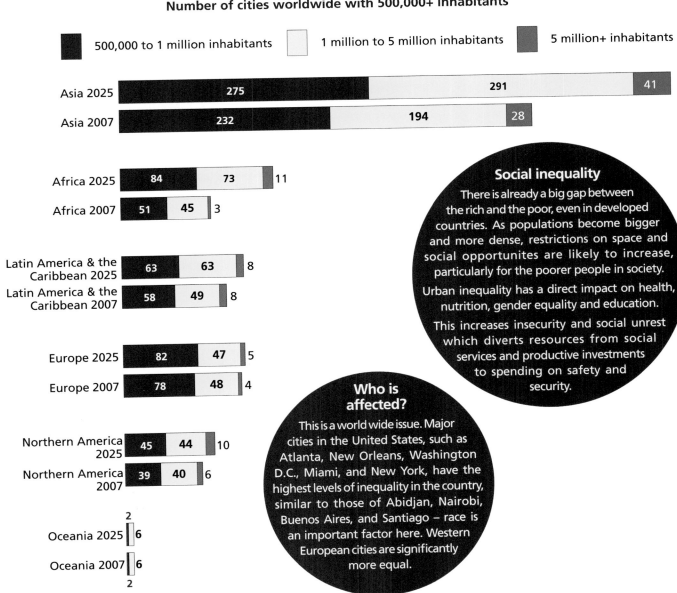

	500,000 to 1 million	1 million to 5 million	5 million+
Asia 2025	275	291	41
Asia 2007	232	194	28
Africa 2025	84	73	11
Africa 2007	51	45	3
Latin America & the Caribbean 2025	63	63	8
Latin America & the Caribbean 2007	58	49	8
Europe 2025	82	47	5
Europe 2007	78	48	4
Northern America 2025	45	44	10
Northern America 2007	39	40	6
Oceania 2025	2	6	
Oceania 2007	2	6	

Social inequality

There is already a big gap between the rich and the poor, even in developed countries. As populations become bigger and more dense, restrictions on space and social opportunites are likely to increase, particularly for the poorer people in society.

Urban inequality has a direct impact on health, nutrition, gender equality and education.

This increases insecurity and social unrest which diverts resources from social services and productive investments to spending on safety and security.

Who is affected?

This is a world wide issue. Major cities in the United States, such as Atlanta, New Orleans, Washington D.C., Miami, and New York, have the highest levels of inequality in the country, similar to those of Abidjan, Nairobi, Buenos Aires, and Santiago – race is an important factor here. Western European cities are significantly more equal.

Source: UN Habitat, State of the World's Cities, 2008/2009
http://www.unhabitat.org

Poor chance

Worldwide, 2,000 children die each day from preventable injuries – most are poor

Global divide

In one year, approximately **950,000** children under the age of 18 died from preventable injuries.

The child death rate from preventable injuries is **3.4** times higher in low- and middle-income countries than in high-income countries.

World death rates per 100,000 children by cause and country income level

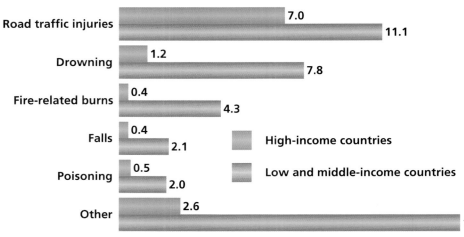

Cause	High-income	Low and middle-income
Road traffic injuries	7.0	11.1
Drowning	1.2	7.8
Fire-related burns	0.4	4.3
Falls	0.4	2.1
Poisoning	0.5	2.0
Other	2.6	14.4

■ High-income countries
■ Low and middle-income countries

Worldwide the death rate for High income countries is **12.2** compared with low and middle income countries which is **41.7**

Source: World report on child injury prevention, World Health Organization, 2008
http://www.who.int

Where?

High-income countries include western Europe, the USA, Australia and New Zealand.

Low and middle-income countries include Africa, southern Asia and South America.

UK divide

In the UK, which is considered a high income country, child injury deaths have declined from about **11** deaths per **100,000** children aged 0-15 years (1981 census) to **4** deaths per **100,000** (2001 census). However, socio-economic inequalities remain. There is a drastic divide between the income groups.

UK injury and poisoning death rates per 100,000 children aged 0-15

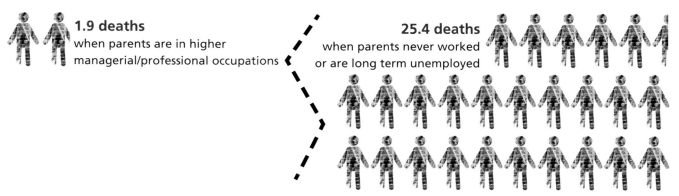

1.9 deaths when parents are in higher managerial/professional occupations

25.4 deaths when parents never worked or are long term unemployed

Source: Injury Trends and Social Gradients, Department of Health
http://www.dh.gov.uk

Worlds apart

Scandinavia leads the world in gender equality

The Global Gender Gap Index measures the gap between men's and women's access to resources and opportunities in individual countries

Global Gender Gap Index, rankings and scores, 2008
Top 15 and bottom 5 countries (ranking shown in brackets)

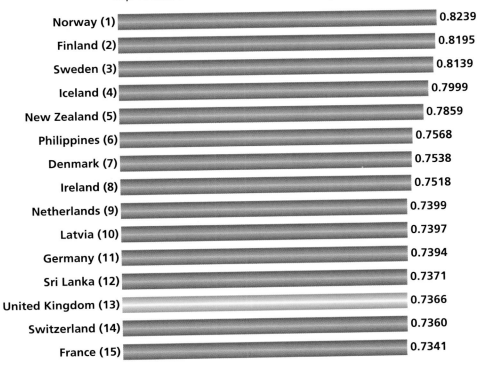

Country	Score
Norway (1)	0.8239
Finland (2)	0.8195
Sweden (3)	0.8139
Iceland (4)	0.7999
New Zealand (5)	0.7859
Philippines (6)	0.7568
Denmark (7)	0.7538
Ireland (8)	0.7518
Netherlands (9)	0.7399
Latvia (10)	0.7397
Germany (11)	0.7394
Sri Lanka (12)	0.7371
United Kingdom (13)	0.7366
Switzerland (14)	0.7360
France (15)	0.7341

Country	Score
Benin (126)	0.5582
Pakistan (127)	0.5549
Saudi Arabia (128)	0.5537
Chad (129)	0.5290
Yemen (130)	0.4664

Each country is assessed in four areas: Economic participation (including wages, employment levels and numbers of women in senior positions), Educational attainment, Health & survival, and Political empowerment.

A score of 1 means that equality of men and women has been achieved in that area, and 0 would mean complete inequality. The overall ranking is an average of each country's scores in the four areas.

How the UK measures up in each area	Rank	Score
Economic participation and opportunity	42nd	0.692
Educational attainment	1st	1.000
Health & survival	69th	0.974
Political empowerment	21st	0.280

Source: The Global Gender Gap Report 2008: World Economic Forum
http://www.weforum.org

Maximum penalty

Countries in Asia carried out more executions in 2008 than the rest of the world put together

Chinese authorities do not release information about executions so the death penalty remains shrouded in secrecy.

In Europe and Central Asia, only Belarus still carries out executions but information is also kept secret.

In the Americas, only the USA consistently applies the death penalty and even there, 2008 saw the smallest number of executions since 1995.

The majority of countries now refrain from using the death penalty, but at least **2,390** people were known to have been executed in **25** countries in 2008.

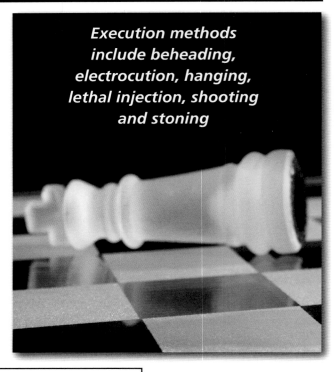

Execution methods include beheading, electrocution, hanging, lethal injection, shooting and stoning

China, Iran, Saudi Arabia, USA and Pakistan accounted for **93%** of all executions

Executions by region, 2008

Middle East & North Africa
Iran (346+)
Saudi Arabia (102+)
Iraq (34+)
Yemen (13+)
Libya (8+)
Egypt (2+)
Bahrain (1)
Syria (1+)
United Arab Emirates (1+)

Sub-Saharan Africa
Botswana (1)
Sudan (1+)

The Americas
USA (37)
St Kitts & Nevis (1)

In 2008 **Japan** had the highest number of executions since 1975

Europe & Central Asia
Belarus (4)

Asia
China (1,718+)
Pakistan (36+)
Vietnam (19+)
Afghanistan (17+)
North Korea (15+)
Japan (15)
Indonesia (10)
Bangladesh (5)
Mongolia (1+)
Malaysia (1+)
Singapore (1+)

The only country to reintroduce the death penalty in 2008 was the state of **Liberia**

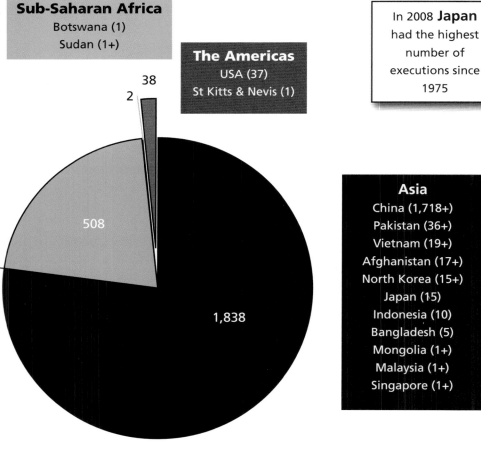

38
2
508
4
1,838

"+" after a number indicates that the figure is a minimum one.
The true figure is **at least** the figure shown

13 countries have carried out executions every year for the last five years: **China, Bangladesh, Belarus, Indonesia, Iran, Japan, North Korea, Pakistan, Saudi Arabia, Singapore, Vietnam, Yemen and the USA.**

Nine countries since 1990 are known to have executed prisoners who were under 18 years old at the time of the crime – **China, Democratic Republic of Congo, Iran, Nigeria, Pakistan, Saudi Arabia, Sudan, USA and Yemen.**

The authorities in **Iran** executed **eight** juvenile offenders in 2008 – it was the only country in the world in which juvenile offenders were known to have been executed in that year.

Saudi Arabia is one of the few states in the world in which the authorities continue to execute women.

25 out of **59** countries that retain the death penalty actually carried out executions.

Other countries may have condemned prisoners to death but the information has gone unreported.

In 2008 at least **8,864** people were sentenced to death in **52** countries

Death sentences by region, 2008

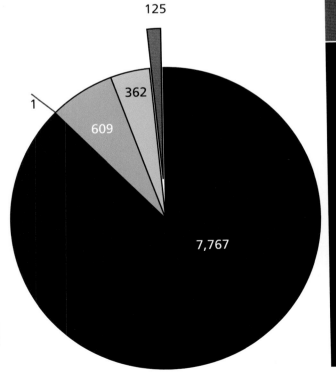

Sub-Saharan Africa
Uganda (114)
Sudan (60)
Democratic Republic of Congo (50+)
Nigeria (40+)
Ethiopia (39)
Mali (15+)
Chad (12+)
Mauritania (8)
Botswana (4)
Ghana (3)
Guinea (3)
Sierra Leone (3)
Gambia (2)
Burkina Faso, Burundi & Niger (1 in each country)
Kenya, Madagascar & Tanzania (more than 1 in each country but figure unknown)

Europe & Central Asia
Belarus (1+)

Middle East & North Africa
Iraq (285+) Algeria (200+) Egypt (87+) Jordan (14+)
Syria (7+) Kuwait (6+) Morocco/Western Sahara (4+)
Libya, Iran & Saudia Arabia (more than 1 in each country but figure unknown)

Pie chart values: 125, 362, 609, 1, 7,767

The Americas
USA (111+)
Trinidad & Tobago (10)
Bahamas (1+)
St Kitts & Nevis (1+)
St Vincent & Grenadines (1+)
Jamaica (1)

Asia
China (7,003+)
Pakistan (236+)
Bangladesh (185+)
Afghanistan (131)
India (70)
Vietnam (59+)
Japan (27)
Malaysia (22+)
Indonesia (10+)
Taiwan (8+)
Singapore (5)
Thailand (3+)
South Korea (2+)
Sri Lanka & Laos (2 in each country)
North Korea (more than one but figure unknown)

NB These figures represent those death sentences known to Amnesty International. All of the figures are minimum estimates only and they use the largest figure that can safely be inferred from their research.

Source: Amnesty International – Death Sentences and Executions in 2008
http://www.amnesty.org/en/death-penalty

Smoking kills

Of the more than 1 billion smokers alive today, around 500 million will be killed by tobacco

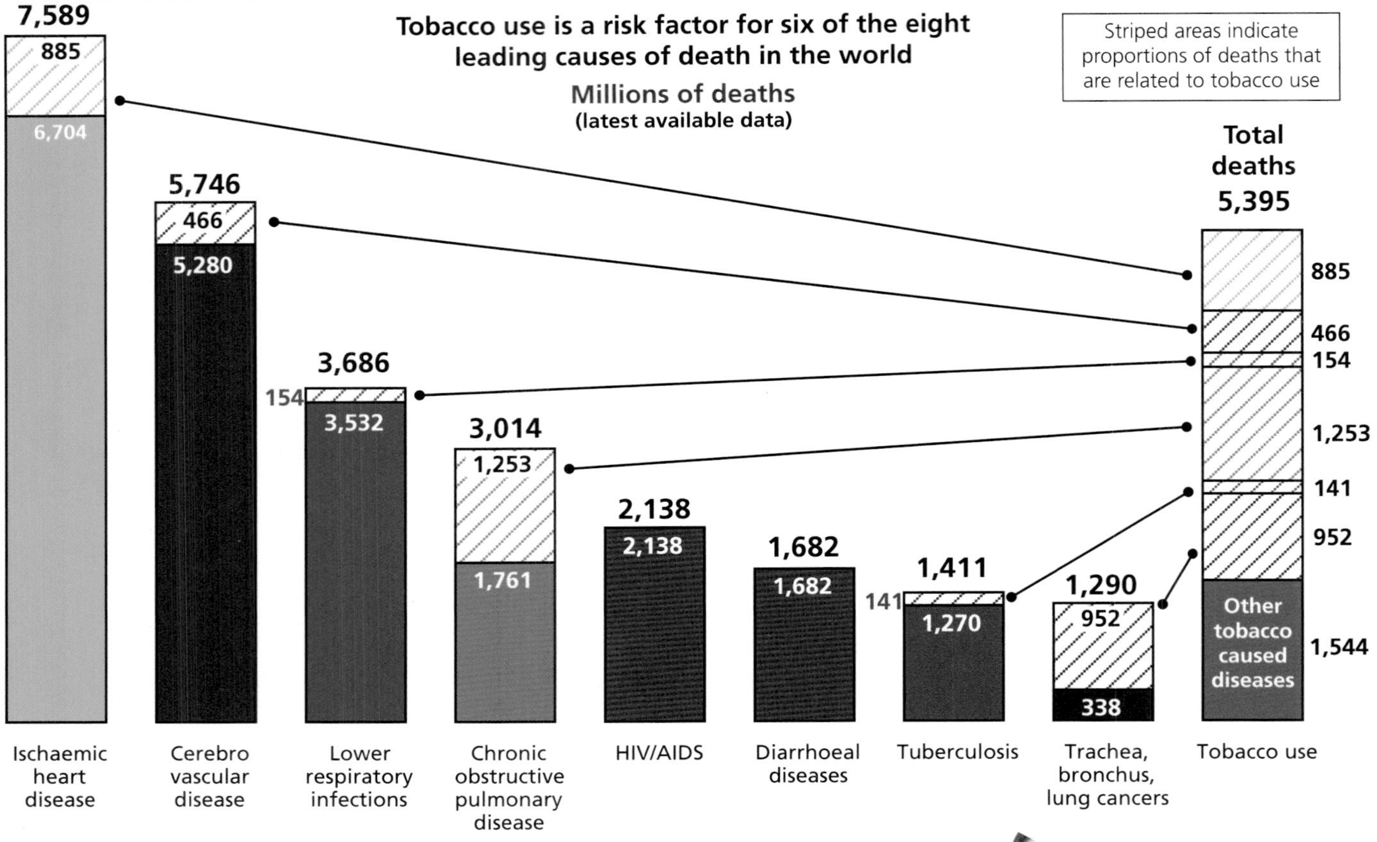

Tobacco use is a risk factor for six of the eight leading causes of death in the world
Millions of deaths
(latest available data)
Striped areas indicate proportions of deaths that are related to tobacco use
7,589
885
6,704
Ischaemic heart disease
5,746
466
5,280
Cerebro vascular disease
3,686
154
3,532
Lower respiratory infections
3,014
1,253
1,761
Chronic obstructive pulmonary disease
2,138
2,138
HIV/AIDS
1,682
1,682
Diarrhoeal diseases
1,411
141
1,270
Tuberculosis
1,290
952
338
Trachea, bronchus, lung cancers
Total deaths
5,395
885
466
154
1,253
141
952
Other tobacco caused diseases
1,544
Tobacco use

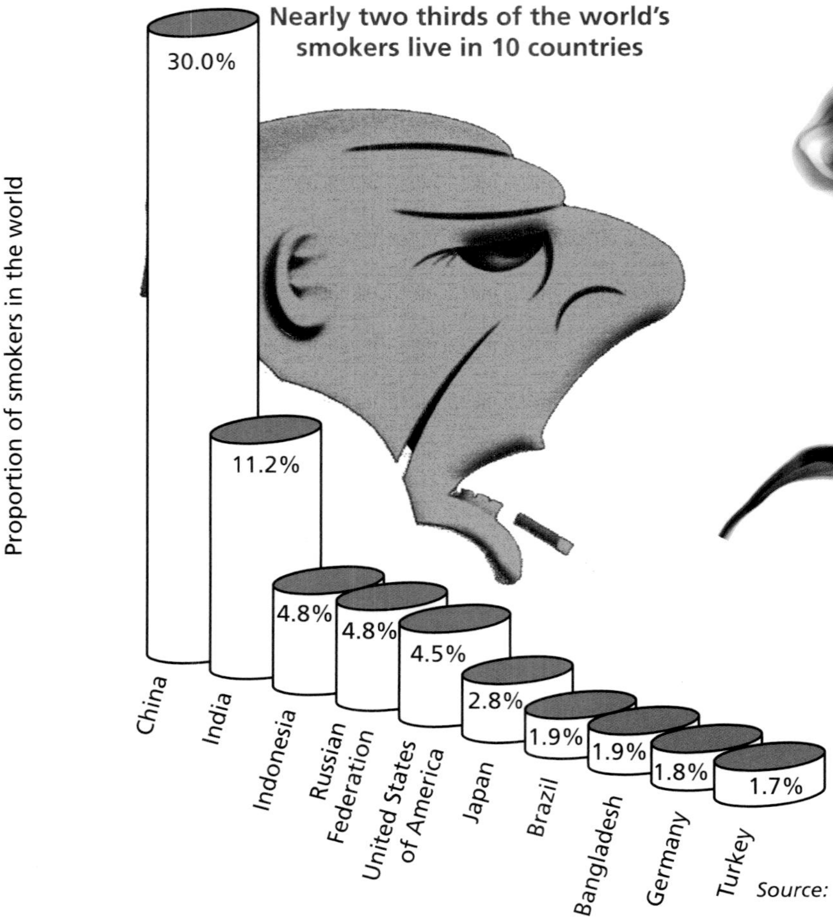

Nearly two thirds of the world's smokers live in 10 countries
Proportion of smokers in the world
30.0%
China
11.2%
India
4.8%
Indonesia
4.8%
Russian Federation
4.5%
United States of America
2.8%
Japan
1.9%
Brazil
1.9%
Bangladesh
1.8%
Germany
1.7%
Turkey

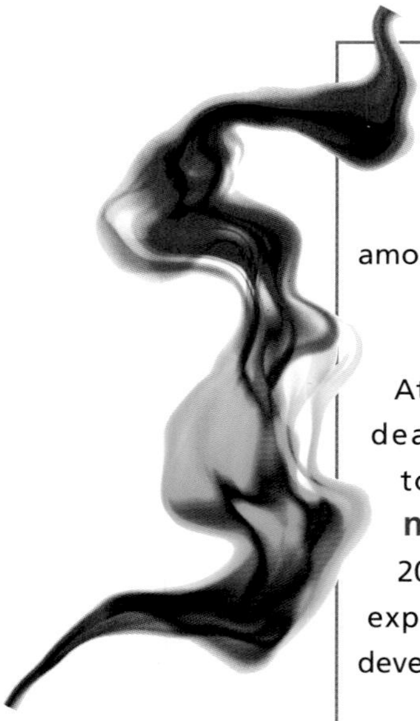

Tobacco is the leading preventable cause of death in the world. It causes **1 in 10** deaths among adults worldwide.

At the current rate, the death toll is projected to reach more than **8 million** annually by 2030, **80%** of which are expected to occur in the developing world.

Governments around the world collect 500 times more money in tobacco taxes each year than they spend on anti-tobacco efforts.

Source: WHO report on the Global Tobacco Epidemic, 2008
http://www.who.int

Dangerous waters

Attacks on the world's shipping have been increasing at an alarming rate

There were **240** reports of piracy during the six months to June 2009 –
almost double compared to the same period in 2008

Actual and attempted piracy and armed robbery attacks against ships

Actual
(boarded/hijacked/detained/missing)

Attempted
(fired upon/attemped boarding)

- 200 — Full year 2008 (Actual)
- 93 — Full year 2008 (Attempted)
- 109 — Six months Jan-June 2009 (Actual)
- 131 — Six months Jan-June 2009 (Attempted)

Full year 2008

Six months Jan-June 2009

In the first six months of 2009, a total of:	
78	vessels were boarded worldwide
75	vessels were fired upon
31	vessels were hijacked
561	crew were taken hostage
19	were injured
7	were kidnapped
6	were killed
8	were missing

> The rise in overall numbers is due almost entirely to increased Somali pirate activity off the Gulf of Aden and the east coast of Somalia

> The attackers were heavily armed with guns and knives in the majority of incidents

Total incidents per region January-June 2009

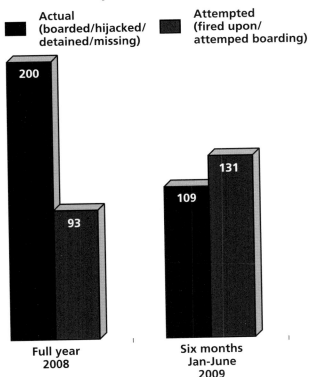

SOMALI PIRATE

- Africa — 172
- America — 22
- S E Asia — 19
- Far East — 12
- Indian Sub Continent — 11
- Rest of the World — 4

> The majority of attacks are against vessels supporting the oil industry

Source: International Chamber Of Commerce, International Maritime Bureau
Piracy and armed robbery against ships report, Piracy Reporting Centre

http://www.icc-ccs.org

Work

Mind the gap

The gender pay gap has been falling since 1998, but rose again in 2008

Mean hourly earnings excluding overtime, UK

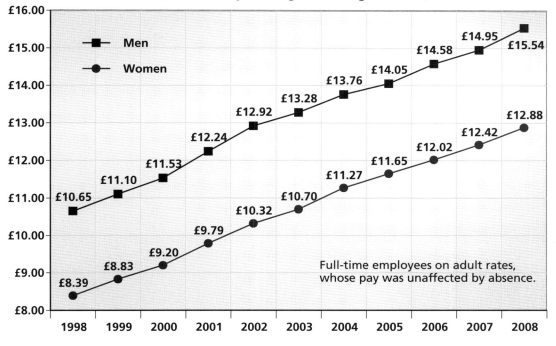

- **Men**
- **Women**

Men:
£10.65 (1998), £11.10 (1999), £11.53 (2000), £12.24 (2001), £12.92 (2002), £13.28 (2003), £13.76 (2004), £14.05 (2005), £14.58 (2006), £14.95 (2007), £15.54 (2008)

Women:
£8.39 (1998), £8.83 (1999), £9.20 (2000), £9.79 (2001), £10.32 (2002), £10.70 (2003), £11.27 (2004), £11.65 (2005), £12.02 (2006), £12.42 (2007), £12.88 (2008)

Full-time employees on adult rates, whose pay was unaffected by absence.

The **mean** is the average calculated by dividing the total by the number of employees.

The **median** is the value below which 50% of employees fall.

The stronger growth in full-time men's hourly earnings excluding overtime compared with women's has meant that the gender pay gap has increased to **12.8%**, up from **12.5%** in **2007**.

Median gross weekly earnings by age, UK, 2008

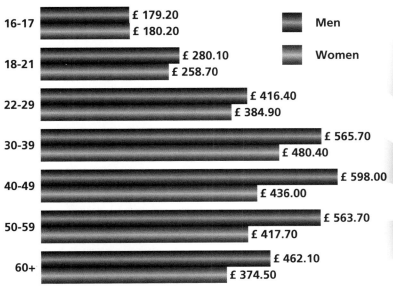

- **Men**
- **Women**

Age	Men	Women
16-17	£ 179.20	£ 180.20
18-21	£ 280.10	£ 258.70
22-29	£ 416.40	£ 384.90
30-39	£ 565.70	£ 480.40
40-49	£ 598.00	£ 436.00
50-59	£ 563.70	£ 417.70
60+	£ 462.10	£ 374.50

Full-time employees on adult rates, whose pay was unaffected by absence. Figures for 16-17 year olds include employees not on adult rates of pay.

Source: Office for National Statistics: Annual Survey of Hours and Earnings 2008 © Crown copyright 2008 http://www.statistics.gov.uk

Healthy attitude

It is working with colleagues – not pay – that most NHS workers find rewarding

How satisfied are you with each of the following aspects of your job?

% satisfied or very satisfied

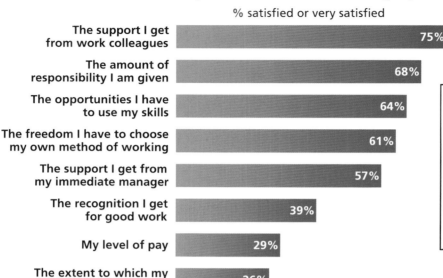

The support I get from work colleagues — **75%**

The amount of responsibility I am given — **68%**

The opportunities I have to use my skills — **64%**

The freedom I have to choose my own method of working — **61%**

The support I get from my immediate manager — **57%**

The recognition I get for good work — **39%**

My level of pay — **29%**

The extent to which my NHS trust values my work — **26%**

In one of the largest staff surveys in the world, 155,922 employees from 391 NHS trusts in England gave their views on how satisfied they were with the different aspects of their jobs. The average score for job satisfaction (ranging from 1 – very dissatisfied staff to 5 – very satisfied staff) was 3.41.

Intention to leave

Despite being generally satisfied with their jobs, 36% of staff agree or strongly agree that they often think about leaving.

24% will probably look for a job at a new organisation in the next 12 months and 18% said that as soon as they find another job they will leave.

Pressure of work

42% of staff felt that they could not meet all the conflicting demands on their time at work and 47% did not have time to carry out all the work. Only 26% felt that there were enough staff at the trust for them to do their jobs properly.

Why are you considering leaving your job?
(Respondents could tick more than one response)

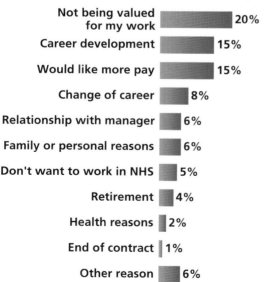

Not being valued for my work — 20%

Career development — 15%

Would like more pay — 15%

Change of career — 8%

Relationship with manager — 6%

Family or personal reasons — 6%

Don't want to work in NHS — 5%

Retirement — 4%

Health reasons — 2%

End of contract — 1%

Other reason — 6%

(Based on those who were considering leaving)

Source: Healthcare Commission National NHS staff survey 2007
http://www.healthcarecommission.org.uk

Ill treatment

12% of people who are disabled or have a long term illness have experienced violence at work

The number of people claiming incapacity benefits in Britain has more than doubled over the last 20 years. The Government intends to reverse this trend and move more disabled people and people with long-term illnesses into employment. However the experience of those who are in work is far from positive.

What type of negative experience have you had at work?

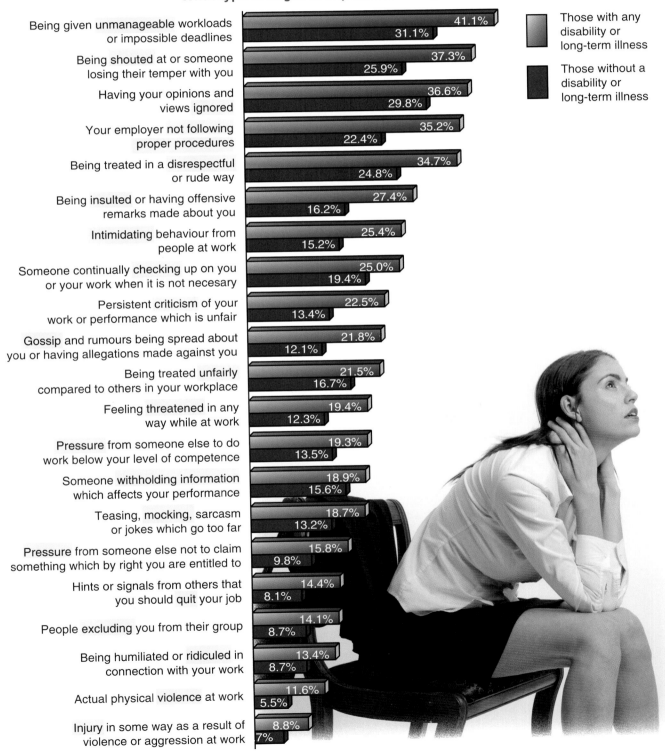

Those with any disability or long-term illness

Those without a disability or long-term illness

Category	Those with any disability or long-term illness	Those without a disability or long-term illness
Being given unmanageable workloads or impossible deadlines	41.1%	31.1%
Being shouted at or someone losing their temper with you	37.3%	25.9%
Having your opinions and views ignored	36.6%	29.8%
Your employer not following proper procedures	35.2%	22.4%
Being treated in a disrespectful or rude way	34.7%	24.8%
Being insulted or having offensive remarks made about you	27.4%	16.2%
Intimidating behaviour from people at work	25.4%	15.2%
Someone continually checking up on you or your work when it is not necesary	25.0%	19.4%
Persistent criticism of your work or performance which is unfair	22.5%	13.4%
Gossip and rumours being spread about you or having allegations made against you	21.8%	12.1%
Being treated unfairly compared to others in your workplace	21.5%	16.7%
Feeling threatened in any way while at work	19.4%	12.3%
Pressure from someone else to do work below your level of competence	19.3%	13.5%
Someone withholding information which affects your performance	18.9%	15.6%
Teasing, mocking, sarcasm or jokes which go too far	18.7%	13.2%
Pressure from someone else not to claim something which by right you are entitled to	15.8%	9.8%
Hints or signals from others that you should quit your job	14.4%	8.1%
People excluding you from their group	14.1%	8.7%
Being humiliated or ridiculed in connection with your work	13.4%	8.7%
Actual physical violence at work	11.6%	5.5%
Injury in some way as a result of violence or aggression at work	8.8%	7%

Source: Insight: Work fit for all – disability, health and experience of negative treatment in the British workplace, Equality and Human Rights Commission 2008

http://www.equalityhumanrights.com

Closed shop

What chance does an ordinary person have of reaching the top?

The majority of those at the top of the leading professions were educated in independent fee-paying schools which remain largely closed to most of the population.

The link between who your parents are and your chances in life is particularly strong in this country, more so than other advanced countries.

School background of leading figures in the professions

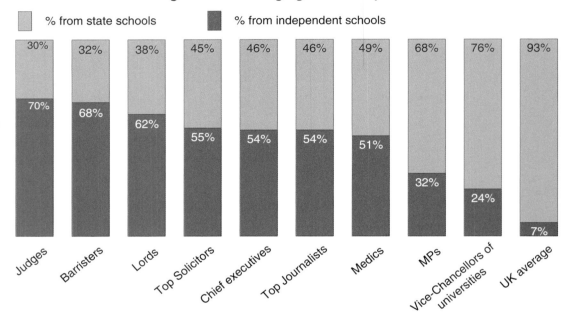

Out of the 30% of Judges who were state school educated, 28% attended a grammar school and only 2% attended a comprehensive school

- % from state schools
- % from independent schools

	Judges	Barristers	Lords	Top Solicitors	Chief executives	Top Journalists	Medics	MPs	Vice-Chancellors of universities	UK average
State	30%	32%	38%	45%	46%	46%	49%	68%	76%	93%
Independent	70%	68%	62%	55%	54%	54%	51%	32%	24%	7%

The key to entry into the professions is entry into university. There have been efforts to increase the numbers of people from lower social and economic groups starting degree course. Since 2003/04, the percentage of young entrants to full-time degree courses from social classes 4 to 7 has only increased from 28.6% to 29.5% in 2007/08. However this comes nowhere near the 47% of the working population who describe themselves as belonging to that social group.

But even entry to university can have a class bias. The Sutton Trust looked at 13 Universities which came top of an average ranking of newspaper league tables in 2000. They are: Birmingham, Bristol, Cambridge, Durham, Edinburgh, Imperial College, LSE, Nottingham, Oxford, St Andrews, UCL, Warwick and York.

The Trust estimates that about 3,000 state school students each year are 'missing' from these universities in the UK. Their places are taken by independent school students with equal A-Level grades. Students in private education make up 7% of the school population and around 15% of those taking A levels.

Top Universities % intake

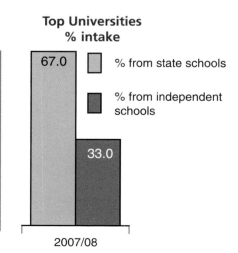

- % from state schools
- % from independent schools

67.0

33.0

2007/08

There is evidence that the situation is getting worse. People in the professions generally come from families where the income is higher than average – and this gap is actually widening.

The chart below looks at the background of professional people in their 30s. It charts their family's wealth at the time when they were 16 compared with the average at that time:

% difference from the average

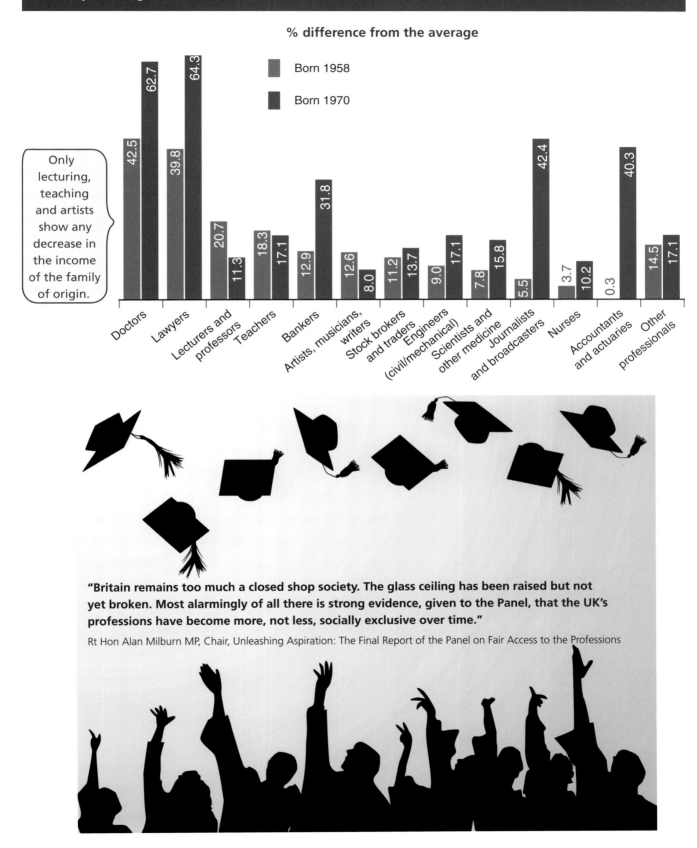

Born 1958

Born 1970

Only lecturing, teaching and artists show any decrease in the income of the family of origin.

	Doctors	Lawyers	Lecturers and professors	Teachers	Bankers	Artists, musicians, writers	Stock brokers and traders	Engineers (civil/mechanical)	Scientists and other medicine	Journalists and broadcasters	Nurses	Accountants and actuaries	Other professionals
Born 1958	42.5	39.8	20.7	18.3	12.9	12.6	11.2	9.0	7.8	5.5	3.7	0.3	14.5
Born 1970	62.7	64.3	11.3	17.1	31.8	8.0	13.7	17.1	15.8	42.4	10.2	40.3	17.1

"Britain remains too much a closed shop society. The glass ceiling has been raised but not yet broken. Most alarmingly of all there is strong evidence, given to the Panel, that the UK's professions have become more, not less, socially exclusive over time."

Rt Hon Alan Milburn MP, Chair, Unleashing Aspiration: The Final Report of the Panel on Fair Access to the Professions

Sources: Sutton Trust - submission to the Milburn Commission 2009; Social Mobility and the Professions, CMPO, University of Bristol

http://www.suttontrust.com
http://www.bristol.ac.uk/cmpo/

Class of 2009

Only a third of 2009's final year students expect to find a graduate job after university

Confidence in the graduate employment market has slumped to a fifteen-year low.
52% of university-leavers described prospects for new graduates as **very limited**

16,357 final year students were interviewed in March 2009 – a **fifth** of the finalists due to graduate from the 30 universities surveyed.

Although overall these students made more job applications, the number who secured a definite job offer during the annual 'milkround' recruitment process **dropped by a third** compared to 2008.

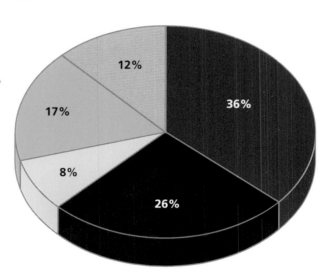

42% of student job hunters feared that even if they **did** find a graduate position, their job **offer might be withdrawn** before they started work.

48% were concerned that they would be **made redundant** during their first year in employment.

Students believe they will either...

- ...start a graduate job or be looking for a graduate job after leaving university
- ...remain at university to study for a postgraduate course
- ...take temporary or voluntary work
- ...take time off or go travelling
- Yet to decide what to do next

Pie chart values: 36%, 26%, 8%, 17%, 12%

The most popular career areas were teaching, media and marketing – this is the first time that teaching has been the top destination for university-leavers

There was a dramatic fall in applications for jobs in banking, finance and property in 2009.

33% of finalists looking for work said that, in the current economic climate, they would have to accept **any job** they were offered.

A sixth admitted that the scarcity of jobs had meant they'd had to apply to employers that they **weren't really interested** in.

One in six job hunters confirmed that they had deliberately targeted employers that appeared to offer the best **job security**, rather than generous graduate salaries or high quality training and development.

A study of vacancies at the UK's one hundred leading graduate employers showed that they planned to hire almost **20,000** new graduates but at least **5,500 posts** were **cut or left unfilled** because of the continuing recession. This amounts to a **28% reduction.**

How graduate vacancies have changed since 2008 and how applications for graduate jobs changed in 2009

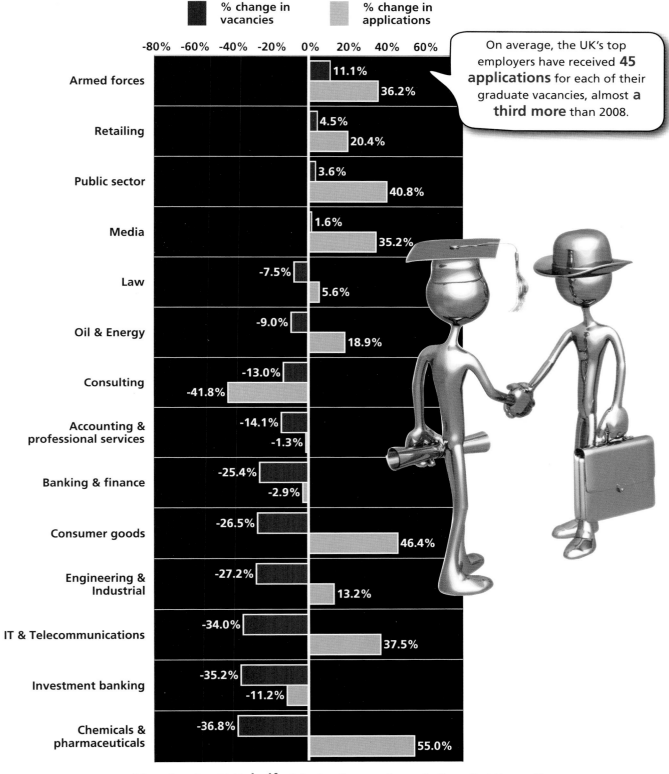

■ % change in vacancies   ▨ % change in applications

-80%   -60%   -40%   -20%   0%   20%   40%   60%

Sector	% change in vacancies	% change in applications
Armed forces	11.1%	36.2%
Retailing	4.5%	20.4%
Public sector	3.6%	40.8%
Media	1.6%	35.2%
Law	-7.5%	5.6%
Oil & Energy	-9.0%	18.9%
Consulting	-13.0%	-41.8%
Accounting & professional services	-14.1%	-1.3%
Banking & finance	-25.4%	-2.9%
Consumer goods	-26.5%	46.4%
Engineering & Industrial	-27.2%	13.2%
IT & Telecommunications	-34.0%	37.5%
Investment banking	-35.2%	-11.2%
Chemicals & pharmaceuticals	-36.8%	55.0%

On average, the UK's top employers have received **45 applications** for each of their graduate vacancies, almost **a third more** than 2008.

Looking ahead to 2010, **half** of the leading employers believe that they will hire a similar number of graduates to this year – a **fifth** believe their intake will increase but almost a **quarter** warn of further reductions in recruitment.

Source: UK Graduate Careers Survey 2009,
The Graduate Market in 2009, High Fliers Research Ltd

http://www.highfliers.co.uk

Chance event

Fatal accidents are often caused by chance – combined with shortcomings in safety precautions

Chance plays a big part in how many accidents occur in a particular year.

Because of this element of chance, it is not easy to draw conclusions about how dangerous it is to work in certain industries or in certain conditions.

To even out the influence of chance, figures are averaged over a five year period.

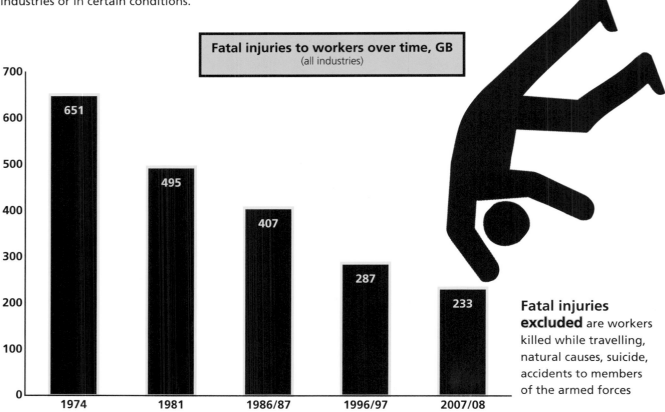

Fatal injuries to workers over time, GB
(all industries)

- 1974: 651
- 1981: 495
- 1986/87: 407
- 1996/97: 287
- 2007/08: 233

Fatal injuries excluded are workers killed while travelling, natural causes, suicide, accidents to members of the armed forces

There has been a general downward trend since the 1990s but the rate for 2008/09 also represents a statistically significant decrease compared to the average rate for the previous five years.

The most likely explanation for this striking drop is that the play of chance has fallen in a highly favourable way – by chance there have been fewer accidents. This has come after two years when the figures were very much in the upper range of what might be expected. The recession could also be having an effect.

Average rate of fatal injury, per 100,000 workers, per year, for the five year period 2003/4 to 2007/08	
Agriculture	9.9
Extractive & utility supply (eg mining and quarrying, extraction of oil and gas, supply of electricity, gas and water)	4.2
Manufacturing	1.1
Construction	3.4
Services	0.3
All industries	0.8

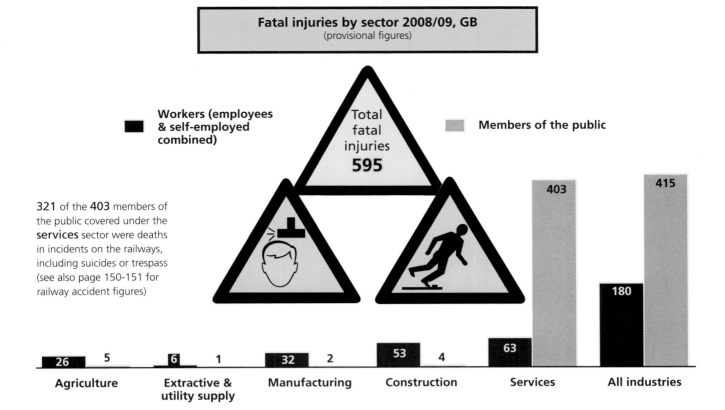

Fatal injuries by sector 2008/09, GB
(provisional figures)

■ Workers (employees & self-employed combined)

▨ Members of the public

Total fatal injuries **595**

321 of the **403** members of the public covered under the **services** sector were deaths in incidents on the railways, including suicides or trespass (see also page 150-151 for railway accident figures)

	Agriculture	Extractive & utility supply	Manufacturing	Construction	Services	All industries
Workers	26	6	32	53	63	180
Public	5	1	2	4	403	415

Comparison with other EU countries over a number of years shows that the fatal injury rate for Great Britain is consistently one of the lowest in Europe – amongst the five largest EU countries, GB has had the lowest fatal injury rate for the five year period.

Rate of fatal injury (per 100,000 workers) in selected countries and EU average

	GB	Germany	France	Italy	Spain	EU Average
2002	1.4	2.5	2.6	2.1	4.3	2.5
2003	1.1	2.3	2.8	2.8	3.7	2.5
2004	1.4	2.2	2.7	2.5	3.2	2.4
2005	1.4	1.8	2	2.6	3.5	2.3
2006	1.3	2.1	3.4	2.9	3.5	2.5

Source: Health & Safety Executive – Statistics on fatal injuries in the workplace 2008/09 © Crown copyright 2009

http://www.hse.gov.uk

Insecure future

79% of employees said their organisation had been affected by the recession

A YouGov survey on behalf of The Chartered Institute of Personnel and Development questioned 3,487 UK employees and sole traders in the summer of 2009 on their opinions and attitudes to work and the recession.

50% of employees said they were worried about the future while 13% were confident of finding work elsewhere.

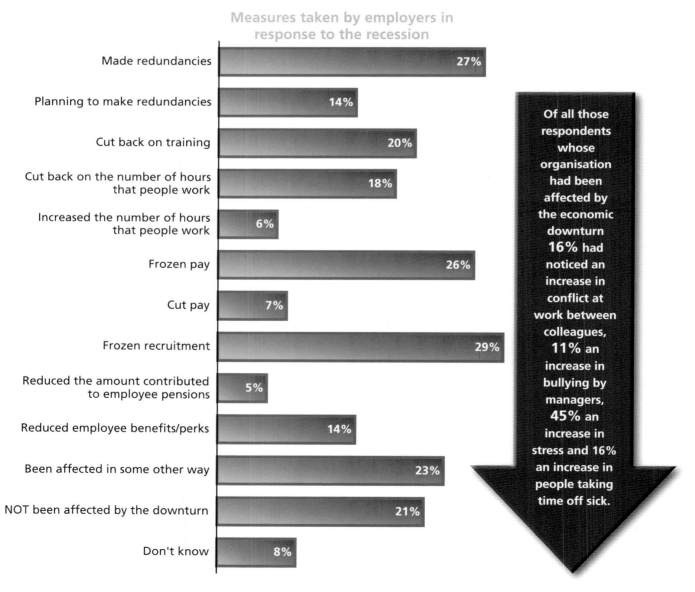

Measures taken by employers in response to the recession

Measure	%
Made redundancies	27%
Planning to make redundancies	14%
Cut back on training	20%
Cut back on the number of hours that people work	18%
Increased the number of hours that people work	6%
Frozen pay	26%
Cut pay	7%
Frozen recruitment	29%
Reduced the amount contributed to employee pensions	5%
Reduced employee benefits/perks	14%
Been affected in some other way	23%
NOT been affected by the downturn	21%
Don't know	8%

Of all those respondents whose organisation had been affected by the economic downturn **16%** had noticed an increase in conflict at work between colleagues, **11%** an increase in bullying by managers, **45%** an increase in stress and **16%** an increase in people taking time off sick.

Fact File 2010 • www.carelpress.com

70% of employees whose organisations had made redundancies said that the job cuts had **damaged morale**

Impact of redundancies on 'survivors'
(% agreeing with statements)

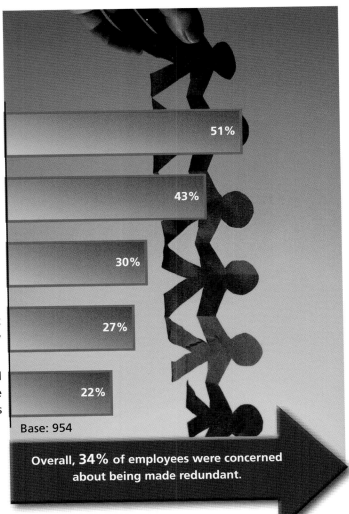

I feel under increased pressure to perform and prove my worth — **51%**

I felt a great sense of shock and loss but realise the redundancies were necessary for the organisation to survive — **43%**

A positive aspect of the redundancies is that it has helped weed out poor performers — **30%**

I am less motivated in my role as a result of losing colleagues through redundancy — **27%**

I feel the redundancies weren't handled well and am looking to change employer as soon as the recession is over and the labour market improves — **22%**

Base: 954

Overall, **34%** of employees were concerned about being made redundant.

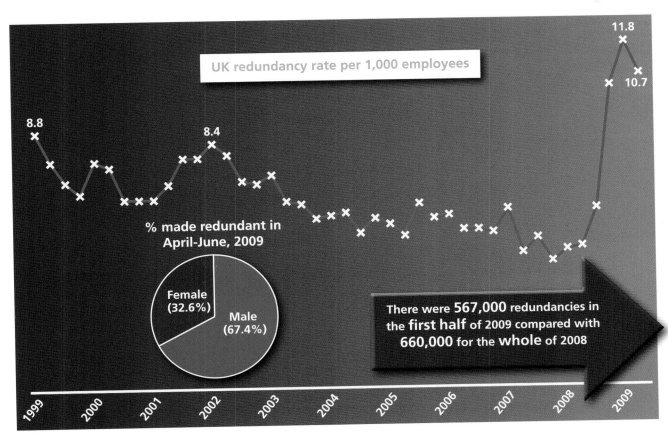

UK redundancy rate per 1,000 employees

8.8

8.4

11.8

10.7

% made redundant in April-June, 2009

Female (32.6%)

Male (67.4%)

There were **567,000** redundancies in the **first half** of 2009 compared with **660,000** for the **whole of 2008**

1999 2000 2001 2002 2003 2004 2005 2006 2007 2008 2009

Source: YouGov on behalf of Chartered Institute of Personnel and Development
ONS labour force survey © Crown copyright 2009

http://www.cipd.co.uk
http://www.ons.gov.uk

Job-less

Unemployment is at its highest level since mid-1995

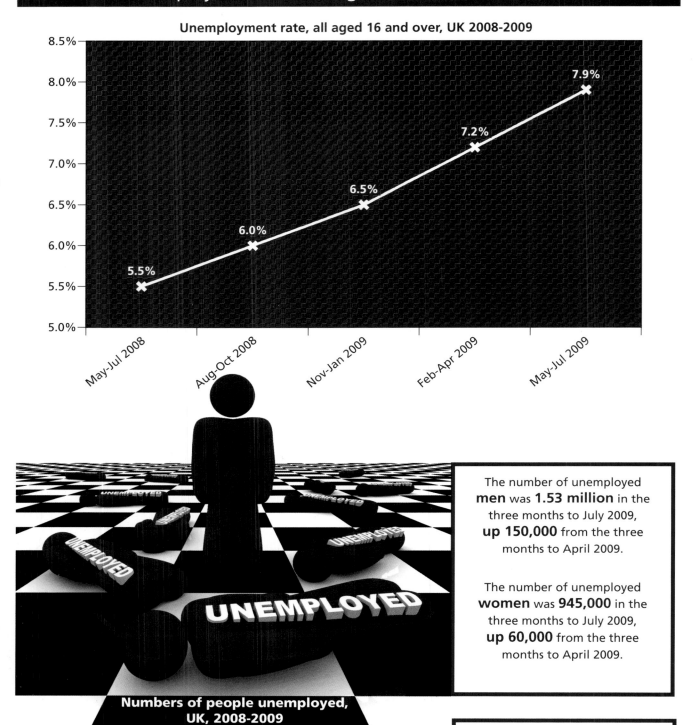

Unemployment rate, all aged 16 and over, UK 2008-2009

5.5%	May-Jul 2008	
6.0%	Aug-Oct 2008	
6.5%	Nov-Jan 2009	
7.2%	Feb-Apr 2009	
7.9%	May-Jul 2009	

The number of unemployed **men** was **1.53 million** in the three months to July 2009, **up 150,000** from the three months to April 2009.

The number of unemployed **women** was **945,000** in the three months to July 2009, **up 60,000** from the three months to April 2009.

Numbers of people unemployed, UK, 2008-2009
(thousands)

May-Jul 2008	1,727
Aug-Oct 2008	1,864
Nov-Jan 2009	2,029
Feb-Apr 2009	2,261
May-Jul 2009	2,470

The number of people unemployed **for over 12 months** was **567,000** in the three months to July 2009, **up 52,000** from the three months to April 2009.

Source: Office for National Statistics: Labour Force Statistics Statistical Bulletin, September 2009 © Crown copyright, Europa http://www.statistics.gov.uk http://europa.eu/index_en.htm

Lost generation

Age 16-24 unemployment rate, UK 2008-2009

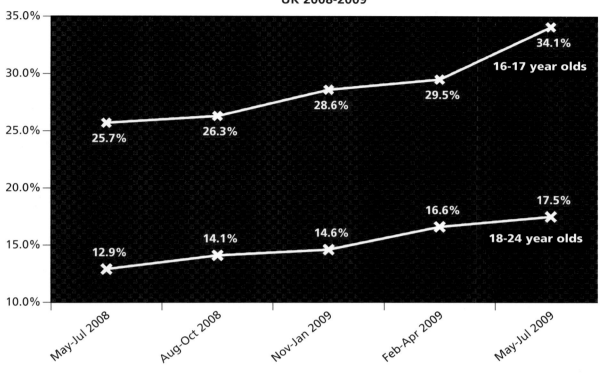

- 16-17 year olds: 25.7%, 26.3%, 28.6%, 29.5%, 34.1%
- 18-24 year olds: 12.9%, 14.1%, 14.6%, 16.6%, 17.5%

(May-Jul 2008, Aug-Oct 2008, Nov-Jan 2009, Feb-Apr 2009, May-Jul 2009)

Number of unemployed 16-24 year olds, UK, 2008-2009
(thousands)

Period	Number
May-Jul 2008	729
Aug-Oct 2008	781
Nov-Jan 2009	818
Feb-Apr 2009	888
May-Jul 2009	947

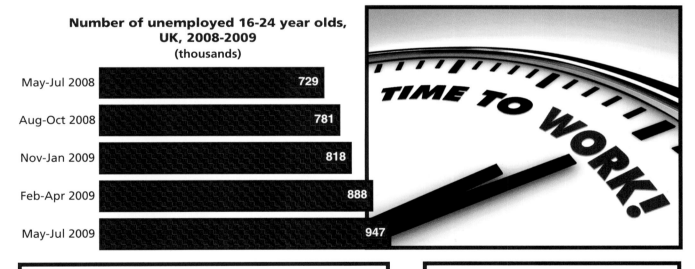

The number of under 25s **out of work** is equivalent to **one in five** of the age group.

The number of under 25s **in work** is the lowest on record at **3.87 million** – down **344,000** over the year.

At the same time the number of **pensionable age** people **in work** is rising – it stood at **1.38 million** in the three months to July 2009. This represents an employment rate of **12%,** also the highest ever.

In the 27 countries of the EU the youth unemployment rate is rising faster than the total unemployment rate.

There were **5 million** young people unemployed in **EU27** in the first quarter of 2009 – the unemployment rate for those aged **15-24** was **18.3%,** significantly higher than the total unemployment rate of **8.2%.**

Source: Office for National Statistics: Labour Force Statistics
Statistical Bulletin, September 2009 © Crown copyright, Europa

http://www.statistics.gov.uk
http://europa.eu/index_en.htm

Index

Entries in **colour** refer to main sections. In the case of double page spreads, references are to the first page